Perfection

Perfection

The Inside Story of the 1972 Miami Dolphins' Perfect Season

Bob Griese and Dave Hyde

WILEY

John Wiley & Sons, Inc.

Photo credits: all images courtesy of the Miami Dolphins
Cover image: © Neil Leifer Collection/Getty Images
Cover design: Jose Alamaguer

Published by John Wiley & Sons, Inc., Hoboken, New Jersey
Published simultaneously in Canada

For general information about our other products and services, please contact our Customer Care Department within the United States at (800) 762-2974, outside the United States at (317) 572-3993 or fax (317) 572-4002.

Wiley also publishes its books in a variety of electronic formats and by print-on-demand. Some content that appears in standard print versions of this book may not be available in other formats. For more information about Wiley products, visit us at www.wiley.com.

Library of Congress Cataloging-in-Publication Data

Griese, Bob.
    Perfection : the inside story of the 1972 Miami Dolphins' perfect season / by Bob Griese & Dave Hyde.
        pages cm
    Includes bibliographical references and index.
    ISBN 978-1-118-21809-9 (hardback); ISBN 978-1-118-28689-0 (ebk); ISBN 978-1-118-28237-3 (ebk); ISBN 978-1-118-28396-7 (ebk)
    1. Miami Dolphins (Football team) I. Hyde, Dave, 1961– II. Title.
    GV956.M47G75 2012
    796.332′6409759381–dc23

Printed in the United States of America

10 9 8 7 6 5 4 3 2 1

To Coach Shula and all those Dolphins fans
who keep the spirit of '72 alive

Contents

Prologue

Let's start with a story. A small story. One that's true and timely and that translates what it was like to be quarterback for the Miami Dolphins on the magic carpet ride of 1972.

It starts in my realty office that off-season. The phone rang. An actress wanted to sell her home, and she asked me to be the listing agent. I was delighted. Listings are the lifeblood of any Realtor, after all, and this sounded like a good one. That meant business for me in an era when most players conducted some form of business in the off-season. We didn't work out every day like today's athletes do. We just worked. Regular jobs. Regular hours. Just like the regular people we were.

Jim Langer, our Hall of Fame center, was a bank teller. Manny Fernandez, the anchor of our defensive line, earned five dollars an hour as a carpenter on construction sites. Larry Little, our Hall of Fame guard, was a substitute teacher, regularly breaking up racial fights in high school hallways during these turbulent times.

You see, lottery money wasn't part of our athletic dream in those days. Nick Buoniconti, our Hall of Fame linebacker, began playing professional football with the modest dream of making enough money to drive a new Buick and to pay off his $20,000 home mortgage. By 1972 he surpassed those dreams, in part because he pushed himself through law school while playing in Boston. He joined a law firm in Miami.

Football, we knew, took you only so far. Half the players on our undefeated team earned $20,000 or less playing pro football. Their earnings were more than doubled by the $25,000 they won in that year's postseason. Dick Anderson, our great safety, tells how he made more money ($120,000) on the Celebrity Golf Tour in 1994 than in his first five seasons combined with the Dolphins ($109,500). And it wasn't just the players who appreciated that additional postseason money. Howard Schnellenberger, our offensive coordinator, took that money and got himself out of debt for the first time in his life.

The millions showered upon today's athletes were unimaginable back then. And not just to us players. To everyone. My aunt Lorraine and uncle Fred were visiting from Indiana at about this time. A limousine stopped before them outside the Miami airport. A man in cap and livery jumped out, identified himself as "Bob Griese's chauffeur," and took their luggage. Another man, in cap and bushy mustache in the passenger seat, identified himself as my butler.

"I'll be taking you to Mr. Griese's mansion," the chauffeur said.

My aunt and uncle were stunned. They knew I made decent money, but this was beyond anything they expected. A chauffeur? A butler? Even a mansion for their young nephew?

The butler turned in his seat to look at them.

"Bob?" Uncle Fred said.

I smiled.

"Bob, is that you?"

I laughed. I couldn't play out the practical joke anymore. I had rented the limo and dressed the part to have some fun. It was fantasy to think in terms of actually having that life.

So after getting the phone call from the actress, I drove to Pembroke Pines and inspected her home. Upon arriving, I was surprised by the revealing outfit she wore.

She's really Hollywood, I thought.

She had lunch waiting for just the two of us.

That's unusual, I thought.

Then, on the tour of her home, she lingered in the bedroom. And lingered. Even my small-town, midwestern, naive sensibilities began to understand what was at work. I explained that I was married, and tried to leave as quickly and quietly as possible.

Needless to say, I didn't get that listing.

But this was when I first realized that fame and the accompanying idea of celebrity were becoming part of the equation of a Dolphin player. In my first few years in Miami, pro football was background music in a resort town. We never had more than four wins in a season. Our games were some of the least-attended in the American Football League, averaging just 35,116 fans in the cavernous Orange Bowl in 1969.

Then Don Shula arrived as coach, and everything changed overnight. He showed how one person can change the entire dynamic of a team. We began winning. We became a show. Our attendance doubled by 1971 when we made it to the Super Bowl. For the 1972 season, 5,000 bleacher seats were added to accommodate the demand. We averaged more than 78,000 fans per game that year. By 1973, we had that many season-ticket holders—the most ever for a pro sports franchise—and the publisher of *Sports Illustrated* wrote, "Possibly no city in the United States is as maniacal about one team as is Miami about the Dolphins."

The city's transit system adopted the Dolphins' aqua-and-orange colors for their buses. A highway was renamed "Dolphin Expressway."

I was one of eight Dolphins who had regular radio shows—nine, if you include Paul Warfield offering his "Thought of the Day" program on one station. We became so associated with winning that at the annual meeting of Manufacturers Life Insurance, the president challenged his salesmen to rise to the top like the Dolphins, even passing out Dolphins T-shirts to the board of directors.

At this time, the sight of a full Orange Bowl was unforgettable. And not just to me. Vern Den Herder walked into it for the first time as a rookie in 1971 and was so awed by the sights and sounds of a place that held thirty times the population of his hometown of Sioux Center, Iowa, that he took a mental snapshot. Thousands of fans waved white handkerchiefs. The noise vibrated from the ground. And the passion at those games? In one telling moment that 1972 season, Buffalo quarterback Dennis Shaw settled under center six times and backed away each time because the crowd prevented teammates from hearing his signals. The game was delayed for seven minutes. Dolphin radio announcer Rick Weaver pleaded to those fans with transistor radios to have their neighbors quiet down. That didn't help. Only when Shula held up his hands for the crowd to lower the volume did it obey. Shaw came to the line, dropped to pass, and was promptly sacked by Manny Fernandez and Bob Matheson. The cascade of boos immediately converted into such a thunderous roar that that held up the game, too.

This was a different town, a different time. In *this* Miami, even Stephanie Noonan, the wife of wide receiver Karl Noonan, who was injured that season, signed a check at a store and heard the clerk ask, "Is this *the* Karl Noonan?" In *this* Miami, controversy came in the form of a North Miami bar owner, Frank Shula, opening a joint called "Shula's" and advertising it as a place to "score after Dophins games." In *this* Miami, Dolphins tight end Jim Mandich could be pulled over by a police officer after leaving his favorite bar, hear the officer say, "Not you again, Jim," and be driven home with no problem or headline.

For much of the previous decade, Miami's national image was captured by a boat speeding across Biscayne Bay each Sunday night as a voice welcomed television viewers to "the fun and sun capital of the world!" But the *Jackie Gleason Show* went off the air in 1970. The turbulent days captured by *Miami Vice* were a decade away. In this intermission, the Dolphins delivered the winning image of their city. Take me as an example of what we were undergoing. I threw a pass (incomplete) on a play drawn up for the Dolphins by President Nixon. I appeared on the covers of *Time* and *Sports Illustrated* in the span of a few weeks. And I was scouted by national security adviser Henry Kissinger during a game against Oakland. Kissinger watched that game closely enough to predict my next play.

"Griese hasn't passed on first down yet," Kissinger said during a break from diplomatic meetings. "He'll throw here."

And I did.

If the national attention showed the reach of our team, there were moments when the local passion spilled like a bucket of water across the floor, unbridled and reckless. It wasn't just me and real estate listings. Here's a story:

Running back Jim Kiick got a call that 1972 training camp from the manager of the Keyes real estate company.

"Mr. Kiick, your checks for $2,500 on the rented house bounced," the manager said.

"I didn't rent a house," Kiick said.

"You rented a $150,000 home on Key Biscayne. My secretary recognized you."

That began the NFL's first investigation into a man using a player's identity for criminal acts. The break in the case came when police received a phone call from a woman claiming to be Kiick's fiancée. She was watching our exhibition game against Atlanta on television that August when the man claiming to be Kiick called her. *Oops.*

Suddenly such incidents were happening across our roster. One of Mike Kolen's college teammates claimed to be him and asked people for money in Atlanta. Another impostor in that city claimed to be

Jake Scott. In South Carolina, a man saying he was Larry Little actually married a woman, though what frosted the real Little was how fat the man was. For Jim Kiick, it went one beyond that. He had a second impostor, who caused such a string of trouble in Los Angeles before the 1972 season that the real Kiick flew there to testify in a court case. The impostor was a Mexican man.

All of this spoke of a shifting era in American sports thanks in good part to the manner in which the game was being captured and marketed by the television camera. In 1966, Dolphins owner Joe Robbie started the franchise and received $500,000 for that season from the television contract. By 1972, he received $1.7 million for that season. Slowly, over the coming years, television's platform and money changed everything around the game.

We didn't see that big picture in 1972. Our world was 100 yards long. It centered around three hours on Sunday afternoons. It involved a roster of forty players who were pushed and prodded and threatened by a staff of six coaches. We'd lost the Super Bowl the previous year, though the city of Miami still wanted to throw us a parade. See how crazy the place was at the time?

"I don't want a loser's parade," Shula said. "Hopefully, we can have a winner's parade in a year."

He spelled out the stepping-stone goals in the first team meeting that training camp: make the playoffs, win the conference, then win the Super Bowl. Larry Csonka's head snapped up from the floor when Shula even mentioned the idea of "going undefeated." Csonka thought, This man is obsessed.

Csonka was right. Shula *was* obsessed.

On some level, entering that season, we all were.

1

Are We Really That Good?

GAME ONE
—at—
Kansas City Chiefs
September 17, 1972

In later years, when the Beatles were asked in what period they did their best work and felt at the top of their musical game, they often surprised people by saying it was back before they were discovered, back when they were nobodies, way back when they were humble and hungry and hoping to be discovered.

I never felt that way about this Dolphins team.

I ran out of the locker room for the season opener in Kansas City's new Arrowhead Stadium full of inner questions and private concerns. I was told constantly that off-season how we were on our way, that the 1971 season's playoff run and Super Bowl loss were a launching point to something special. There was merit in that idea. And I agreed with it to friends, to teammates, to reporters, to strangers, to anyone who asked.

To myself, deep down, even as we ran onto the field for this opener, I wasn't so certain.

Was that past season a fluke?

Were we really that good?

These nagging questions settled like dust on my mind. I knew we had talent. I knew we were well coached. But fortune kissed us on that run through the playoffs last year starting right here, in Kansas City, against a great Chiefs team. Jan Stenerud, a placekicker headed to the Hall of Fame, had missed a short field goal at the end of regulation and had another blocked in overtime. That allowed one playoff win. Then the greatest quarterback of his era, John Unitas, didn't throw for a touchdown and had an interception returned for one as Baltimore was shut out for the first time in 97 games. Sure, at thirty-nine Unitas was getting older. But were we that good?

Then came the Super Bowl itself. A 24–3 loss where the fundamental strengths of the team didn't hold together. We managed three points. Three measly points. For forty years since then, no team has scored that few points in a Super Bowl. Dallas read our offense like some flimsy pamphlet. They even diagnosed things I didn't know existed. In their postgame comments, Dallas players mentioned how our wide receivers crept in a few yards closer to the linemen during running plays to have better blocking lanes. Was that true? Was such a telltale sign that obvious?

A month after the loss, I finally and uncomfortably brought the Super Bowl game film home and watched it in the privacy of a spare bedroom I made into my home office, just as I did with film during the season.

"Oh, no," I said, watching myself play. "Why did you do that? What were you thinking?"

In one sense, that was just me. I always talked about the mistakes I made instead of the good plays. I remembered the fumbles I made, the checkoff I missed, the passes I overthrew. My philosophy was that you learn more from losing than you do from winning. Winning is what you work for all week. Losing means something was wrong and needed correcting. And a whole lot went wrong that Super Bowl against Dallas.

Down the roster, all of us still came to grips with the same questions over the off-season. Manny Fernandez considered that Super Bowl so physically crushing, so emotionally emptying, that he had to stop while walking back to the hotel that day. He sat on the bumper of a car. For ten minutes, he put his hands in his face and cried uncontrollably. He felt he let everyone down—family, friends, teammates, maybe himself most of all. He said it was the worst feeling he ever had in sports.

Larry Csonka didn't cry—hadn't cried since watching *Old Yeller*, he said—but he fell into a dark frustration, even an anger, at the way the day played out. He hadn't fumbled all season. Not once in 234 carries. But he and I fumbled a handoff exchange that day, early in the game, that set the tone for everything to come. That stayed with him. It unsettled him, bothered him. Just as it bothered me.

Most players found similar motivational fuel from that game that they carried into the next season. Cornerback Tim Foley taped a picture in the back of his locker of that final scoreboard: Dallas 24, Miami 3. The clock read all zeroes. He made a point to look at it each day before practice.

Nick Buoniconti cut out a quote from a newspaper of Dallas cornerback Cornell Green. "The difference between the Miami Dolphins and the Dallas Cowboys," Green said, "was Miami was just happy to be in the game, and Dallas came to win the game." Buoniconti tacked it to the locker room bulletin board, where it stayed all season. He made a point of noticing it when he walked by.

Perhaps only Paul Warfield, a veteran of championship teams in Cleveland, looked at the assembled talent and young careers inside our locker room and decided that that initial Super Bowl came too early for most of us. We weren't ready to win a game like that in the timelines of our development, he thought. Too young. Too raw. We played a mature, focused, and talented Dallas team that went through its own periods of disappointment to achieve that Super Bowl win. Warfield thought the loss would help everyone understand what it took to win on that stage. He thought that only now, after feeling the sting of such a high-profile loss, were we ready to win a Super Bowl.

Years later, I could reflect with the same understanding of time and place. In that off-season moment, however, I had doubts and questions that grew one February night after my three children went to sleep and I watched film of that game. I rewound plays. I reworked matchups. I saw again how both Dolphins lines—offensive and defensive—had trouble. Dallas schemed against our best players. Again and again they took Warfield out of the equation with a double-team of cornerback Cornell Green and safety Mel Renfro.

What I noticed from the start was the start itself. Could it have been any worse? Our first possession was three downs and out. Our second possession saw the fumbled handoff to Csonka. On the third possession came the play that blinks in neon forever for me. I went to pass for what I expected to be a quick, controlled play. The running backs released to the flats. The receivers ran quick slants, then broke upfield, if necessary. I took a three-step drop, set, and threw to the most open receiver. Simple, right?

Well, I took that three-step drop, set to throw and . . . Dallas defensive end Larry Coles jumped in front of me. I retreated a few steps, turned the other way, and . . . Bob Lilly was in my face. I retreated a few more steps, turned back the other way and . . . nearly ran into the referee, Jim Tunney.

Then there was Coles again. I retreated again.

"Griese chased back to the 20 . . . the 15," network commentator Al De Rogatis told the national audience that day.

Lilly finally tackled me for a 29-yard loss.

In my Hall of Fame induction speech, I said how it was the only Super Bowl record still in my possession. That day in New Orleans, out of breath, I called a time-out and went to the sideline to talk with Coach Shula.

"Okay, you always want to call plays," I told Don. "Third and thirty, you can call this one."

"Oh, no, you got us into this mess," Shula said. "You get us out of it."

There was no spark all day. No fire. No spring in any of our steps as I sat watching the film. Finally I turned off the projector, put the final reel of film back in its canister, rubbed my head, and asked the question I was still asking on opening day in Kansas City: Are we really that good?

We started to find out that first game. Shula warned us how prepared the Chiefs would be. New season. New stadium. They had stewed for eight months after their playoff loss to us. They also knew that the only reason we were scheduled for the game was so national television could take advantage of the rematch, building it up, replaying the previous drama right down to showing Garo Yepremian's winning field goal as the broadcast began in Kansas City.

If you listed the necessary ingredients for a classic, that playoff game supplied all of them. The consequence of a playoff game; the stage of Christmas Day. It contrasted a Super Bowl champion in Kansas City and our young, rising franchise. Thirteen future Hall of Famers were involved in the game, including both coaches, quarterbacks, and middle linebackers. There were in-game twists and unexpected turns, epic heroes and unlikely goats, giveaways, comebacks, and such drama that the normal four quarters couldn't contain the script. Nor could five. History, a crucial ingredient for a classic, was made that day as the game lasted 82 minutes, 40 seconds and was tagged with a name that identified its uniqueness: The Longest Game.

Everyone involved recognized its special quality even as it played out. The players realized it. So did the TV announcers. Even the refs knew. "This is a helluva game," backfield judge Adrian Burk said to several Dolphins on the sideline early in the first overtime period.

Before the second overtime, I came to the sideline and took the clipboard from David Shula, the coach's teenage son who maintained it. On the top sheet was the list of plays the Dolphins ran and Kansas

City's matching defenses. Beneath that was a list I drew up before each game of plays I wanted to call. I saw one we hadn't used. I didn't want to call it early on, thinking the veteran Kansas City defense would be looking for it. Later, I simply forgot about it. After Kiick ran 5 yards to the Dolphins' 40-yard line, I called the play that became a part of Dolphin lore: "Roll right, trap left."

The play relied on timing, subtlety, and ultimately Csonka's brute strength. Kiick and I flowed to the right. Csonka took a fake step to the right, then moved against the flow to the left. Left tackle Doug Crusan posted up the Chiefs' defensive end. Larry Little and Norm Evans pulled in unison from the right side to the left. Csonka followed them through the hole. And what a hole it was. Little ran through it with no one to block and kept running downfield. Csonka grabbed Little's belt as he followed him.

"He's faster than I am, and I had to hold to keep up," Csonka said.

Csonka ran 29 yards before being tackled at the Chiefs' 36-yard line. Over the next few plays, I made careful calls that moved the ball to the 30-yard line. Everyone was exhausted. Csonka lost 18 pounds that day. He still had enough strength to lift Yepremian off the ground before his 37-yard field goal attempt and say, "You little bastard, if you miss this field goal, I'll kill you."

As the ball left his foot, Yepremian knew it was good. He turned and jogged upfield without watching it, as he always did, when the silence of the crowd made him shudder momentarily. Had he missed it? Why was there no noise?

Then he realized that it was a Kansas City crowd that was silent. And now here we were for a season opener that shared nothing from our earlier game against the Chiefs. We were in the heat of summer, not the cold of winter, at the start of a season, not the end of one.

And this time we dominated Kansas City.

My months of questions and concerns? They began to be answered that day—good answers—right from the start when we moved the ball down the field and I threw a 14-yard touchdown to Marlin Briscoe. In a one-minute span in the second quarter, Csonka scored a touchdown from a yard out and Yepremian kicked a 47-yard field goal.

It was 17–0 at the half. And it was over. You could sense that just by looking over the line. Kansas City wanted nothing more to do with the hottest day I ever played in. Shula once reached into his shirt pocket that day for his game plan, and the ink had mixed with his sweat to not only make the plan unreadable but put an inkblot on his shirt as well. We were used to hot days in Miami. Bob Kuechenberg celebrated cloudless game days at the Orange Bowl, knowing the weather would melt him but just might kill his opponent. And sometimes it nearly did. Just a year earlier, the San Francisco 49ers made an emergency landing in Denver on their way home to treat more than a dozen players for dehydration.

In a snapshot that became the day's full portrait, guard Larry Little began sprinting after the end of the third quarter in boiling heat down the field . . . 10 yards . . .

What's he doing? I thought.

. . . 20 yards . . .

All right, Larry, I thought.

. . . 30 yards . . .

The other Dolphin offensive linemen began running, too, in a manner that made the entire stadium notice.

. . . 40 yards . . .

"Oh, my God, I can't do that," Kansas City defensive tackle Buck Buchanan must have thought.

Little led his lineman on a 60-yard sprint of intimidation from where the Dolphins ended the third quarter at one 20-yard line to where they started the fourth quarter at the other 20-yard line. The heat? Game fatigue? Just plain energy conservation? Little told everyone that didn't matter. They were bigger, stronger, fitter. Earlier in that game, the Dolphins watched Buchanan wobble to the sideline after one series, overheated. They talked about it. They saw other Chiefs flush from the temperature. They knew the physical strain of this weather.

They also knew the mental game to be played, which is why Little took off sprinting down the field and the other linemen followed his lead. It was daunting to the Chiefs. It was energizing to the Dolphins.

And to Little?

He strutted around at the other end with a look of invincibility as he waited for the other players. Tired? Him? His body language said it was a walk in the park. The truth said something else entirely. Little was breathless. His legs were butter. It took all the strength of a strong man to act as if that downfield sprint were nothing, that he had plenty of energy left where that came from. It worked, too. The entire stadium sagged a bit at seeing Little apparently sneer at the heat. Or maybe the rest of us in the huddle just felt emboldened by his spirit. I know I did. The dismantling of Kansas City continued to the point that the final score of 20–10 didn't do the day justice.

That first Sunday, we left with a completely different emotion than in our previous visit. Instead of a giddy celebration that continued all the way to Miami airport where twenty-five thousand fans met us, there was a more businesslike satisfaction to the win. We dominated a good team. We answered questions about who we were. Already, I felt some off-season concern melt away on this opening day.

"I don't think either team played with much enthusiasm," Kansas City coach Hank Stram said. "It was a listless game throughout."

Shula, told by reporters of Stram's comments, offered a small smile.

"I was happy with our enthusiasm," he said.

2

Three Men and the Backfield

GAME TWO

———

Houston Oilers
September 24, 1972

One day in practice that summer, Mercury Morris took a handoff, accelerated around the end, and that was it. He was gone. Untouched. Uncatchable. That speed to the outside was the precise gear our offense lacked the previous year. I turned and looked at Don Shula. He looked at me. Neither of us said anything, but no words were necessary.

Our thought was the same: "This guy's got to play."

It wasn't that simple, though. For as fast as Mercury ran, he couldn't block like Jim Kiick, the starting running back for the past four seasons. And as a receiver, Morris had hands of granite. He never caught more than 15 passes in a season for his career. Kiick, meanwhile, was perhaps the best receiver out of the backfield in the league. He led our team in receiving in 1970 and was second his other three years.

So Shula's challenge was how to incorporate both players' talents into the same position. It didn't just require innovative thinking. It demanded a revolutionary thinker given the time and place of football in the early 1970s. Up to this point, the idea of "situation substitution," where specific players with specific talents were introduced at specific points in a game, was unheard of. Teams had starters who played all the time, and teams had reserves who played only when a starter was hurt or tired. That was it. That's how the game was played. That's the box everyone thought in . . . until 1972.

Shula was like Columbus sailing to the New World with what he introduced that season. It actually was an issue Shula and the coaching staff had been wrapping their minds around for a while. It wasn't just the backfield, either. We had a dominant blocking tight end in Marv Fleming, who wasn't a great receiver, and a great receiving tight end in Jim Mandich, who wasn't much of a blocker. Wide receiver Howard Twilley was an excellent route-runner inside the 20-yard line. But out in the open field, Marlin Briscoe had the speed and quickness to stretch the field.

The issues Shula faced ranged from strategic ones of using players to their best advantage to practical ones of how to get each player in the game at the proper time. I was the guy calling the plays, too. How would I call for the necessary player to enter the game for the play I wanted to run in the short time between plays? Another thing no one had mastered before.

Then there were feelings inside the locker room and outside in public. This is where everything could have sunk a weaker team with selfish players. Through the previous four years, the one constant I had in this offense was Kiick and Larry Csonka in the backfield behind me. Kiick led the team in rushing in 1968 and 1969, with Csonka second. Csonka led in 1970 and 1971, with Kiick second. They were tough, productive, and dependable, fumbling only once in a combined 448 carries in 1971.

"Kiick and Csonka," an anonymous AFC coach told *Sports Illustrated* before the 1972 season. "You can't spell 'em and you can't stop 'em."

Their on-field partnership reflected an off-field friendship that began in proper fashion at the 1968 College All-Star Game in Chicago.

Each separately left the team hotel by a back fire escape to sidestep curfew, stumbled across each other in a bar, and stayed out until 4:00 a.m. Married and with young children by 1972, Csonka and Kiick still believed in partying hard at night and playing hard the next day. As such, their careers, social lives, and public personas became intertwined. They often greeted assistant coach Tom Keane, who did curfew checks the night before games, with an invitation to the party in their room. "Come to the party and fix yourself a drink, Tom!" one would say. They spent the night before a rainy game in Boston with a bottle of Jack Daniels. When Kiick was facedown in a puddle during the game, Csonka said, "Don't swallow, Kiick, or you'll spoil all that good whiskey."

Stories involving them stacked up like so many cans on a shelf. Once, Csonka noticed Kiick biting the arm of a New York Jets player and asked in the huddle why he did that.

"Because he was twisting my leg," Kiick said.

"Did you bite him hard?" Csonka asked.

"Hard enough to make him stop."

Miami Herald sportswriter Bill Braucher, entertained by their antics as much as their football, hung a nickname on them after attending a movie matinee starring Paul Newman and Robert Redford: "Butch Cassidy and the Sundance Kid." Kiick and Csonka loved the nickname. The movie characters were the perfect fun-loving, good-looking reflection the running backs saw in themselves. They played up the arrangement for self-entertainment and modest profit. Kiick, buried under a pile of Los Angeles Rams, looked at Csonka and quoted a line from the movie: "Listen, kid, find out who these guys are. We ain't coming back here again." Teammates hung signs on their lockers with movie references such as "Where's Peru?" Posters were sold of them posing as Redford and Newman. A TV special was made of their adventures, featuring them on horseback, riding into the sunset down a Miami Beach road.

They hired the same high-powered agent, Mark McCormack, and held out of training camp in 1971 before signing matching three-year contracts for $60,000 per year. Upon their return to the team, Shula took the unusual step of inviting them out for beers to assure them that all problems were gone. (He also suggested that Kiick get a haircut.)

Kiick and Csonka wrote a book, *Always on the Run*, together. They appeared with Johnny Carson on the *Tonight Show* together. They were featured together on the cover of *Sports Illustrated* before the 1972 season. Csonka, seated by a standing Kiick on the magazine cover, provided the spirit of their persona by placing his middle finger over a crossed leg. It was supposed to be a spoof, one of dozens of photos left on the editing floor, but it made the cover and resulted in Csonka receiving hundreds of letters from angry parents worried about their children's role models. Later, Csonka and Kiick were pictured to far less controversy in derby hats and suits on the cover of *Esquire*. ("You're looking good, Mr. Kiick," Csonka says in the caption. "God knows I try, Mr. Csonka," Kiick answers.)

They were legitimate characters, too. I once came up to the line in the Super Bowl against Minnesota, thinking what play I'd change to if they showed a certain defense, and I forgot the snap count. Just forgot it. I turned to Csonka. "What's the snap count?" I asked.

Csonka had his head down, not hearing. I asked again. He raised his helmet slowly.

"It's on two," he said.

I turned back around.

"It's on one," Kiick said.

"It's on two," Csonka shot back.

Here we were, in front of eighty thousand people with millions more watching on TV in the biggest game of the year, arguing over a snap count. I had 30 seconds total to get the play run; I knew time was running out and put my hands under center. On "one," the ball came up from center Jim Langer. But nobody moved. Not the offense. Not the Vikings' defense. Either Langer was confused by the conversation between Kiick and Csonka, or everyone else was.

"What the hell's going on out there?" Shula asked when I came to the sideline.

I didn't have the heart to say. But Kiick and Csonka were such national names, the president of a woman's club in Washington, D.C., entered the Redskin offices to buy five thousand tickets to an exhibition game that 1972 season. When asked for which game, she answered, "I want to see Butch Cassidy and the Sundance Kid."

They were strong enough personalities on their own. Each week, Shula asked each of us on the offense to suggest an opening play for the game against the upcoming opponent. I measured the defense's strengths against our strengths, factored in any injuries, and considered what was working best for us before suggesting a play.

"P-10," Csonka always said.

The linemen fired out. Csonka took the handoff up the middle. That was P-10. As subtle as a punch to the gut. If they couldn't stop that, he figured, why get cute with the play calls?

Shula's favorite scene of Csonka came from the 1971 highlight film. Csonka lumbered into the end zone, his helmet viciously twisted, his uniform slathered in mud, his expression set in stone. He turned impassively after scoring, flipped the ball over his shoulder, and jogged to the bench.

"The image of manhood," Shula called it.

Nor was it an image in the cultivated sense with which later generations of athletes marketed themselves. That was Csonka at his core, and his ruggedness resonated through the team. Players sat in film sessions each week, watched him purposely run into opposing defenders, and joked, "Way to find the safety, Zonk!" Once, when Buffalo safety John Pitts had an angle to push him out of bounds, Csonka smashed a right forearm into Pitts's head, leveling him and becoming perhaps the first running back penalized for a personal foul while carrying the ball.

"When he goes on a safari," line coach Monte Clark said, "the lions roll up their windows."

That was Csonka.

Kiick was called a "cowboy from Wyoming" in a newspaper story upon arriving as a fifth-round draft pick in 1968 with the Dolphins.

"I'm a pool shark from Jersey," Kiick told the reporter.

That wasn't the first time anyone misread him. Or the costliest. At the College All-Star Game, the assigned college coach, Norm Van Brocklin, wanted him to play fullback. Kiick declined, pointing to Csonka.

"I won't be playing fullback with the Dolphins," Kiick said.

"You should want to play anywhere," Van Brocklin answered. "You've got a bad attitude."

Van Brocklin didn't play Kiick a down that game. The most contact he had, Kiick later joked, was when Curley Culp accidentally bumped into him on the sideline while making a tackle.

In Miami, Kiick seemed destined for such disappointment when two backs ahead of him were hurt in training cmp. He quickly showed his game. He led the Dolphins with 621 yards rushing as a rookie, and added 421 yards more on 44 receptions. These were the kind of productive and versatile statistics Kiick provided through the first four years of his pro career. He also played one game with a broken toe, a broken finger, a hip pointer, and an elbow that needed an in-game cast so he could play. When he broke his ankle playing basketball one off-season, the X-ray revealed that it had been broken once before, in another place.

"Imagine how I'll play now," Kiick told the doctor.

That was Kiick.

This, then, was the good friendship and business partnership they developed. Even Shula wasn't quite certain how it would work over the course of a long season. It involved thought, imagination, and all his developed diplomacy to make it a success. Three running backs in a two-back offense? Who did that? And why?

"I've heard of it, but I don't know what it is," Kiick said that training camp. "I've never seen it. We've never practiced it. Ask Coach Shula."

Shula was asked daily about it by reporters. He explained the idea of mixing Morris's speed and Kiick's receiving skills. He talked of creating matchup problems for the defense. For a team loaded with talent,

Shula's novel idea represented a brilliant use of it, I always thought—
the kind that received the highest praise possible in the NFL in coming
years as teams quickly copied it. But like most new ideas, it was
accepted with doubt and, even then, condensed to a common denominator everyone understood.

"Who's starting this week, Kiick or Morris?" reporters constantly
asked Shula.

When Morris started in the Kansas City opener (gaining 67 yards
on 14 carries), Kiick was outside Shula's office on Monday morning,
wanting more playing time than the 4 carries he got, for 11 yards. When
Kiick started the second game, against Houston (carrying 9 times for
55 yards), Morris was outside the coach's office despite getting 17 carries
for 79 yards. It became a scheduled part of Shula's workweek and the
season's conversation. Fans took sides. Teammates watched it play out.
And the media? It became a never-ending story.

"Kiick's Pride Stung by Lack of Activity," a *Miami Herald* headline
read one week.

"Morris Wants More Carries," a *Fort Lauderdale Sun-Sentinel* headline read another week.

"Jim Kiick Gripes and Shula Understands," a *Miami News* headline
read yet another week.

Kiick told reporters, "I've got to play more in order to get better."

Morris heard this and came back with his own line: "The more I
play, the better I get."

Back and forth it went. And back again.

Morris grasped how pivotal a time this was for him. He was talented, to be sure, with the kind of raw speed our offense lacked. He
also earned a reputation in his first three NFL seasons as lacking the
discipline to put those skills to use. Just as I left practice each day with
game film in hand, Morris later joked that he left each day with a different beautiful woman on his arm.

His mind-set about football began to change in the moments
immediately after the Super Bowl loss to Dallas. Uniform on, arms

folded, voice angry, Morris sat at his locker in New Orleans and loudly questioned the Dolphins' run-between-the-tackles strategy to reporters. That played into the strength of the Dallas defense, Morris said. Why hadn't they used his speed to run to the outside? Why didn't he have a carry all day?

Morris turned so upset that day watching his former West Texas State teammate Duane Thomas gain 95 yards rushing for Dallas that he kicked over a sideline table during the game. "The only time I got off the bench was for the kickoff and the national anthem," Morris told reporters.

A season's worth of frustration poured from Morris that day. He wanted to be a running back, he said over and over to each wave of reporters, not just a kick returner. Or he wanted to be traded.

"Hell, no, I wouldn't mind going somewhere else," he said. "I want to play. I can do it in this league if I get a chance."

Shula, already upset over the loss, heard Morris's quotes and immediately found him in the locker room. He warned that there would be trouble if Morris said anything inflammatory without first discussing it with the coaches. Fine, Morris said. And there they stood, glaring at each other. It was a high-noon scene from the Wild West, Morris remembered, as two headstrong men tried to deal with a tough day.

Morris considered that postgame rant and its predictable public fallout his first emotional step toward gaining a deserved place in the offense. There were other steps. A couple of weeks later, Morris went as a kick returner to the Pro Bowl. The elected running backs, Floyd Little and Leroy Kelly, didn't want to expose themselves to further injury by playing the complete game, so Morris played at running back as well. He gained 55 yards on 5 carries. Both coaches, John McCaffery and Tom Landry, wondered aloud why he wasn't used more in that role with the Dolphins. Morris, whose self-belief needed little strengthening, felt encouraged by their words nonetheless.

That summer, Morris was summoned to Shula's office and heard the words he wanted to hear: he would get an extended chance as a running back in the upcoming exhibition season. Shula advised Morris to report in shape. Be ready to compete. In his first three seasons, Morris had a total of 140 carries—or fewer than the 162 for Kiick and 195 for Csonka in just the 1971 season alone. The exhibition season, Shula said in that summer meeting, was a time for Morris to get ready for the regular season.

"This is your shot," Shula said.

So for the first time in his football career, Morris dedicated himself completely to his craft. He worked out on the new-age Nautilus weight machines to build up body armor. He plotted what was necessary to win the job. He counted down to the start of training camp. This represented the first genuine chance in his career, and he came into camp noticeably more focused. I saw it. Everyone did.

Morris never was the kind of personality to shrink from confrontation or the public spotlight. He gained a measure of national recognition when *Life* magazine saw a local sportswriter reference the "mercurial Morris" and photographed him as if he were the Roman god of speed. Wings were on his helmet and shoes. His body was suspended in midflight—feet off the ground, legs churning, upper torso twisted and straining. "Mercury" was born.

If his nickname was unorthodox, it fit his personality. He constantly had new cars—in 1972, it was a yellow Corvette he bought and an upscale El Dorado he received through an endorsement deal. And he talked as loud as he lived. One of his first public ventures as a Dolphin rookie in 1969 was to attend an annual Chamber of Commerce breakfast. The coach, George Wilson, spoke first and told the assembled group of businessmen and civic leaders that his hope was to win half the games that season.

"Did I just hear our coach say it was okay to lose seven games?" Morris asked when it became his turn to talk. "Well, that's not okay with me. I'm here because I want to go 14–0. If we lose the first game, I want to go 13–1, and if we lose the second, I want to go 12–2. But I certainly want to do better than 7–7."

For his first three years, Morris was used primarily as a special-teams return man. He topped out at a modest average of 4 carries a game in those seasons. What wasn't so modest was his 5.9-yard rushing average. That suggested an underutilized talent. Morris saw it. Shula saw it. That exhibition season, anyone with an open mind could see it, too. Morris led the team in rushing and provided the offense with a faster gear. After three years of not dedicating himself completely to football, he appeared ready to assume a bigger role. When asked before the Kansas City opener if he expected to play more that season, Morris, direct as ever, said, "You're damn right."

I liked that new attitude. We all did. Well, not everyone. At first, Jim Kiick wasn't upset over Morris receiving most of the work in the 1972 exhibition season. Upset? Kiick loved it. His body rested. His mind stayed fresh. After four years of starting and coming off his best statistical season—one that ended with his team in the Super Bowl—losing his job ranked far down on Kiick's list of concerns.

Later in life, as he considered Shula's decision to use Morris more and looked back on its strategic effectiveness, Kiick agreed with it in a manner he didn't in the moment. To the younger Kiick, it wasn't a decision of strategy by Shula; it was one of personal penalty, of control—a coach showing who was boss simply because he was the boss.

Kiick even pinpointed the precise moment he "lost" the job. One of his quirks was a dislike of exercise. Sit-ups? Weights? He didn't embrace such things. But a special place in his mind was reserved for the 12-minute run that Shula made a part of each training camp. The drill was simple enough: players ran as many times around a football field in those 12 minutes as possible. Each player position had a minimum distance to run. If a player didn't finish that minimum distance, he had to run the full distance the next day.

"If I'd wanted to run," Kiick told the media on the eve of the run in 1972, "I'd have run cross-country in school."

He quit eight minutes into the run that day. The flu, he said. He couldn't breathe. Csonka stopped beside him while the rest of the players continued to the end. Shula came running across the field.

"What the hell are you doing, trying to defy me in front of everyone?" he asked.

This became the moment he lost the starting job, Kiick thought all that '72 season. He was punished for not following the coach's program.

"Shula is the one who stuck it to me," Kiick wrote in *Always on the Run*, his book with Csonka that was released after the season.

"Jim shouldn't have been subjected to somebody taking his position," Csonka wrote. "The way I saw it, Shula handed Merc the opportunity at Jim's expense. Not only handed Merc the opportunity, but stepped on Jim's pride with no qualms. Step on Shula's pride and see how he reacts."

If they felt that way during the season, I never saw it. It didn't get in the way of their work or our winning.

Shula began using situation substitution in its most elementary ways in 1972. As time went on, we refined it. I used hand signals to bring in the players I wanted. I'd put two fists in the air, for instance, for a two tight-end package. Three fingers in the air meant I wanted three receivers.

If switching players was new to those of us running the offense in 1972, it was entirely unrecognized by the defenses playing against us. They never caught on to what we were doing. It sounds impossible by today's thinking, I know. But other coaches' thoughts remained contained by the idea that starters always played unless they needed a rest or were hurt. So when Morris replaced Kiick in a game, they didn't think to watch for the sweep. They just thought Kiick was tired. Or when Mandich came in for Fleming at tight end, the defenses didn't expect a pass to him. They just thought Fleming needed a break.

At game's end, Houston coach Bill Peterson, normally the most lively of personalities, sat down before the media, then immediately stood up and left. "Gentlemen, I'll be right back," he said in a shaky voice caused by our 34–13 win in which his team was never a factor. We crushed them in what became our formula against our opponents that season. We set a team record for rushes (52) and rushing yards (274). I threw just 17 passes, completing 12 for 161 yards and a touchdown. We had entire drives—eight plays, nine plays—where we ran the ball up Houston's gut.

Peterson returned to reporters from his needed break and said using Kiick and Morris in that shared manner was like "having twelve men on the field." It was like having two quarterbacks, he said, "a guy who can sprint out and one who can drop back and pass. It's awfully hard to prepare for a team like that."

We found that out as the season went on. My appreciation of Kiick grew, too. It's easy for fans and the media to discuss concepts such as sacrifice and unselfishness in general terms. The more difficult part is doing so as Kiick did in the prime of his productive career.

Kiick didn't like his new role. Who would? But he kept helping us win, and he didn't complain in public. And Shula wasn't deaf to his running backs' feelings. He tried to smooth egos without reducing his team's chances. He talked to both players constantly to explain his thinking. Morris was happier in this expanded role, but he wasn't content. In 1973 Morris had a defining game against New England with 197 yards on 15 carries—a whopping 13.1-yard average. Before the next game, against Kiick's hometown New York Jets, Shula came to him and said, "Hey, I'm starting Jim."

Morris, surprised, asked why.

"His people are in the stands," Shula answered. "Remember, I started you in Pittsburgh when your people were in the stands."

You've got to keep everyone happy. And there was only one way for that not to be an issue, I knew.

Win.

3

The Education of
a Quarterback

Before being a Hall of Fame selection, before owning Super Bowl rings, before being nicknamed the Thinking Man's Quarterback, before directing a winning team, before I was even secure as an NFL starter, I was assigned a nickname that spoke of a different player: the Scrambler.

It was more reflection of the one-year-old team I went to in 1967 than any embraced talent. The roster was thin, and the coaching, I thought, was minimal. The Dolphins' first head coach, George Wilson, was a good man riding out the back end of his career with an assembled staff of friends. Sometimes the coaches broke for lunch at Johnny Raffa's restaurant, just down the road from the Orange Bowl, and returned for the afternoon practice breathing alcohol into the huddle.

Sometimes I'd see a weakness in a defense during a game and have no play in the Dolphin system to attack it.

Always, the first thing to do when dropping back to pass in those years was to guess where the offensive line would leak on that particular play. That's why I developed a reputation as a running quarterback. Running for my life, maybe. But I certainly wasn't running by design.

"I want you to stay in the pocket," Don Shula said at our first meeting in 1970.

"Make me a pocket, and I'll stay in it," I said.

Those first few years before Shula came on board were a long and, at times, a painful process. I threw more interceptions than touchdowns. Whatever improvement came was self-taught. I became my own worst critic, prodded others for thoughts, and broke down film for hours in my home.

I didn't have the talent of a Joe Namath to carry a team. But put talent around me, and I'd draw the most out of it. When Shula provided a professional attitude, as line coach Monte Clark provided structure, and as Larry Little, Jim Langer, and Bob Kuechenberg blossomed into dominant linemen, my talents were magically revealed.

By the 1972 season, my education as an NFL quarterback was complete. No game showed that more than the third victory of the season, against Minnesota. Players agreed that this was our most physical game of the year. A bar fight. A back-alley brawl. The Dolphin defense sacked Fran Tarkenton five times and intercepted him three times. Minnesota's defense had three sacks and two interceptions of their own.

Our offensive linemen punched few holes through what they agreed was the toughest of defensive lines, the Purple People Eaters. And hard-hitting? Larry Csonka caught a swing pass with his back turned to the defense and seemed to snap in half when hit by linebacker Roy Winston. Johnny Carson replayed it the next night on the *Tonight Show* for chuckles. And if you define comedy as a man being grotesquely bent in two, it was hilarious. Csonka could hardly breathe.

He couldn't stand up. He crawled, groaning, to the Dolphin sideline just a few yards away.

"Get up! Get up!" Shula yelled at him. "They're going to think you're hurt!"

"I *am* hurt," Csonka said.

What did everyone say about Shula? That he had a high tolerance for another man's pain?

With four minutes left, Minnesota led, 14–6. Garo Yepremian had kicked field goals from 38 and 42 yards for our only scores. On fourth-and-one deep in Dolphin territory, Shula went for it. Morris gained two yards to keep hope alive. When that drive stalled, Shula had to decide whether to try a 51-yard field goal. He turned to Yepremian on the sideline.

"Can you make it?" he asked.

"Sure," Yepremian answered.

Why not? When you believe in yourself, as Yepremian did, you don't believe halfway. Shula waved on the field-goal unit. Yepremian kicked the longest field goal of his career to that point.

When we got the ball back with 2 minutes left, I threw a couple of passes to Howard Twilley and navigated the running game to the Vikings' 3-yard line. There were 19 seconds left. Standing in the huddle, Jim Mandich later said he knew what play was coming. Everyone did. Give Csonka the ball. Give Csonka the game.

"I-19 split delay," I called.

This was an era when quarterbacks called their own plays in the NFL. Mandich wondered if he heard right. That wasn't the punch up the gut with Csonka. It was a pass to Mandich. He didn't show his surprise. No one did, really. That's part of the code on the inside. Run the play. Run it without doubt, question, or often even thought when it came down to it.

Later, turning the decision over in his mind, Mandich understood the thinking to the play. Everyone *knew* Csonka would get the ball. Sometimes the best play is the simplest one, where you dare the defense to stop you. But against a great defense like Minnesota's, when great players knew exactly what to expect, that's the time you drop in a surprise. This was the place to do it, too.

I had developed two rules for goal-line offenses. The first was not to change plays at the line of scrimmage. The noise, the demands, the utter urgency of the moment worked against an audible. Players couldn't be assured of hearing the change with the end-zone crowd noise. Plus everyone was so geared up for the moment, they might just move at the quarterback's voice instead of waiting to hear the call.

The second rule was strategic: First down is the best time to throw. That provided the best element of surprise. There also was the lack of space in succeeding downs if you move in closer and make the end zone easier to cover.

This I-19 split delay wasn't a new play. We'd used it previously. Minnesota knew about it. And I knew they knew about it. But surprise was an ally here, and we could use every ally possible.

At the line, as I surveyed the Minnesota defense, it was clear the play would work just as drawn up. At the snap, I turned as if to hand off to Csonka, who ran up the middle like he was going to take the handoff. Mandich mock-blocked for an extended second on the line—the "delay" part of the name.

Csonka barreled empty-armed into the line. Mandich slid past the line and moved into an open area of the end zone. I then stood up and threw to an open Mandich for the simplest of touchdowns. Mandich jumped up and down, celebrating. Marv Fleming ran to him, jumping. Csonka loved it.

Shula stood there at the sideline, extending his hand, a smile on his face.

The Scrambler? Not anymore.

I was the middle child of Sylverius and Ida Griese in a very close and relatively poor family in Evansville, Indiana. Sylverius (whom everyone called Slick) had a plumbing business. He stretched the budget so my older brother, Bill, and I had enough equipment to play sports. My dad put up a basketball hoop in an alley behind our home.

Sports were something fun for us to do, a reward for chores and keeping grades up, not something pushed. My dad was a fan more than a demanding parent. A family story about what may be my first hit in youth baseball shows that.

"That's my boy!" Dad yelled. "That's my boy who got that hit!"

Still elated, still yelling, he didn't realize what happened after I rounded first base and kept running until Mom yanked him back into the seat.

"Sit down, Slick. Your boy just got thrown out at second," she said.

I was small and scrappy, and Dad saw something in me that no one else did. One day at a game, he leaned over to his wife, pointed at me, and said, "This boy is going to be a great athlete someday."

Mom chuckled. "That little bitty boy is going to be a great athlete?"

Still, the moment that defined my youth didn't come on an athletic field. It arrived one morning when I was ten. I awoke to find that my father had suffered a heart attack during the night and died. Mom, raw with shock, sat down Bill, me, and my younger sister, Joyce, and told us. Mom was lost in its immediate aftermath, and her children were, too.

As family and friends gathered at our home that day, Mom suddenly realized I was missing. She searched through the house. Soon people were running all over the neighborhood looking and calling for me. Mom then heard a thumping noise from upstairs in one of the bedrooms. She opened a closet door. There I was, sitting on a cedar chest in the dark, alone, thumping my heels against the chest. Evidently that was how I chose to deal with the pain.

One moment stayed with me forever from my dad's funeral. Mom walked us up to the coffin just before it closed. "Take one final look at your father," she said. "You won't see him again."

The entire episode traumatized me to the point that years later, when I was losing my wife, Judi, to breast cancer, I gave considerable thought about the best manner to shepherd our three sons through their grief. My youngest son, Brian, was twelve. I felt awful for him and for our family history repeating itself. But we got through it, depending on each other. When Brian became a NFL quarterback in Denver, he started a charitable foundation to help children deal with the emotional loss of a parent. You know how proud that made me feel?

There was no such support when I lost my father. Everyone suffered terribly. Beyond trying to keep her emotions afloat, Mom dealt with the financial implications of raising three children. She kept the plumbing business alive for a while. Eventually she sold it, and she became a secretary to support the family.

Looking back with an adult's perspective, Dad's death impacted my personality deeply in a couple of ways. It made a young boy pull deep within himself. It made me change from a normal, outgoing child to the reserved, introspective personality that people have seen since.

A second outgrowth became something of a benefit in sports. I became coachable in the best sense of the word. While friends received fundamental sports lessons from their fathers—hold your hand this way; move under the ball like this—I relied on coaches to impart such lessons. As a result, I became a world-class listener. I trusted what people with more knowledge than I said. I loved playing sports and wanted to learn more, and my youth coaches became the main avenue to help.

When this trait of being coachable combined with a midwestern work ethic and a natural athletic talent, I became a three-sport star at Rex Mundi High School in Evansville. Baseball, the first sport I played, was my first love. I was a pitcher from the start of Little League at age eight, and played on every age-group team through my senior high school season, when Evansville advanced to the American Legion World Series in Keane, New Hampshire. My pitching record was 11–0 that summer on the heels of a 6–0 high school season record. The day before Evansville's opener in the World Series, a Baltimore Oriole scout introduced himself and inquired about any interest in signing a contract with the team. This was the year before the baseball draft was introduced, and teams signed any prospect they wanted.

I told the scout I was attending Purdue on a football scholarship and planned to get an education. I then promptly went out and pitched awfully, and we lost the game. I figured the scout was happy there was no signed contract. A couple of weeks later, I was at Purdue for the start of the football workouts when a senior lineman knocked on my door, upset at performing an errand for a lowly freshman.

"Rook, there's a phone call for you," he said.

It was the Orioles' scout again.

"You're really going to school and playing football?" he asked.

As a kid, I never aspired to be a quarterback, probably because I rarely played the position. Until high school, I only played pickup football, often with my older brother's friends. That meant I often was the last player chosen in games and typically was reduced to snapping the ball before running a pass route.

Rex Mundi was a new high school with new, young players when I was a freshman. It was so new, my brother was allowed to finish his time at the traditional neighborhood school. That set up an intrafamily rivalry during football games. As a freshman, I tried out for the football team. The coach, Ken Coudret, asked what position I played.

"Receiver," I said.

"Don't you pitch in baseball?" he asked.

The new school needed a quarterback. It needed everything, actually. As a freshman, I passed the football, ran with it, kicked extra points and field goals, and even punted. Coudret was a good fundamental coach who taught me what football was about. He also was a former collegiate defensive lineman who had three passing plays in his offense. That explains in part why I was better known in high school as an all-around athlete. I was named all-state in basketball. Baseball was perhaps my most developed game. But football presented the only scholarship offers, limited as they were. Indiana and Purdue. That was it. My mom's boss, an Evansville businessman named Ferris Traylor, was a Purdue alum. He called the coaching staff. As much as anything, his connection to Purdue helped make my decision to go there.

At first, I saw college as an athletic extension of high school. I wanted to play everything at this higher level of competition, not just football. Purdue head football coach Jack Mollenkopf said while recruiting that I could play baseball. With nothing to do in the winter, I went out for the freshman basketball team. We often practiced against the varsity team, and it became clear early on that I fit in with collegiate talent. I was a starting guard as a sophomore on Purdue's basketball team, with a trademark of shutting down the opposing team's perimeter scorer. In fact, years later, Mark Rudner, the Big Ten's communications director, approached me about a surprising radio interview he heard. Cazzie Russell, by then a retired University of Michigan and NBA star, was asked by the show's host to name the best defender he ever faced.

"College or pro?" Russell asked.

"Either one," the interviewer said.

"Bob Griese."

"Bob Griese, the football player?"

"He wouldn't let me get the ball," Russell said. "It's hard to score when you don't have the ball."

After my sophomore year, I dropped basketball. Baseball already had gone from view as a freshman when Mollenkopf said, "If you play baseball, you ruin any chance to compete for the starting quarterback job in spring practices."

The quarterback job seemed beyond hope at the time anyhow. Six quarterbacks were ahead of me. Since freshmen were ineligible, I had spent the fall season shuffling between quarterback and defensive back while coaches decided on which position was better. The most questionable part of my game was a sidearm throwing motion, a souvenir from baseball pitching. My passes sometimes wobbled. Some veered. With their defensive backgrounds, my high school coaches never corrected it.

Still, I began rising on the depth chart as Purdue's spring practices progressed. What did I do to achieve that? Whatever I was told. I threw to the right receiver. I called the proper plays against the given defense. I moved the offense. In short, I demonstrated an understanding of the role of my position. All the intangibles coaches look for in quarterbacks were my strengths: leadership, smarts, game. And command of the huddle? I might be a freshman still growing accustomed to college life and, after practice, would carry upperclassmen's pads off the practice field as the rite of passage demanded. But in the huddle it didn't matter if I was the youngest or the weakest. I barked at seniors. I demanded better play from the line. Leadership skills at a leadership position, the Purdue coaches quickly realized, were something I had.

By the end of spring practices, I was Purdue's starting quarterback. The offensive coordinator, Bob DeMoss, understood that I was raw and that he was a gifted coach who had the ability to teach quarterbacks. Len Dawson, who by then was an NFL star, developed at Purdue before my time. Mike Phipps, who also played in the pros, came after me.

DeMoss saw something in this skinny kid from Evansville. But he was stumped through spring practices at the mechanical problem in my motion. What exactly was wrong? And how could it be corrected?

Early that summer, DeMoss had a visit from his mentor, Cecil Isbell, a former Green Bay Packer quarterback famed for throwing to Don Hutson. As they talked, DeMoss mentioned the undetected flaw.

"This kid knows how to play quarterback, but he can't throw the football," DeMoss said. "I don't know what's wrong."

DeMoss turned on a film projector. Isbell watched two plays and said to turn off the projector. He saw the problem.

"He's not turning out his wrist when he throws," Isbell said.

I was called in and shown the problem. They gave me some drills to correct the motion. Remember how well I listened? I worked all summer on those various drills. Kneeling on a step. Throwing the ball from behind my ear. Following through. Checking the elbow. Again.

And again. When we reported for practice that August, the flaws were gone. I threw spirals. I was more accurate.

DeMoss taught me the next progression in a good quarterback: how to read defenses. Start with the safeties' positioning. Are they up close, threatening blitz? Back in two-deep coverage? Move to the cornerbacks. Are they bump-and-run on receivers or playing off? Finally, look at the linebackers' eyes. Sometimes they'd tip what back they were covering or an upcoming stunt with a defensive lineman.

This habit caused me to feel a pulse of panic as a Dolphin rookie in my first exhibition game. I looked across the line into the eyes of Chicago linebacker Dick Butkus.

Butkus glared back.

"What the fuck am I out here for playing against a goddamn rookie from Purdue?" he shouted across the line.

Flustered, I didn't settle behind center. I put hands under guard Larry Little.

"What you doing, rookie?" Little said.

At Purdue, there was no such learning curve. In my first game, I scored every Purdue point in a 17–0 win against Ohio University. Ran for two touchdowns. Kicked two extra points and a field goal.

That started four fun years in college. As a junior, I led an upset against top-ranked Notre Dame, completing 19 of 22 passes for 283 yards and 3 touchdowns. "The greatest single performance I have ever witnessed," Notre Dame coach Ara Parseghian called it.

I was named to the All-America team my final two years at Purdue and finished college with a 15–14 win in the Rose Bowl against junior O. J. Simpson's Southern California team.

That was it. Football was done. In 1967, there wasn't the buildup to the draft and pro football like today. With a degree in industrial management, I planned to find a job at a blue-chip company like Procter & Gamble or Johnson & Johnson. I was getting married to Judi immediately after graduating, too. My mind was full of those ideas, not the NFL draft.

I wasn't even sure when the draft was being held. March? April? This was years before draft combines, draft gurus, wall-to-wall draft coverage, and teams being put on the clock. The idea of being drafted was out there, but I never had workouts with teams or was visited that spring by scouts.

Then one day in March, I entered the Purdue football office and someone mentioned I was drafted by the Dolphins.

"Oh, I was?"

The more I thought of it and heard about the money, the more it made sense. I'd give it a try. That's as far as it went in my mind. A try. One or two years before moving to the real world of business.

I had no idea how to read a pro defense or attack that caliber of athlete. But quarterback Rick Norton, the Dolphins' number-one pick the year before, later said he saw me work in the opening practices and that that marked the end of his career. Of course, he also noted one other substantial difference.

"Two steps," he said. "Bob was quick enough to get out of bounds after being chased by the rush. I was two steps slower, and the defense would knock the hell out of me."

The plan was to break in slowly and get accustomed to the pro game. That changed in the opening minutes of the opening game. John Stofa broke his ankle.

"You're on the offense," Wilson told me on the sideline.

That first game worked like a dream. We played a weak Denver team, led the entire game, scored the most points in franchise history—okay, the franchise was just a year old—and won easily, 35–21.

Unfortunately, the next week's opponent was a powerful Kansas City team just off a Super Bowl loss to Green Bay. We were beaten, 24–0. I felt like a kid lost in the mall. It wasn't simply the scope of the Kansas City talent. I hadn't called plays at Purdue, and that was a big part of the job in the pros. I called plays without consideration of blocking schemes or tactical matchups. I didn't know what it meant when the cornerback shaded over the inside shoulder of the receivers or the free safety lined up behind the weak side linebacker.

"What's he doing that for?" I thought, watching the defensive nuances of a great team.

After that loss, I vowed it would be the last time I went unprepared into a game. Maybe we wouldn't win. Maybe I wouldn't play well. But lack of preparation would not be the problem. I got a movie projector the next week, set it up in my home office, and began a routine of bringing home game films to study that lasted the rest of my career.

On Tuesdays, the offense went over film of the previous game with the coaching staff. I then took the film home, sat in that office at night, and projected the film on a wall. I ran plays back and forth, again and again, and fully critiqued every play. Options that weren't seen during the game became obvious now. Decisions were second-guessed. I also read teammates' strengths and weaknesses in ways beyond the more general tone discussed in the coaches' film sessions. This is how I taught myself and evolved from a young, relatively untutored quarterback into a knowledgeable professional.

On Wednesday nights, a different film canister came home with a different lesson. This was the film of the upcoming opponent. In school, I enjoyed the process of applying mathematical formulas to solve problems. Anyone could turn to the back of a textbook to read the answer. But to understand the answer meant unlocking the proper concepts and following them to the correct solution. It was much the same at quarterback, I thought. Fans saw quarterbacks throw to open receivers. But the thinking that was required for a quarterback to find the proper receiver, play after play, game after game, required unlocking football formulas unknown to the casual fan.

Midway through my rookie year, I was studying the New York Jets' defense when something clicked. On some plays, by focusing on the free safety, I understood the coverage of the entire secondary. On other plays, I understood how cornerbacks were shading receivers to the inside, expecting a teammate's help there. These were simple keys that applied to every defense in some form. And I began to apply them.

On Thursday nights, a deeper analysis of the defense was studied. What did the defense do on third downs? How did it set up inside the 20-yard line? What tendencies did it have?

I saw that defensive coordinators didn't attempt to hide their schemes or vary their calls too much—at least when you knew what you were looking for.

Such discoveries made a job filled with all sorts of pressures and difficulties much simpler and less threatening. When Earl Morrall arrived in 1972, he was struck by how I could look at a defensive alignment and describe what each defender would do even before the ball was snapped. He said he'd never seen anyone play quarterback that way. And Morall worked with plenty of great quarterbacks in his eighteen years, including Y. A. Tittle, Fran Tarkenton, and John Unitas. Like them, Morrall simply waited for the snap of the ball, made a few quick reads, and allowed a veteran's feel for the game guide him. He couldn't describe precisely what he was doing from defense to defense. He just knew how to do it very well.

It was an art form as Morrall played it, and more of a science the way I did. Without coaching to guide me those first years, I invented ways to improve my craft that fit my personality. No nuance was too little. Each week, our players received the game plan on a sheet of paper organized by formations. I-formation plays were under one column, for instance, and split-back formations under another. I cut out the individual plays and taped each one over the offensive lineman's position where it was designed to run. A split-back play where Larry Csonka ran between the center and right guard was taped on the paper between the center and that right guard. A Mercury Morris sweep around right end would be written on the sheet wide of the right end.

That way, in the middle of the game, while needing a play to attack a certain area, I visualized the plays to do just that.

Just as I was scouting defenses, they were scouting me.

I need to know what they know, I thought.

A sideline attendant began charting plays I was calling on each down in addition to the opposing defensive scheme. The plays were written in different colors—blue for first-down plays, green for second downs, and red for third downs. Thus, on the sideline, I could make a quick read of the third-down defenses being played. I looked for patterns to attack and clues of game plans.

"It's like he's looking in my head," Buffalo safety Pete Richardson once said about me.

I was trying, anyhow.

I also came to understand that a prime job during the week was gathering information. That led me to something that was rare for quarterbacks at that time: Sit in on offensive line meetings. Listen to their assignments.

"Give me a play that you think will work," I'd say.

Armed with that knowledge, I made play calls with blocking assignments in mind, never wanting to put a lineman in a position to fail, a fact the linemen appreciated. A block that might work for tight end Marv Fleming, who was a great blocker, might not with Jim Mandich, who was a better receiver.

I regularly asked teammates for updates as games went on, too. Was a defensive lineman soft? Was a pattern open? Had someone on their line hurt a knee or a shoulder? And again: What plays do you think will work?

That took knowing my teammates, too. Guard Bob Kuechenberg always had such a long list of effective plays that a different tack was taken.

"Bob, tell me what plays you don't like," I'd say.

Paul Warfield went the other way, as befitting his quiet personality.

"Well . . ." he would say if I asked whether he had been open on a certain play.

That was enough. I understood it was Warfield-speak for the fact that he was open and to get him the ball. Guys learned to provide good information, too.

"Hey, I thought you said you were open in that game," I'd say the next week in a film session. "Run that film back."

We'd watch it again.

"Does that look like you're open?"

That put across my message to make sure you didn't exaggerate or call for the ball without merit. The manner in which I led and motivated, some teammates came to think, was through knowledge. I studied so much and read defenses so well that they trusted whatever play I called. Mercury Morris thought that in my first few seasons, my reserved nature coupled with my knowledge carried an intimidation factor. Once, I noticed as I stood under center that Morris lined up wrong for a play. With no time to change the play and not wanting a delay-of-game penalty, I had to call a time-out. I turned and glared at Morris for an extended second, saying nothing. Morris felt worse than if he had been chewed out.

My talent wasn't my arm, legs, voice, or motivational karma. It was incorporating some great players into a winning offense. With this powerful offensive line and potent running-back combination in 1972, I understood that the best way to win was with a ball-control ground game. We ran the ball more than two times for every pass that season. We set the record for most rushing yards in a season.

That led people to say I couldn't pass. Maybe I didn't have the strongest arm. But maybe I just thought the number-one idea was to win. Later that decade, with Csonka, Kiick, and Morris gone, my arm became a more integral part of the offense. In 1977, I threw a career-high 22 touchdowns, including 6 in a win against St. Louis. *Sport* magazine asked five All-Pro defenders to rate the NFL's quarterbacks on thirteen different categories. I received perfect scores on reading defenses and play-calling, as well as a near-perfect score on short-to-medium passing. Two seasons from retiring, I received my lowest scores on throwing the deep ball, but I finished with 269.5 total points. Roger Staubach was voted the NFL's best quarterback in the magazine's poll, with 270 points.

Joe Thomas probably had it right in comparing me not to Namath or Billy Kilmer or any of the quarterbacks who carried themselves with a big arm or a swaggering personality. Thomas thought I was closer to an efficient quarterback like Green Bay's Bart Starr, right down to how we carried ourselves.

"Listen to them talk, you'd think they were twins," Thomas said.

Shula was a crucial key for my career. He organized and disciplined a team in a manner that allowed his preparation to count. He also backed me in a moment when my career could have gone either way. After a 4–1 start in 1970, we were shut out in consecutive games. When I threw a careless pass in the next game against Philadelphia that was intercepted, I was benched. Stofa rallied the offense to two fourth-quarter touchdowns. All the ingredients for a quarterback controversy were on the table. Doubts. Competition. And public debate?

Fans chanted, "We want Stofa." *Miami News* columnist Al Levine wrote a column about Griese titled, "Is This the Quarterback to Bring Miami a Title?" Another local columnist listed the names of fifty quarterbacks who were better than Griese. Among them were retired quarterbacks Eagle Day, Sammy Baugh, and Eddie LeBaron, even New York sports columnist Stan Isaacs. "All these are better than the Dolphins No. 1 quarterback. Now," Levine's column read.

Howard Schnellenberger, our offensive coordinator, remembers this as a significant moment for Shula. And for me. "It wasn't a decision he [Shula] asked anyone about," Schnellenberger said. "Don had to settle it for himself."

Before the first practice following that Philadephia game, Shula said in a team meeting that Griese was his starting quarterback. And he didn't just say it. He underlined it to his players so there would be no misunderstanding.

"I don't care what any of you say, what the press says, even what the owner says," Shula said. "Bob is our quarterback. He will remain our quarterback. He will be the quarterback the rest of the year no matter what."

That was that. Shula could focus any complex situation into a simple thought, and the simple thought here was that the franchise needed to get fully behind me.

The speech had its intended effect. Warfield, who saw my confidence at a low point in this stretch, noticed an immediate difference even in how I carried myself. And maybe since Shula believed in me, I believed in myself again. The next game, I completed 15 of 19 passes for 225 yards and was named the AFC's Offensive Player of the Week as the Dolphins beat New Orleans.

"I saw a guy who stood in there and proved he was the quarterback everyone thought he was," Warfield told reporters after that game.

From that point, I felt secure. We finished that regular season winning six straight games before losing to Oakland in the playoffs. I was named to the Pro Bowl team that year. I was the Pro Bowl starter by 1971.

And by 1972?

Shula's handshake as I came off the field in Minnesota said enough.

4

The Color of Miami

My education as a young quarterback didn't include just breaking down film at home or working overtime with the new coaches. In the summer of 1970, I walked into my assigned dorm room at Biscayne College for training camp and found a new roommate holding out his hand.

"Hi, I'm Paul Warfield."

I chuckled. "I know who you are."

Know? I had admired Warfield from afar for years. The speed. The grace. The professional ethic. Warfield was considered by most football people to be the best receiver in the league when he was traded from the Cleveland Browns to Miami that off-season. He led NFL receivers in touchdowns in 1968. He was in a six-year run of averaging more than 20 yards a catch. His talent immediately provided our offense with a new, downfield dimension defenses had to fear.

Plus, I figured, Warfield was someone to learn from, especially as roommates. But then everyone wanted to learn from him. Veteran receivers Larry Seiple and Howard Twilley studied Warfield each practice to glean anything to apply to their games. Stretching. Route running. Body angles. Anything. And the defense? They gauged themselves each day against him. The first time cornerback Lloyd Mumphord went against Warfield, Mumphord was beaten so badly on a simple 5-yard pattern that he became flustered.

Warfield's reputation was so respected that when tight end Jim Mandich was traded to Pittsburgh in 1978 he was quickly cornered by its young receivers Lynn Swann and John Stallworth. They wanted to know how Warfield practiced. What drills he did. How he ran the down-and-out pattern. The post? What about his homework? His footwork?

Greatness wasn't an accident, Mandich told them. He told them what every Dolphin saw right from that first training camp. Twilley, a twelfth-round pick who forged a career through hard work, was stunned to see Warfield putting in extra work after most practices.

"He works as hard as I do," Twilley said to me.

The manner of that work fascinated me, too. Warfield intellectualized football. At Ohio State he studied anatomy, kinesiology, and psychology to focus his football mind. In anatomy, for instance, he examined how the abductor and adductor muscles work in the hip rotation of a receiver making a cut. This type of detail, he was certain, allowed him to develop and concentrate on those muscles and thus improve his athletic movement on the field. Although Vince Lombardi's famous line stated that "fatigue makes cowards of us all," Warfield thought differently. In one class he hooked a frog's muscles to a machine that worked them repetitively until they were fatigued. Lombardi was wrong in his thinking, he concluded. Muscles simply fatigue at some point and nothing could be done about it.

Warfield was meticulous in his habits, too. As a world-class long jumper, he ranked fifth internationally in the early 1960s despite competing only during the spring season. He became part of a U.S. national team that competed against the Soviets before sellout crowds at Stanford Stadium. His long jump there of 26 feet, 2 1/2 inches that year was only 3 1/2 inches less than the gold-medal-winning jump by Lynn Davies of Great Britain at the 1964 Summer Olympics. Warfield would have been part of that team, too, except he was entering his rookie pro season and couldn't risk losing the time or the money.

In long jumping, Warfield measured his stride so that on a 130-foot, 5-inch run his left foot always hit the takeoff board perfectly. He brought this same discipline to running pass patterns in football. He ran the same initial four steps every play to prey on the defender's mind. Run. Pass. Deep pattern. Short pattern. The first four steps never changed. Warfield could be heard the first couple of weeks of any training camp counting steps out loud as he ran—"One, two, three, four"— to find his invisible grass board for a 5-yard hitch pattern or 15-yard down-and-out.

After practice, Warfield didn't just run patterns against an imaginary cornerback. If he was covered one-on-one, Warfield considered that completion a sure thing. A gimme. He always practiced against various forms of imaginary double coverage. He always talked everything through with me, educating me on what he was doing and where he thought the ball should be thrown. I'd often line up under a mock center in these sessions, ready to run the play, and see Warfield walking in from the receiver's position to explain in detail what he planned to do.

"Okay, Bob, we're going against a double zone, and I'm going to release inside, get downfield 15 yards to where I'm upon the safety and pressure him, threaten him, to where he doesn't know if I'm running a square-in post, square-out, or corner," he'd say. "I'll put a move to the outside and . . ."

These were lessons delivered in Warfield's methodical manner of speech. That provided amusing sidelights later when I asked receivers in game huddles what routes were open. Warfield would begin explaining how he noticed a cornerback's technique and provide involved details of why he could get open until, pressed to call a play, I had to interrupt.

"Paul," I'd say, "just tell me what's open."

That fourth win of the '72 season, against the New York Jets, revealed again that there was plenty open. This was one of those rare games where we loosened the valve of the passing game some. I completed 16 of 27 passes for 220 yards and a touchdown. That might not sound like much. But in the five years from 1970 to 1974 comprising our great run, in any given game I threw more than 27 passes only once.

Warfield, of course, was the prime target. In this game against the Jets he caught a season-high 5 passes for 71 yards against a secondary pointed to stop him.

"He was just too good," Jet coach Weeb Ewbank said. "The worst part is he not only made the catches against double coverage a lot of times, but he opened up the rest of the passing game for other guys."

Double coverage didn't bother me with Warfield. Other receivers wondered sometimes why more throws weren't at the single coverage they received. It was because of those practice sessions, I came to understand. Warfield reduced the danger of double coverage by walking me through his thoughts and precisely explaining his plan of attack. I understood what a benefit it was to know exactly what the receiver intended to do against complex coverages. We weren't just on the same page, we often were reading the same words on that page at the same time.

What I noticed was how Warfield never acted like the superstar he was. He carried himself like another guy just trying to make the team.

"Did I run that right?" he'd ask me after a play in practice.

"Was that better?" he'd ask later.

"Nice throw," he'd say.

As roommates, we'd carry on-field discussions off the field. How to run a post. How to set up coverages. Warfield was full of thoughts from the moment he arrived. I lapped up the knowledge. This, of course, was partially why Shula came up with the rooming assignments before that training camp in 1970.

The other reason?

I'm white.

Warfield is black.

And Shula was concerned about a problem inside the team.

The racial component didn't matter to Warfield or to me. We were both from the Midwest. We both played and lived among the other race. We didn't even know this was some type of social experiment, really, until someone pointed it out to us.

Even then, we shrugged.

Shula, however, gave this a lot of thought. He noticed that sports weren't simply moving with the shifting social currents of the times, they sometimes set the pace. Sports often had been a principal vehicle over the previous decade to address racial inequities. The St. Louis Cardinals bought a hotel in the mid-1960s so blacks and whites could live together in the segregated city of St. Petersburg during spring training. American sprinters Tommie Smith and John Carlos created an international incident by raising black-gloved fists on the medal stand at the 1968 Summer Olympics in Mexico City. Black students at Penn State aired their grievances on the field at halftime of a football game in 1970. *Sports Illustrated* ran a cover story detailing prejudice titled, "The Black Athlete—A Shameful Story."

A move to Miami at this time was met with caution by many black players. It was a city rooted in the Deep South. Less than a decade earlier, a skinny black kid jogged daily in predawn hours from the black streets of Overtown across MacArthur Causeway to the lily-white town of Miami Beach. Police often stopped him. Blacks needed an identification card after dark, according to the laws of Miami Beach.

"Yes, that's Cassius Clay, that's our guy," boxing trainer Angelo Dundee told police when they called to verify the kid's story.

"A Caucasian town," running back Hubert Ginn called the Miami he found upon arriving to the Dolphins in 1970.

It was changing slowly, however, and no one measured that change better than Larry Little, the team's star guard. Little grew up in Overtown and saw a different world in the 1950s and early 1960s than most of his Dolphins teammates. He rode in the back of buses. He sneaked sips from "white only" water fountains to see if it tasted different. Every school he attended was segregated, as were his athletic games throughout his youth. The only public beach he legally could visit was Virginia Key on Key Biscayne. When he walked a few blocks from home to attend University of Miami football games in the Orange Bowl, he sat in bleachers designated for blacks. The all-city teams published by the newspapers were only for white players. In his entire youth, the only whites Little saw in his world owned a corner store or did the monthly bill collecting in the neighborhood.

But Little never thought of what he was denied or didn't have. He grew up happy, and if there was a white world he didn't see, the opposite held true as well. There was an entire world full of successful blacks that whites didn't know anything about. His parents—his mother worked as domestic help; his dad labeled himself the "Superintendent of Services" for a hotel—imbued their children with a healthy sense of self. His older brother, George, was Larry's hero growing up. He attended Howard University on an academic scholarship and became an actor and singer. His younger brother, David, became a standout linebacker for the Pittsburgh Steelers.

The fact that none of Florida's major colleges recruited black players at the time didn't enter Little's thinking when he graduated in 1963 from Booker T. Washington High, one of Miami's five black high schools. His dream of playing in the NFL was attainable. Sunday afternoons showed him that on a grainy black-and-white television set. The closest NFL teams to Miami were Washington and Baltimore, and there were televised role models to watch on each of those teams. Baltimore had standout black players like Big Daddy Lipscomb and Jim Parker. Washington added Bobby Mitchell in 1958. When Little became an All-American nose tackle at Bethune-Cookman, he wore number 76 in honor of Lipscomb.

What's more, many of these black college teams were better than the white college teams he grew up watching in the Orange Bowl, he was certain. Teams such as Florida A&M, Tennessee State, and Grambling had too much speed and athleticism to be contained by Miami, Florida, or Florida State.

A more tangible problem for Little out of high school was that these upper-level black football programs didn't recruit him. They didn't consider him talented enough. He found out later that his high school coach, who attended Florida A&M, said he couldn't make it. Little went to Bethune-Cookman in Daytona Beach, where he became a standout defensive lineman and remained insulated in a blackcentric world.

"The first white guy I ever hit in football was when I went to the San Diego Chargers' camp," Little said.

That was as an undrafted rookie 1967. Two years later he walked into an Overtown bar during the off-season and saw his former high school teammate and Dolphin cornerback Mack Lamb.

"I've been traded to the Dolphins," Little said.

"That's great. We'll be teammates again," Lamb answered.

"No, Mack, I've been traded for you."

Little returned to live in Miami and saw that the closed world he knew as a kid was opening some. Cubans moved into the city and settled in the Orange Bowl area. Blacks and whites mingled more freely than in his youth. The next generation didn't draw the lines so definitively on racial barriers, though it still was the Deep South, a fact that was apparent in ways big and small, especially for many of the other Dolphins.

Warfield had lived his entire life in Ohio, and was concerned upon being traded to the Dolphins about his family moving so far south. His grandfather had been a sharecropper on the Kentucky-Tennessee border, after all, and Paul heard some family stories about the South. When the time came to go to Miami, he decided to keep his family in Cleveland. He'd go south alone at first.

• • •

Shula wasn't concerned about the social evolution of blacks and whites in the broader America. His world consisted of those 100 yards. But he cared about anything that affected his team's unity and thus, he felt, its performance. His eyes were opened after a trade for tight end Marv Fleming in May 1970.

Shula stood in the locker room before players he had known only a few months and introduced Fleming as a player most of them knew, a winner of two Super Bowl rings, and the kind of veteran this team could use.

Fleming then stepped forward and introduced himself.

"Hey! Hey! Hey!" he yelled. "What is this here?"

He pointed to one side of the locker room.

"All the blacks over here!"

He pointed to the other side.

"All the whites over there!"

He looked slowly from one side to the other again. He shook his head. He chuckled in a way that didn't sound like a chuckle. Fleming was the first black tight end in Green Bay Packer history, but joked that Vince Lombardi recognized only three colors: gold, green, and Italian.

Black? White? No one had any issue with that inside the Packers. That was one element, Fleming was sure, that helped them become the NFL's dominant team. So this first trip into the Dolphins' locker room was revealing to him, even if it wasn't surprising.

When Fleming was traded to the Dolphins and heard the contract terms that would double his pay, he hugged his agent. He understood the business of football better than most players. He knew how to play the game off the field, too. So in the first meeting with Dolphins' owner Joe Robbie and general manager Joe Thomas he said, "It's a nice contract, but I have reservations."

His agent stepped on Fleming's foot under the table. Reservations? But it was true. Fleming did have reservations. He grew up in a racially tranquil environment in California, playing sports with and against racially diverse teams. He attended the white-bread University of Utah, where he roomed with George Seifert, the future coach of the San Francisco 49ers and the Carolina Panthers. He also had white roommates with the Packers. But there's one thing he had never done in football, something he would have to do now, something he did with a certain measure of trepidation.

"I've never played below the Mason-Dixon line before," he told Robbie and Thomas.

Thomas and Robbie were silent. What exactly did that mean? Was it a problem? Would he refuse to report? Could they work out a deal?

Over the next several minutes, Thomas and Robbie gained insight into the business mind of their new player. Fleming allowed how his reservations about the South might go away if he got a new car in the deal. A Buick, to be precise. The Dolphin brass quickly looked at each other and agreed. Fleming got the car.

But it was one thing to know there might be issues with living in the South. It was another to stand below the Mason-Dixon line for the first time and see a fault line inside the team. The Dolphins wanted veteran leadership from him? Well, he dropped his equipment bag that day in the middle of the Dolphins' locker room. He looked again at his new teammates.

"You don't mind if I dress right here, do you?" he asked.

He began to change into his workout clothes right there, too. Right in the middle of the locker room. Shula watched this scene unfold and understood this was a bit of inheritance he needed to change immediately in his first season as Dolphins' coach. Truth is, this racial divide bubbled inside the team for years. Even if it didn't cause open problems, all the ingredients were there for one.

"There's a sticky situation here at Dolphin camp," Mercury Morris wrote in a rookie diary for the *Miami News* in 1969. "I've been doing my best to get rid of it. There's de facto segregation being practiced here, and it's as much my Black brothers' fault as anyone else's."

The dining hall, Morris noted, was broken down by race. Blacks sat with blacks. Whites with whites. Maybe that was understandable, given that people sat with whom they were most comfortable. But the idea stretched into every avenue of their worlds.

"One day I walked into the shower and saw all the Black fellas crowded into one area, and the whites off to another side," Morris wrote. "I said, 'Oh, no, we can't have this stuff.' So I moved them all about, mixing them up. I want us to be a team. All that dirty water rolls down one drain."

It wasn't just blacks and whites clumsily feeling their way through these times like a person in a dark room. Sometimes it broke down to players from the North and players from the South. Morris grew up in Pittsburgh and was considered brash, even abrasive with his words, by many black and white players alike. Eventually he and Larry Little would become best of friends, a relationship that carried through life so that into their sixties they might talk a few times a day. But that first year together showed how uncharted the times were. Morris wanted to effect immediate change inside the team. He often pointed out problems, directly and loudly, like in the newspaper column he wrote. Little thought Morris was a know-it-all who spoke out too loudly. And not just on racial topics. On everything. Music. Weather. Football. So the two clashed regularly, even in the team huddle in games.

"Shut up, Merc!" Little would shout.

"You can't shut me up!" Morris would shout back.

But if Morris could be dismissed by many players as a loud kid when he arrived, Fleming was someone else entirely. He reeked of success and carried himself accordingly. It wasn't just football. Fleming earned his stockbroker, real estate agent, and pilot's licenses while a player. He took acting lessons and went on to become accomplished enough for a speaking role after football in the 1978 movie *Heaven Can Wait* ("Mr. Farnsworth, have you ever played college ball before?" he asked Warren Beatty's character).

While a Packer, Fleming also befriended John Y. Brown and invested $8,000 in one of the business mogul's new ventures called Kentucky Fried Chicken. In just the first six months, Fleming made $200,000.

Most of all, Fleming had those Super Bowl rings and his Green Bay heritage to reinforce his introductory words to the Dolphins. To Shula, perhaps most of all. The next day when players arrived to work, they found the locker room changed.

Offensive players were on one side.

Defensive players were on the other side.

They weren't defined by colors anymore. They were organized by units. That was Shula's plan anyhow. And in the coming days he would carry it further. He put hair care for black players, such as picks and Afro Sheen, in the locker room.

"How's that working out?" he once asked the white fullback Larry Csonka.

"How would I know?" Csonka answered.

The black players appreciated Shula's effort more than the actual benefit. It said he was trying. It suggested that a new and better mind-set was coming in with the new coach. Slowly, over time, concerns diminished, prodded by strong personalities such as Fleming, who was interested in all the players he worked with becoming not just better teammates but also better people.

"Wait a minute," Fleming once said upon hearing several white players talk about the previous night's party. "You had a party without me?"

The players looked at him. Among his other attributes, Fleming was known for a healthy social life, even being voted as one of *Ebony* magazine's most eligible bachelors.

"Were there any black guys there?" Fleming said.

The players said there weren't.

"Was this a private or a team party?" Fleming asked.

A lot of players were there, the players said. Fleming said nothing more. His point was made. And a few days later he heard a white player's voice come across the locker room: "Attention, Marvin Fleming! We are having a party tonight and you are invited!"

That night, Fleming was the last to leave the party.

The roommate assignments became an outgrowth of Shula's desire to address any racial issue before it became a serious concern. He also fostered football talk by matching players by positions. Defensive backs Curtis Johnson, who is black, and Tim Foley, who is white, were put in the same room. Fleming, a tight end, and reserve quarterback John Stofa roomed together. Like Warfield and me, these were players from the North to whom interracial rooming wasn't an overriding consideration.

But in 1971 a pair of rookie defensive linemen with similarly long odds of making the team brought together two, separate Americas from the moment they stepped into the room together and shook hands.

"Nice to meet you," Maulty Moore said.

"You, too," Vern Den Herder answered.

The truth was, neither was quite certain about that. It wasn't that either harbored any personal prejudice. It was more institutional ignorance. Neither had been around the opposite race much in their young lives.

Moore, who is black, was a genuine product of the Deep South, as he grew up in Brooksville, Florida, with segregated schools and separate water fountains. For two years after high school in 1964, he earned ten dollars a day as a migrant farm worker, picking melons, cucumbers, oranges, and other seasonal crops up the harvest highway from Florida to New York. He quit that to lay sod along Florida highways. It paid a little better. It provided a more regular income.

He was done with work one day in 1967 and playing basketball in Daytona Beach when the football coach of Bethune-Cookman noticed his large frame and fluid footwork. He approached Moore and asked if he wanted to play football. Moore figured it beat picking fruit or laying sod. He would even get to attend college, something he never expected, and he developed a grand plan to parlay the education into a coaching job.

So for the next four years Moore played football for a black college in the South against other black colleges in the South. He never had a white teammate. He never played a white opponent. There might have been token whites in the stands watching a game, but to his young mind it was a completely black universe.

With little football background, Moore didn't dream too hard of a pro career. He remained a talented but raw player through college and went undrafted by the NFL. But the Dolphins saw enough to offer him a free agent contract in 1971.

"Hey," Moore thought after listening to the call, "it beats picking fruit."

Den Herder's background, meanwhile, was everything Moore's wasn't. He grew up in Sioux Center, Iowa, a farming town of twenty-five hundred people. No blacks were in the community. None were in his high school. He then attended Central College in Iowa, where it was a similar story. So through high school and college, Den Herder had no black teammates and played against only a handful of black opponents. He showed just enough at that small college to be drafted in the ninth round by the Dolphins and so made the long trek south in the summer of 1971.

Suddenly Moore and Den Herder were roommates. And rookies. And defensive linemen with equally long shots of making the team. They woke at the same time. They went to the same daily meetings. They did the same drills in practice. They came back to the room each night with the same level of exhaustion and concern about making the team.

They didn't become fast friends right away. They didn't talk deep into the night about personal matters or social issues. They didn't talk much at all that first training camp, actually. But somewhere across the daily routine it struck Moore how he wasn't just living with a white man for the first time in his life. He actually felt something in common with one.

"I started to realize you had to get to know someone as a person before you understood them," he said. "That changed the way I had thought all my life. It opened me up. Just getting to know Vern a little, and seeing him do everything I did in pretty much the same way, allowed me to see a white person as a person for probably the first time in my life."

Both Moore and Den Herder beat the odds and made the team that summer. For the next few years, they remained roommates. And as the days turned to months and then to years, they became more than just teammates. They became friends, even if their separate universes weren't always aligned.

On the night before the Super Bowl that 1972 season, they lay in their hotel beds sharing how they would spend their bonus money from the playoffs. It wasn't a small reward. For each, the $15,000 winner's share came close to doubling their salaries.

"I'm going to take that Super Bowl check and buy a ranch and a bull," Den Herder told Moore that night.

Moore nodded and said, yep, that sounded good. And he kept nodding as Den Herder spelled out his grand plan for back home in Iowa. But Moore also thought, "A bull? Why is he talking so much about that?"

Den Herder didn't think to explain how it wasn't any ordinary bull he meant to buy. It was a prized, stud bull. He saw it in a catalog. He researched it. He studied its bloodlines. He would use it to start a herd of cows on his new ranch. Anyone knew what he meant, he figured from his worldview.

"What are you going to do with your money?" Den Herder asked.

"I'm going to buy an air-conditioned house," Moore said.

Den Herder nodded and said that sounded good. And he kept nodding as Moore spelled out his grand plan. But he thought, "What's the big deal about an air-conditioned house?"

Just as Den Herder with his bull, Moore didn't think to explain that no one in Brooksville he knew growing up had air-conditioning. They couldn't afford it. If he got a house like that, it would mean he had achieved something in life. He would be somebody. A success.

Moore even had the home picked out in Lauderhill. He drove by it occasionally for motivation. He'd stop in the street and look at it. Four bedrooms. Two bathrooms. And that wonderful air conditioner.

As everything worked out that season, both players achieved their dreams. Moore bought his house with air-conditioning that defined him as a success story in his world. And Den Herder bought that farm and bull in Iowa. In fact, forty years later, he was still living on it.

When training camp opened in 1972, Marlin Briscoe unpacked at his third team in five years and, beyond measuring how he could fit in this Dolphins offense, measured the climate inside the team. What he saw as the days went by lifted his weary hopes. The Dolphin players weren't just more talented than any team he had played on, they also were more mature, more professional.

What struck Briscoe most was that the players—black and white—were comfortable together in friendships, working relationships, and general locker-room demeanor. That didn't translate into everyone liking each other or mean that the entire roster hung out together. A good team did not have to be composed of pals. But it meant that there was a professional standard on how to act and what was important. This, in turn, was important to Briscoe. What was equally important was how the best players on the team and the strongest personalities inside the locker room were pointed toward winning in a manner that took everything else out of the equation. Ego. Statistics. Selfishness.

And especially race.

In his first days as a Dolphin, he felt like a great personal search was finished. This team had everything he hoped to find. Everything he never expected to find, too.

Because at a time when racial issues hung heavy over much of America, they hung heaviest over Briscoe. His dreams were scarred by this point, and he carried a disproportionate level of anger with him for good reason.

"The Quarterback," Joe Namath called him decades later whenever their paths crossed.

That meant something of significance to Briscoe. It told him that an important peer understood what happened.

In 1968, in Denver, in the final embers of the American Football League, Briscoe was drafted in the fourteenth round as a defensive back. At five-foot-nine, he expected that to happen, even if he was an All-America quarterback at the small college of Omaha-Nebraska. He understood that his size and color weren't prototypes for an NFL quarterback. A few blacks in the league's early years threw a handful of passes in cameo roles at quarterback. But no black quarterback had been on an NFL team since 1953, and all the stereotypes that kept blacks from playing the position—too dumb, too undisciplined, not clutch enough—held firmly in place.

Briscoe was young, confident, hopeful, and a touch naive, and the racial issue didn't concern him. A native of Omaha, he was the first black quarterback everywhere he played. Junior high. High school. College. He won each of those places over quickly with the exciting manner in which he played the position. He even earned a nickname: "The Magician."

He did not intend to fail at this next step. Briscoe negotiated his own contract to include an unusual clause guaranteeing him three days of training-camp practice at quarterback. That's all he needed to show off his arm, he figured. Denver seemed an ideal franchise for him. It not only had no proven quarterback, but also was one of the few teams with practices open to the public. Visibility would be a positive force, Briscoe thought.

Briscoe spent that summer putting himself through punishing workouts to assure that when camp started he would be in top form.

When his three days came to play quarterback, he thought he threw the ball and represented his game well. But that was it. Head coach Lou Saban moved him back to defensive back at the end of those three days with no discussion. And there Briscoe stayed until a succession of injuries and offensive miscues left the Broncos 0–2, trailing 20–3 in their third game, and trying a succession of no-name quarterbacks.

Desperate, Saban tried Briscoe, who completed his first pass. He scrambled for a touchdown to end his first drive. He led another scoring drive on the next possession. Denver lost the game, 20–17, but the team found a spark, the crowd found a favorite, and the coach saw he had no choice. At least that's how Briscoe viewed it.

Saban had to start him the next game.

"Not that he wanted to," Briscoe said.

On October 6, 1968, Briscoe became the first black quarterback to start in the NFL to no fanfare at all. If there was no appreciation for what Briscoe achieved, his disappointment came from struggling enough in the game to be replaced by halftime. That started a revolving operation at quarterback between Briscoe and veteran Steve Stensi the rest of the season. In seven games that year, Briscoe threw 14 touchdowns (still a Denver rookie record) against 13 interceptions. He ran for 3 more touchdowns. He wasn't a polished product, as his 41.5 percent completion percentage showed, but considering that he was a rookie and the general lack of talent on the team, Briscoe thought it was a good start to his quarterback career. He anticipated an off-season's worth of work to improve.

That off-season, Briscoe was home in Omaha when he received a phone call from a friend inside the Denver organization with some ominous news: Saban was holding meetings with the other quarterbacks. He was purposely excluding Briscoe from the camp. Briscoe was never one to swallow his anger. He immediately got in his car, drove to Denver, and confronted Saban.

"He couldn't look me in the eye," Briscoe said.

Stensi, whom Briscoe considered a good man, apologized for being part of that situation. But Saban never apologized. He later said it was Briscoe's small stature, not his color, that ended his quarterback days. That didn't explain the secret end-around the coach attempted, though.

Upset and understanding that this obstacle could never be removed, Briscoe asked for his release. He then wrote every professional team asking if they needed a quarterback. And he waited. In the days and weeks of anxious waiting that followed, he learned a second lesson about the NFL: his anger at Denver resulted in him being labeled a difficult young black man around the league.

No team considered him a quarterback. Buffalo, however, replied that it needed a receiver, if he wanted to try that position. Briscoe had never played receiver, but with no other offers, he eventually signed there. He immediately got film to study who he considered the two best receivers in the league: Warfield and San Diego's Lance Alworth.

He started that first season in Buffalo and quickly made himself into a dangerous receiver. By the following year, he was named All-Pro. But after his third season in Buffalo, he read the news that Buffalo had named Lou Saban as its new head coach. Briscoe knew what that meant. Sure enough, he was traded to the Dolphins in June 1972 for a first-round draft pick. And so, he later noted with irony, the very man who attempted to wreck his career was responsible in some manner for his being the first black starting quarterback and the winner of two Super Bowl rings.

Years later, the residue of bitterness over his career didn't leave him when he left the game. The anger bubbled to the surface. He got into crack cocaine. He lost his family and his money, even hawking his Super Bowl rings for drugs. He derisively was called "17–0" on the street for our 1972 team's record. Dolphin teammates helped him at various times and after several years, he found his way into a drug rehabilitation clinic, where he rediscovered his path.

"The Dolphins were the good years," he said. "The players, on and off the field, only cared about one thing: winning. That's how it should be. But that was the only team I found it to be like that."

5

My Sunday Nightmare

GAME FIVE

———

San Diego Chargers
October 15, 1972

Every few years, when we attend annual Hall of Fame functions in Canton, Ohio, the great defensive end, Deacon Jones, approaches me with a half-joking request: "Hey, Bob, you need to tell everyone the truth again."

"What's that?" I ask.

"People are still giving me hell about breaking your leg. Can you tell everyone it wasn't me?"

The tenth play against Jones's San Diego team was a perfect storm of ugly for me, and it didn't start with the blocking on Jones or on anyone else. It started with my arm. Let's be clear about that. I knew my arm wasn't the strongest. I could throw the ball a moderate 55 yards downfield—maybe 60 yards with a helpful breeze.

To help on deep passes, I released the ball a split second earlier than a quarterback with a stronger arm might. That way, the ball reached the receiver before he ran too far downfield. I also took a mighty step forward as I threw, allowing my entire body to get behind the pass on the follow-through. A quarterback with a strong arm needs to take just a baby step forward while throwing. Brett Favre's arm actually allowed him to step back while throwing the ball downfield, lessening his risk of injury from a rushing defender. It's a move I didn't have.

Stepping forward as I did maximized that risk. And on that play against San Diego, the odds—and several hundred pounds of misfortune—finally fell on me. I moved left and looked downfield for Paul Warfield, my first option on the play. He was covered. I then saw Kiick moving straight down the field. Deep. And open.

To this point, my career was relatively free of injury. A knee sprain in 1969 cost me five games. That was my only significant injury. But as I stepped forward and put my body into the throw, San Diego defensive tackle Ron East busted through two future Hall of Fame linemen, Jim Langer and Larry Little. It happens.

East stumbled low into my firmly planted leg. That was the cause and effect of the injury. East was near the ground, hidden by the cover of big bodies, so people thought Jones, who arrived a second later and hit higher, did the damage.

Norm Evans, responsible for blocking Jones, heard on the radio driving home after the game that I'd broken my right leg and dislocated my right ankle on the play. He immediately pulled his Chevy station wagon to the side of I-95, got out of the car, and began crying. His wife got out to comfort him. His children sat in the car, watching.

"I cost us the season," Evans thought as he stood there along the highway, his shirt damp with tears.

Those are the kinds of teammates we had. It's really what made us the team we were. It would take days for the films to show Norm what actually happened, and weeks for the guilt to lift off him completely. But he had nothing to do with the injury.

As soon as East hit me, I felt a riot of pain in the lower part of my right leg. The stadium went silent. I reached down for the ankle and knew immediately that it was broken. I ran my hand up my leg but didn't feel anything else wrong. I sat up, but the leg wasn't moving with me. It was an odd sensation. I looked down at the leg, which was bent at an angle that didn't make sense. Even before the trainer and the doctor arrived, I guessed what had happened and calculated how many regular-season games remained: nine.

"My season's done," I thought.

Shula walked onto the field. The pained look on his face confirmed my thoughts. "I wanted to throw up," he later said.

I was wheeled off the field on a stretcher and driven a few miles to Mercy Hospital in Coconut Grove. My ankle was swollen. My leg pulsed with pain. The doctors huddled. Sitting there, wondering what it all meant, where it all would go, I did what anyone would do at that point.

I watched the game on television.

When my wife, Judi, and Howard Twilley's wife, Julie, entered the room, I pointed at the television. "Hey, what are you doing here, Julie?" I asked. "Your husband just scored a touchdown."

As I was carted off the field, Earl Morrall moved to the Dolphins' huddle with all the anxiety of a man walking out the front door to catch the morning bus to work. That was Earl. If anyone understood and mastered the use of surprises in sports, it was the thirty-eight-year-old now in the middle of the huddle. He had been ushered in and out of so many situations and lineups, teams and trials, across eighteen seasons and six franchises that his teammates' dire thoughts never pierced his world.

As I was carried off the field, Jim Mandich later told me he said to himself, "Hell, it's over." Mercury Morris heard the questions in his mind and studied his teammates' sagging body language and thought, "We're in trouble." Down the roster, similar thoughts went.

Meanwhile, Morrall, being the good pro he was, immediately grabbed the sideline clipboard to study the chart of plays called and ones he preferred to be called. He checked in with the coaches. He considered the down and distance to decide what play to call, because he immediately understood that this season was in his hands. He began throwing on the sideline to warm up and smiled upon hearing Bill Stanfill say, "Old man, get those cataracts in motion, turn up the hearing aid, and let's go!"

Morrall stood in the huddle with neither panic nor excitement in his manner or voice.

"Come on, let's keep it going," he said to the offense crowded around him, and called a bread-and-butter running play to Morris. Simple. Smart.

Morris gained 5 yards.

In Detroit, in New York, and most famously in Baltimore, Morrall had said similar words at similarly anxious times when he replaced an injured starter. After the Morris run, Morrall threw a safe and short pass to tight end Marv Fleming. That gained 4 yards. That put the Dolphins short of the first down, but Morrall held the ball as Garo Yepremian's 37-yard field goal gave us a 3–0 lead.

All in all, it was a good way to start, Morrall figured as he walked to the sideline. And it stayed that way most of the day. The big play was safety Dick Anderson picking up a fumble and returning it 35 yards for a touchdown to give us a 10–3 lead. But the spotlight was on Morrall. He threw 19 yards for Paul Warfield's first touchdown of the year. He later connected on that 18-yard touchdown pass with Howard Twilley. For the day, his numbers were a modest 8 completions in 10 attempts for 86 yards and the 2 touchdowns. He was named the NFL's Offensive Player of the Week in the Dolphins' 24–10 win.

"The mark of a good team is how it plays under adverse circumstances," Shula told reporters after the game. "They can't get much more adverse than when you see your quarterback laying out in front of you."

Shula had come to me that winter and said he was going to sign Morrall as an insurance policy. And what a move that proved to be. No one knew that then. No one really trusted it. Oh, everyone used all the good and proper sports clichés that players are supposed to use when calamity struck a team. They trusted Earl, they said. They wouldn't miss a beat, they said.

"Everything will be fine," Bob Kuechenberg said.

"There are no problems we can't handle," Nick Buoniconti said.

In truth, their words masked a team full of questions. Everyone liked and enjoyed Earl Morrall the man. But that was a different proposition than trusting Earl Morrall the quarterback.

On his first practice as a Dolphin that summer, Morrall took his first snap from center, moved back to pass, and . . . fell down.

"Whoa," he said.

Players laughed. How couldn't they? With his crew-cut and phrases such as "dagnabit" and "cheesie-weesie," Morrall was the Man from a Different Era. Modern quarterbacks turned their hips and performed a quick crossover step to set up in the pocket. Morrall backpedaled from center, like in those black-and-white films from the 1950s. Then there were the passes. They wobbled. They misfired. And Morrall talked to his passes.

"Up, up, up," he'd say when one was underthrown.

Morrall didn't complete a pass in the preseason, hampered by an abdominal muscle strain. So when he officially was named the backup quarterback by Shula, and the former reserve, Jim Del Gaizo, was demoted to the taxi squad, some players privately wondered if that was the correct decision.

One Sunday's win didn't change that. Players privately feared their season now had a ceiling. Buoniconti told the defense it had to play even better. Monte Clark gathered his offensive linemen around him that next Monday and said they needed to work harder, to protect the quarterback even stronger. If human nature is to relax in good times, my injury and Morrall's entrance suggested to this team that a

5–0 record didn't reflect their standing. Their margin for error was smaller now. Their individual demands were bigger.

All they could do was support Morrall, the players decided, and in this sense Morrall made it easy to do. He was perhaps the most likable player on the team, a man without pretense. He might not have much in common with many teammates—his wife was pregnant with their fifth child that fall, after all—but he enjoyed the camaraderie of a locker room. He drank beers with teammates after practice. He told of bygone stars, such as San Francisco 49er tackle Bob St. Clair, who ordered raw meat in restaurants.

"Rare?" the waiter would ask.

"Raw," St. Clair would answer.

A young black defensive tackle such as Maulty Moore felt as impressed that Morrall would lean against his truck, talking away an afternoon with him, as veteran white receivers such as Howard Twilley and Karl Noonan enjoyed joking with him in front of *Fort Lauderdale Sun-Sentinel* columnist Bill Bondurant.

"You're getting old, Earl," Twilley said.

"No, I'm not," Morrall shot back.

"When I was a kid, I used to save bubble gum cards with your picture on them," Twilley said. "You were with Pittsburgh."

"I saw the same cards, Earl," Noonan said.

"You're almost thirty," Morrall told them.

"That's just it," Noonan said. "We're the old guys on the team and we still remember your cards." It was Morrall's good personality to include rather than exclude, and he accepted that his age was a good conversation point for teammates. They called him "Old Bones." He had a rocking chair placed at his locker, courtesy of equipment manager Danny Dowe, who also once hung an intravenous bottle off it so Morrall "could get his Geritol." Once, at a public dinner, Garo Yepremian dressed in Morrall's number 15 and sang to the tune of "Old Man River," "Old man Morrall . . . that old man Morrall . . . he must know somethin' . . . he don't say nothin' . . ."

Such stories told how comfortable Morrall made everyone. A regular event of entertainment became Morrall running the timed, 40-yard sprint while teammates watched in good humor.

"What time did I run?" he asked David Shula, the coach's son, who had the stopwatch.

"You don't want to know."

"Was it that bad?" Morrall asked.

"Yes."

If I mastered the science of playing quarterback from a technical aspect, Morrall did from a human standpoint. Howard Schnellenberger thought Morrall's strength was in understanding the craft of the position. What to see in the defense. How to relate to teammates. When to say something and how to express it. In 1979, Schnellenberger became the University of Miami head coach and hired Morrall simply to talk daily with a young freshman named Jim Kelly. Morrall performed none of the detail work of other assistants. He appeared half an hour before practice, looked at the schedule, and spent the practice relating to Kelly what he saw in certain situations on the field.

Morrall was born in Muskegon, Michigan, during the Great Depression. His youth was colored by World War II. His father worked intermittently, and his mother held a regular job, which was unusual at the time. He had a youth of early-morning paper routes and afternoon sports practices. If he wanted sports gear, he bought it himself. He didn't even consider attending college. Who would pay for it? He was a high-school junior when he heard about the idea of athletic scholarships. When dozens of schools actually began offering him one the next year, a newspaper reporter asked if he was impressed.

"I'm bewildered," he answered.

He could play sports? *And* go to college? *And* not pay a cent? It was a dream scenario to him. Morrall chose Michigan State, where he became an engineering major and one of the top quarterbacks in the country. He led Michigan State to a Rose Bowl win as a senior. He was named All-America. By then he knew pro football was an option, though when confirmation came it didn't come through a scout or a coach. He received a telegram on November 29, 1955, that read:

> Happy to inform you that you were our first draft choice. Our head coach, Red Strader, has spoken to Coach Daugherty and I will contact you by phone. Best of luck in the Rose Bowl.

It was signed by Lou Spadea, the San Francisco 49ers general manager. Morrall didn't know he was the second overall pick in the draft. He just heard that engineers made as much money as football players and had more stability. But when San Francisco offered $14,000 with a $2,000 bonus, it was double what an engineer could earn.

That began the first leg of a football journey where Morrall regularly found himself on the wrong team at the wrong time. When he arrived in San Francisco, Hall of Fame quarterback Y. A. Tittle was the starter and in midcareer. Then, with the third overall pick the next year, San Francisco drafted John Brodie, a local favorite from Stanford. Morrall's wife, Jane, drove across the country with a three-month-old baby and a full U-Haul trailer. Shortly after arriving, the team's new general manager, Frankie Albert, phoned and wanted to visit them. The Morralls thought he was sympathetically checking on their housing conditions. To save money the previous year, they lived with a teammate and his wife in a one-room apartment, with a second bed that pulled out of the wall.

Albert instead handed Morrall an envelope.

"Here's a plane ticket to Green Bay," Albert said. "You've been traded to Pittsburgh, they're in Green Bay, and they want you to start on Sunday."

He was named to the Pro Bowl that year in Pittsburgh. He was seen as the future of a building team where Len Dawson and Jack Kemp were reserve quarterbacks.

"You'll be here as long as I am," Pittsburgh head coach Buddy Parker told Morrall the next year in training camp.

He was traded the next week to Detroit for another Hall of Fame quarterback, the aging Bobby Layne. "Morrall will never make it in this league," Parker told the Pittsburgh writers.

Detroit head coach George Wilson, whose next stop would be the expansion Dolphins, seemed to share that idea. Morrall went from a rising star in the league to a part-time starter sharing time with the likes of Tobin Rote, Jim Ninowski, and Milt Plum. It became an especially trying time in the life of a quarterback who expected more. The problem, Morrall felt, was that Wilson didn't understand quarterbacks. Jane Morrall once drove to a game with Rote's wife and commented that she was excited because Earl was starting.

"Earl's starting?" Betsy Rote asked. "George told Tobin he was starting."

For his seven years in Detroit, that's how it was. This week's starter was next week's reserve. Sometimes Wilson shuffled quarterbacks in midgame. Once he was so indecisive on who to start, he summoned Morrall and Plum half an hour before kickoff. Wilson tossed a coin in the air.

"Call it," he told Plum.

"Heads."

It was heads. Plum started. Morrall developed a reputation as a relief pitcher. "The quarterback who cannot start," one writer began calling him. All he wanted was for Wilson to hand him the ball and say he was the quarterback for a stretch of games.

In 1963, Wilson did so. He had no choice. Plum was hurt five games into the year ("Plum out; Lions stuck with Morrall," read a headline Morrall remembered years later). With his role defined, it became better for him, perhaps because he had experienced the worst. He developed strength in self-reliance. He had one of his best years, throwing for 24 touchdowns against 14 interceptions.

"I felt I proved a lot to myself that year," he wrote in his autobiography, *The Comeback Quarterback*. "But I guess I didn't prove anything to Wilson."

In another of his early career disappointments, he arrived at training camp the next summer, and Wilson said the job was up for grabs again. It hardly mattered, the way it played out. Morrall separated his shoulder early that year. The recovery was so difficult, he nearly retired, thinking he wouldn't be able to throw the ball again. But he rejoined the Lions the next training camp. One night, after a game and dinner, he was driving home with his wife when they heard a radio report that he was traded to the New York Giants.

In New York his football career wavered again among great success, great inactivity, and great disappointment. He threw 22 touchdowns against 12 interceptions for a rebuilding team one season. At thirty-one he looked on his way again. The next season he struggled, then broke his wrist in such a harsh manner that doctors warned he would never play again. He rehabilitated the wrist and worked his way back into shape, only to find a familiar story at training camp: the Giants traded for Fran Tarkenton. Morrall was a backup again. He threw a career season-low 24 passes.

It was approaching 1968, Morrall was thirty-four, and wondered if this was the end. His auto parts business in Detroit was going well. He had four young children whom he didn't want to keep moving (his oldest, Matt and Mardi, would attend twelve schools through ninth grade). He didn't lack faith in his talent as much as in the people deciding on that talent.

He saw Don Shula, then the Baltimore coach, at a golf tournament that off-season.

"How'd you like to play in Baltimore?" Shula asked.

"I'm not coming to Baltimore to sit on the bench in another city," Morrall answered.

John Unitas was rooted as the starter and wasn't just an icon in the city but also the face of it. The only thing Unitas hadn't accomplished, Baltimore columnist John Steadman wrote, was walking across the waves of Chesapeake Bay. "Of course, he's never tried," Steadman wrote.

Playing in Baltimore behind Unitas, Morrall figured, would be no different than playing in New York behind Tarkenton.

"Well, you might not make the team anyway," Shula told him that day at the golf tournament.

Shula knew what he was doing. That small burr stuck with Morrall. Training camp began. Morrall waited. When Baltimore suffered an injury to Unitas's reserve in the exhibition season, Shula made his move. He was an assistant in Detroit when Morrall was there. He remembered Morrall beating his Colts with 13 seconds left in the game one Sunday. He also knew one more thing: Morrall could be had cheaply. New York didn't want to pay his veteran's salary. The initial trade made the cost a fourth-round pick. That later was amended to a straight-up trade of Morrall for Butch Wilson, the Colts' second-string tight end for the previous five seasons. Either way, Shula got what he wanted for a discount price.

The night Morrall's plane landed in Baltimore, Shula took him on the field for a personal practice session. Unitas was coming off a great year in 1967, despite a nagging elbow injury. The elbow remained sore in training camp. Then, in the final exhibition game, Unitas came to the sideline holding his elbow. He'd torn the muscle fibers in it.

Suddenly Morrall was the quarterback of a contending team. This was the opportunity he'd never expected to arrive, and he promised to make the most of it. All the lessons from a career of adversity and misfortune became advantages now. They gave him motivation and desire. San Francisco didn't give him a chance. Pittsburgh gave up on him. Detroit misused him. New York preferred someone else.

Each of his old teams was on Baltimore's schedule. In the opener against San Francisco, Morrall completed 16 of 31 passes for 198 yards and 2 touchdowns. Baltimore won. That began a redemptive second act to Morrall's career where he beat all his former teams, including San Francisco twice. Baltimore had a 13–1 record. Morrall led the league in passing with a career-high 26 touchdowns. One day he entered assistant coach John McCafferty's office to hear him say, "Congratulations."

"What for?"

"You've been named the NFL's Most Valuable Player."

Unfortunately, it's not remembered as that. Baltimore advanced to the Super Bowl against the New York Jets in one final showdown before the two leagues agreed to merge. If this was a changing time in football, it was across America, too. Joe Namath represented that change. Namath's interviews became must-hear events for reporters that week. He became the first trash talker in American team sports history. Beyond a famous "guarantee" of victory, Namath enjoyed the public spotlight and shooting his mouth wherever the conversation led.

Often that was at his Colts' counterpart.

"Earl Morrall would be a third-string quarterback on the Jets," Namath said. "There are maybe five or six better quarterbacks than Morrall in the AFL."

"Who are they, Joe?" a reporter asked.

"Griese. John Hadl. Daryle Lamonica. And myself."

When a reporter suggested that such words might fire up Baltimore, Namath shrugged. "If the Colts have to use newspaper clippings to get up for a game, they're in trouble," he said. "And if they're football players they know Lamonica can throw better than Morrall. I watch quarterbacks. I watch what they do. You put [Jets' backup] Babe Parilli with Baltimore, and Baltimore might have been better. Babe throws better than Morrall."

Morrall didn't have the personal weapons to respond. For that Super Bowl, they became the faces of their leagues, the old, crew-cut Morrall and the shaggy-haired, fresh-mouthed Namath. When Shula defended Morrall, Namath said, "I'm sorry that Don Shula took what I said about Morrall as a rap. I only meant it as a statement of fact."

Worse was the game itself. It humbled the Colts, and ate at Shula and Morrall for years. Morrall completed 6 of 17 passes for 71 yards before being replaced by Unitas. The symbol of Morrall's misfortune came at the end of the first half with a bit of razzle-dazzle that would have swung on a luckier day. Morrall handed the ball to Tom Matte on a sweep. Matte stopped and threw a long lateral across the field back to Morrall. They ran the play earlier in the year, and Morrall threw to an open Jimmy Orr for a touchdown. As Morrall scanned the Super Bowl field, Orr jumped up and down and waved his arms frantically near the end zone. Morrall could not find him. He threw a pass over the middle that was intercepted.

"Earl just didn't see me," Orr said. "I was open from here to Tampa."

Rarely does one play come to define a championship game. For Morrall it extinguished a brilliant season, perhaps the best of his career, and led to a predictable fall from grace. He returned to backing up Unitas, his MVP season forgotten, his career seemingly drifting toward its end. He played sparingly, starting three games over the next two years and only when Unitas was hurt.

Two seasons after the loss to the Jets, Morrall did receive the Super Bowl spotlight again with Baltimore, and he won a ring this time. Unitas broke a rib in the first quarter of the game. Morrall completed a 26-yard pass on his first play and a 21-yard pass on his second to the Dallas 2-yard line. He was on the verge of gaining redemptive-hero status. But in keeping with a career under the radar and a Super Bowl called the Blunder Bowl, Baltimore fumbled away the score. As the game played out, Dallas fumbled down the stretch and Baltimore ran a couple of plays into field-goal position. As time ran down, Morrall held the ball for Jim O'Brien's winning kick.

Entering the 1972 season, Baltimore general manager Joe Thomas said the team couldn't have two old quarterbacks. He prepared to release Morrall unceremoniously when head coach John McCafferty intervened. Given all Morrall did for the franchise, McCafferty asked to deliver the news in person. He flew to Michigan and met with Morrall at his home with the news.

"I've got no choice, Earl," McCafferty said.

"I understand the situation," Morrall replied.

Because a gentleman never forgets his manners, Morrall sent a handwritten letter to the *Baltimore News-American* to have printed in the newspaper. It thanked his coaches and teammates as well as fans and sportswriters for "the best four years of my football career."

Again, at thirty-eight, he contemplated retirement, and again the game decided it wasn't time.

Any team could claim him for the $100 waiver fee. The worst teams got the first chance. To his dismay, New England general manager Upton Bell claimed him. Bell had drafted Jim Plunkett the year before with the first overall pick and no doubt wanted Morrall to hold the rookie's hand. What's more, the Patriots were awful. Morrall told Bell he didn't want to play there. Thirty minutes before the waiver deadline, New England rescinded its claim to him.

That's when Shula grabbed him.

Morrall saw benefits in Miami. He was back with a familiar coach in Shula, and in the familiar position of backing up a star in Griese. The Dolphins obviously were a team on the rise, as their Super Bowl appearance the year before showed. What's more, at this point in his career, he was content with playing backup.

When he arrived in Miami, Morrall had played for five teams and four Hall of Fame quarterbacks, and had seriously considered retiring at least three times. He instantly recognized the Dolphins as a new-age team, not just because of their youth but also in how they conducted themselves. These players in their twenties went about their work in a more businesslike way than the veterans he had left in Baltimore. They joked some. They practiced hard. Afterward, some might go for a beer as all the Colts did. But compared to the previous generation's players, these Dolphins left practice like they were leaving the office for the day, Morrall thought.

The morning after beating San Diego, I woke up in the hospital, and Morrall arrived at the Dolphins' camp as the starting quarterback.

That's sports. "No use crying over it," I thought. I even considered that if this was the type of injury that ended my career, I could live with that. There was life beyond football.

Meanwhile, oddsmaker Jimmy "the Greek" Snyder thought the quarterback exchange to be worth a point on the Dolphins' point spread. He downgraded the Dolphins from a 15- to a 14-point favorite against Buffalo that week.

6

Pain and Other Inconveniences

GAME SIX

———

Buffalo Bills
October 22, 1972

I wasn't the only Dolphin to spend that Sunday night after the San Diego game in Mercy Hospital—or the Mercy Hilton, as we players called it. Mercy was that common a destination given our jobs. A home away from home, if you will.

Manny Fernandez felt sick in the days before playing San Diego. When he reached the locker room for that game, he felt bad enough and breathed hard enough that X-rays were taken of his lungs. Team doctor Charles Virgin performed an extended physical. He then patted Fernandez on the back and told him to have a good game. Immediately upon returning to the locker room after the win, however, Virgin summoned him. He didn't examine him.

"You've got pneumonia," Virgin said. "You need to get in the hospital."

Fernandez wasn't a football virgin. He understood what had just happened. Two years earlier, he was in the hospital, dehydrated and with a 102-degree fever, when his bedside phone rang at 5:00 a.m. He was told to get dressed. A ticket awaited him at the Eastern Airlines counter in Miami's airport. The Dolphins opened against New England that day. Fernandez was told to catch the assigned flight and take a cab to the Yale Bowl, where the game was to be played. He entered the locker room as teammates warmed up on the field. He quickly got taped and dressed. Don Shula told Fernandez that he planned to use him only in specific, pass-rush formations due to his health. The first time the Patriots faced a third-and-long, Fernandez was put on the field. He wasn't taken out for a defensive play the rest of the day. Upon returning to Miami that night, he was told to return to the hospital, where he stayed a couple of more days.

And now he was in the hospital again after the San Diego game. I was released Monday on crutches. Manny stayed until Saturday. He played the following day, in the sixth game, against Buffalo. This was the pressure everyone was under—coaches players, even doctors. As players, we understood that. In his first training camp, Fernandez was a day from being released when two defensive linemen blew out their knees.

"Any of you rookies think you can play?" defensive line coach Les Bingaman said to a group on the sideline.

"You're goddamn right, if you let me," Fernandez said.

"Okay, Mexican, see what you can do."

He wasn't Mexican. He couldn't even say "adios in Spanish," as he once told Johnny Carson on the *Tonight Show* after Manny's name went up in lights. But that practice exchange led to Fernandez gaining a nickname for life: Taco. It also led to him sprinting on the field that day and not coming out of the Dolphins' defense for the next seven seasons. He became the anchor of the defensive line. Sickness? Aches? Minor injuries? Being jerked into and out of hospitals without regard for health?

Just part of the job.

It's what almost all of us understood, really. The prototype of this team's roster was of a tough, recklessly aggressive kid even by the sport's high standard for toughness and reckless aggressiveness. Most of us were kids in 1972, too. Sixteen of the twenty-two starters were twenty-six years old or younger. I was more mature than they. I was twenty-seven. And your mid-twenties is the perfect age to play pro football. We had enough experience to know what we were doing. We also didn't have the mental and physical scars of football that came later. Aside from, ahem, breaking or dislocating bones, we could do anything to our bodies in that time and place without remorse and, more than often, did exactly that.

Before the 1973 season opener, defensive end Bill Stanfill was hospitalized with a lacerated liver, the result of teammate Curtis Johnson's helmet in a practice collision. This wasn't his first liver scare. That happened in 1971, when he ran so hard into Chicago quarterback Bobby Douglas on the final play of the game that Stanfill was taken by ambulance to the Mercy Hilton. This second liver problem put him in the hospital for ten days, right up to the opening game of the season. Virgin visited Stanfill at 8:00 a.m. the morning of the first game, took tests, and said the player's white blood count was too high.

Less than an hour before kickoff, he received a call from Virgin, who was at the Orange Bowl.

"Do you have your car there?" he asked.

"Yes," Stanfill answered.

"Come to the game, I want to talk with you," the doctor said

Stanfill entered the locker room as the Dolphins were on the field warming up. When he asked what Virgin wanted to discuss, the doctor said, "Get undressed and get taped. You're okay to play."

Stanfill played eighteen pass-rushing downs that afternoon. As he cut the tape off his ankle after the game, he noticed the hospital tag still on it. He asked Virgin to do the honors by cutting it off. Virgin instead told him to keep it on and return to Mercy. Stanfill stopped for a twelve-pack of beer before checking into the hospital. He remained there until later that week, when he left to pack his bags and board the team flight to Oakland, where he played the entire game.

That was part of the code on the team: anything it takes, anything at all. The team joke was that Jake Scott had so many screws holding various bones together that he couldn't get through a metal detector to fly to away games. Dick Anderson played two years without an anterior cruciate ligament in his left knee. Nick Buoniconti went two seasons with a cast over his right wrist and hand, the result of two surgeries and a bone graft that didn't take (years later, arthritis in the hand prevents him on some mornings from picking up a coffee cup). Jim Mandich's hand was shattered catching a touchdown pass in the 1973 playoffs. Eighteen screws reassembled the bones. A cast was put over it. The next Sunday, he shot it up with the numbing agent Xylocaine and played on.

Xylocaine was the players' ally, most discovered. I was shot up just once in my career, for sore ribs. For others, getting a shot before a game was as common as pulling on your socks. Virgin and his son, Charles, moved across the locker room with trays of shots before games.

"Over here, Doc!" players called.

Anything was shot up: shoulders, knees, ankles, feet. Jim Mandich once took a shot in his neck ("I turned white," he said. "It was a freaky experience.") Tim Foley once had a broken ankle and a pulled stomach muscle, and the father-son doctor team began to administer him shots at the same time.

"Hold on," Foley said. "Let's slow down here.

So many shots of it were given so quickly in the pregame locker room that reserve quarterback Jim Del Gaizo always stepped outside until the doctors were finished. All the needles made him queasy.

It wasn't just in the locker room: Fernandez had defensive teammates surround him on the bench between defensive series in the 1974 playoffs when doctors shot up his shoulder with Xylocaine to keep him playing. Nor was it just Xylocaine: near the end of his career,

Fernandez tried to coax some final football out of a body decimated by a separated shoulder, reconstructed knee, torn-up ankle, and a back that made him walk like an old man. He began rotating large doses of four anti-inflammatory drugs: Butazolidin, Motrin, Aristocort, and Indocin. Virgin administered the drugs, controlled the use, and moved from one to the next when side effects became too grave.

"One would drive your white blood count up," Fernandez said. "You'd switch to another that ate your stomach lining. You'd then switch to another that affected your prostate. I just kept alternating them in hope of controlling the side effects and being able to play."

Butazolidin later was linked to serious health problems and banned by the Food and Drug Administration. However, it remains legal to use on racehorses.

This irrational, unbreakable addiction wasn't just to football. It was to that moment, that singular moment in our lives, and that became central to the success of this team. When three screws loosened in Jim Langer's right knee during another season, Virgin said the problem could be corrected internally or externally. Langer asked what he meant by internally. Surgery, was the answer. He would be out for the year in that case.

Langer said to treat it externally without asking what that meant. Virgin set a piece of wood atop Langer's knee and hammered against it so furiously the screws reset in the knee. The hammering also split open a five-week-old scar, so his year was done anyhow. A couple of passersby, curious about the noise from a doctor's office, stopped at the door and turned away at the sight.

"I just wanted to play, period," Langer said.

That was the mind-set. No one thought of consequences beyond the next scoreboard. So when Mercury Morris was told he just had a sore neck in 1974, he continued playing out the final six weeks of the season with it. Then he went to the Pro Bowl, where the routine pregame physical showed that his neck was broken. Bob Heinz was diagnosed with a knee sprain before the final regular-season game of 1974. The knee was shot up with Xylocaine so he could play. After the loss ended the season, Heinz was told in the locker room that he had torn ligaments in the knee. He was put in a cast right there in the locker room.

There was this locker-room culture that pain was negotiable but victory was everlasting. Bob Kuechenberg broke his arm on the opening kickoff of a December game in Baltimore in 1973. He went to Virgin on the sideline.

"Doc, you've got to tape me up or something," Kuechenberg said.

Virgin remembered feeling the end of the broken bones "go crack, crack, crunch, crunch, grind, grind. I took him out of the game. He was very angry with me."

The next week, Kuechenberg demanded that the doctor invent something to allow him to play in the coming playoffs. So Virgin did: he drilled bone marrow out of Kuechenberg's broken arm and pounded a quarter-inch, steel-alloy rod into it. A cast was put over the arm on the morning of games. In the Super Bowl that year, Kuechenberg pounded Minnesota defensive tackle Alan Page with the cast so viciously that it was pulp by the end. It was effective, too. Page became so frustrated that he got ejected in the fourth quarter for a cheap shot on me. Kuechenberg could drive an opponent crazy like that.

When Virgin extracted the steel rod from Kuechenberg's arm, he broke three tools because it was so entrenched. Kuechenberg kept it as a souvenir. For years, he mixed drinks for house guests, telling this story of his broken arm and football as he did. He finished by pointing to the stirrer used to mix the drink the guest was sipping by then.

"That's the steel rod that was in my arm, right there," he would say.

Near the end of his career, Kuechenberg's demands on his body became the subject of a *Nightline* segment with Ted Koppel. It began with the camera panning up Kuechenberg's body, giving a tour of the physical harm he accepted in the name of football. A dozen broken toes. A left ankle broken in seven places. A right arch once crushed to the point that he needed Xylocaine administered before each game and at halftime. ("Never mind, Doc, he made it," Kuechenberg said as a shot was about to be given in overtime when San Diego kicker Rolf Benirschke's field goal ended the 1981 playoff game.) Kuechenberg's left knee, *Nightline* viewers were told, suffered a torn medial collateral ligament. Four back vertebrae were broken (he wore an upper-body brace in 1977 but didn't miss a regular-season game). His neck suffered such severe "stingers," or nerve shortages, that Dr. Barth Green, who later headed the Miami Project to Cure Paralysis, warned Kuechenberg that there was a risk of paralysis if he continued playing. He continued. His career ended in the 1985 training camp when fifteen seasons of using his head as a bumper car took its toll. His optic nerves frayed. He got double vision after one final hit on the practice field. He walked off the field right then.

"My attitude was pure and simple: I'm going to play today," said Kuechenberg, who still saw double after his career when he looked up. "That was it. Whatever it takes, I'll do it. Tape me. Shoot me up. Whatever it takes. I've read where a champion racehorse will run itself to death. I was the same way. My attitude was always that every Sunday was a dream come true. The truth is, if they fed me and paid my rent I'd have gone out there for nothing."

That was the norm on the team. But that thinking wasn't normal even by football standards. Many discovered that later in their careers upon finishing with another team. After a decade with the Dolphins, Langer completed his career with a season near his home in Minnesota. He was stunned by the different mind-set. If a Minnesota player hurt anywhere, Langer discovered, he sat out the game. Football, sacrifice, winning, the gladiator life—it didn't mean anything there. "Our bunch of guys in Miami would crawl across broken glass with no clothes on to get on the field," he said.

That didn't make the players in our locker room heroes. It framed the attitude, however. It said what this team was, how much the game meant to everyone on the roster, and what they would do to win. There were other common ways beyond Xylocaine.

Above one player's locker, beside the sign about not gambling on games, a jar was kept. And in the jar were pills. And in the pills were various stimulants.

Before most games, many players reached in the jar and took a couple. Green pills for energy. Brown pills for more energy. I didn't take any. I needed all my senses. Before cold games, other took them to take the edge off the weather. That's what they said, anyhow, because they took them before home games, too, simply to feel that they were tapping into some primal form of energy.

Greenies, they called them. Uppers. On teams in this era, they were as common as pregame tapings. Mercury Morris was introduced to them in a different manner. The night before the Dolphins' opener at Kansas City that 1972 season, he told a team doctor he was having trouble sleeping. The doctor gave him a pill. That put him to sleep. But it caused a problem before the game.

"Doc, I'm groggy, I can't wake up," Morris said upon reaching the stadium.

He was handed two green pills and a brown pill.

"What are these?" Morris asked.

"Mood pills."

"What do they do?"

"They get you in the mood."

"Mood for what?"

"Mood to play."

He took the pills. He kept taking them in that combination all that season. Games, he found, were in a bit of a haze. Postgames weren't much better. He chewed gum madly for hours. He stayed awake beyond normal hours. This wasn't unique to the Dolphins, as Morris discovered. After the 1973 season, Morris went to the Pro Bowl. He was sick all week. O. J. Simpson worried about playing too much if Morris was out.

"Hey, man, you can't leave me out there by myself," Simpson said before the game. "Here, take one of these."

"What is it?" Morris asked.

"It's a black beauty."

"A black beauty?"

"I take two before every game."

Morris took the pill at four o'clock on Sunday afternoon. He didn't sleep again until Tuesday morning. He wondered as he waited for sleep to come: And O. J. took *two* of these?

Morris quit taking pills after the 1973 opener. He didn't like the feel. Free of their sway, he immediately felt better, more natural. The pills, he felt, hurt his intuitive style of running. That return to a mentally natural running style, he felt, helped him to have his best statistical season as a professional that year.

There was an unseen toll for such big, strong men who felt bulletproof in their twenties and early thirties. Tim Foley thought only a crash-test dummy for car tests could relate to the violent abuse football players subjected their bodies to over a long career. "And that's if you looked in on the dummy after he got some age on him," he said.

In later years, as we reached our sixties, some of us began paying the price of Sundays in ways we never considered: worthless knees, replaced hips, bum shoulders, elbows that refuse to open, fists that never close, wall-to-wall backaches, and numbness in arms and legs caused by pinched nerves from wayward discs.

Buoniconti got a titanium hip. Anderson has an arthritic neck, a bad shoulder, a worse back, and a left knee that feels most mornings like it was whacked by a tire iron. Vern Den Herder gets headaches if his neck moves too much. Morris receives a message about football every time his neck moves, and he has a nerve deficiency that makes "everything on my right side smaller than my left side—shoulder, deltoid cap, biceps, triceps, forearm, pectorals, lat, everything," he said.

When Stanfill collided with Den Herder in a 1975 exhibition game, Stanfill's neck was so damaged it effectively ended his career. Doctors warned that he risked paralysis, even death, if he continued. But just because he was done with football didn't mean football was done with him. Less than two decades into retirement, his degenerating neck discs caused such pain he couldn't sleep. His right arm ached. He couldn't use his right triceps. His thumb couldn't even button his pants. Three operations fused four neck discs so it felt like he had "swallowed Viagra that got caught in my throat." He left soda cans a third full because his neck couldn't tilt enough to take any more.

That was just the beginning of Stanfill's problems, too. "Stretch," as his teammates called him for his six-seven frame, was an oversized farm boy from Cairo, Georgia, who won the Outland Trophy in 1968 after recording 67 1/2 sacks in his three-year career at Georgia. Until the pros, he had no use for modern science to help his football. He was young, strong, active. He didn't lift weights. As he said during his College Hall of Fame inauguration speech, his farm background developed him perfectly for football. Milking cows every morning strengthened his hands to throw off blockers. Lifting two-hundred-pound cotton sheets taught him how to handle running backs. Walking peanut fields for hours developed his legs. Getting knocked down by steers taught him how to get back up and immediately take them on again.

With the Dolphins, Stanfill discovered an actual use for modern science. To soothe aches, to mask pain, and sometimes just to improve a 90 percent body to a 100 percent machine, he began taking what players called a "Xylocaine cocktail." It was a medical shot of the numbing agent mixed with cortisone. Stanfill took one in midweek to soothe joints. He took another in the pregame to summon his body's best feeling. As his career moved on, he upped his intake to the point that at the 1972 season's Super Bowl he managed the pain of two broken ribs by taking three Xylocaine cocktails—one in the pregame, one at halftime, and one after the game to soothe his joints. Over his eight Dolpins seasons, Stanfill took an estimated one hundred Xylocaine cocktails with the doctor's help in almost every part of his body: Back. Knees. Shoulders. Ribs. Ankles. The one area he never was injected into was his hips, which became one of life's small jokes in later years.

Virgin later compared administering cortisone in such doses to sending the earliest miners underground for coal: the eventual consequences weren't known at the time. Cortisone was considered a miracle drug to many. The doctors who discovered it in 1950 won a Nobel Prize. Its ability to reduce swelling in joints and relieve pain for days, even weeks, made it a drug of choice among NFL players in the 1960s and early 1970s. By the mid-1970s, however, the bill began coming in. Oakland's Jim Otto had the first of more than two dozen surgeries because of his heavy cortisone use. Chicago's Dick Butkus was awarded $600,000 in 1976 and San Francisco's Charlie Kreuger collected $1 million for their teams' liberal use of cortisone. A Ball State study showed that more than 55 percent of players who retired before 1990 used cortisone.

Stanfill's cortisone settled in his hips, as it commonly did. It caused avascular necrosis, which cut off the blood supply near the end of a bone, causing it to deteriorate and die. His left hip crumbled first in 1991 and was replaced. Eight months later, his right hip needed replacing. He put the deteriorated right hip in a mayonnaise jar filled with water—his answer to Kuechenberg's metal rod. When a local charity once asked for something of his to auction, he offered the hip, saying the auctioneer could start bidding by asking, "Who wants a piece of Bill Stanfill?"

No member of the 1972 Dolphins paid a price like a forgotten member of our team, Mike Kadish. When there was a twenty-fifth reunion of the team at a *Monday Night Football* game, TV announcer Dan Dierdorf announced that every living member of the team was present. A few seconds later, at Kadish's home in Ada, Michigan, the phone rang.

"Are you alive?" a friend asked.

"Yes," Kadish said.

"Okay, just checking."

Kadish was a rookie that 1972 season, a number-one draft pick out of Notre Dame meant to bolster a thin group of defensive tackles. He had the portfolio. He led Notre Dame in tackles and sacks and was voted a consensus All-America. There were all the normal quotes in the draft's aftermath. Personnel director Joe Thomas, overseeing his final draft for the Dolphins, said he was "happy as hell, because we never expected to be there" at the twenty-fifth overall spot. Kadish said he "couldn't have been happier" to be the newest Dolphin. Don Shula said he was "exactly what we need" to supplement a thin defensive line.

When Kadish arrived at the Dolphin training camp that summer, however, there was more to him than expected. He weighed 285 pounds. Shula wanted him at 260. When Kadish's agent said the added weight might be the result of a recent wedding, Shula said, "What'd he marry, a refrigerator?"

Looking back later at what went wrong in Miami, Kadish settled on this fundamental concept of weight. His body, he thought, wasn't built to be 260 pounds. He ran and sweated before the Friday weigh-in. Sometimes he didn't eat for a full day. He felt weak that full season.

Still, each week, Kadish practiced like any player. He prepared to play. He studied the opponent. He thought he could help the team, too, because the disciplined scheme the Dolphins used was something he thrived on. He wasn't a freelance type of player. But before each of the seventeen games that year, Shula came to him and said they had deactivated him for the game. It was all the work of professionals. There was no grudge or malice involved in the manner that can happen in sports, Kadish thought. It still was an intensely frustrating year for him. For that entire 1972 season, Kadish never played one down—never even dressed in a uniform for a game. He watched those games from a stadium seat, dressed like any other fan.

The next season, planning to prove his talent, Kadish arrived motivated and at the prescribed 265 pounds. The Dolphins, he understood, didn't have a defensive system built on bulk. It was built on speed, athleticism. He attempted to become that player in his second training camp. Everything went as he hoped until in making a tackle in the second week of practice he suffered a terrible concussion. Kadish had a history of concussions already. His first one came while covering a kickoff in high school. Two more came at Notre Dame. But this one in the Dolphin training camp was the worst he ever had. His mind went dark, fuzzy. He suffered terrible headaches. He spent a week in Mercy Hospital and did not practice for nearly another week.

Upon returning to the team, he quickly was inserted into the lineup for an exhibition against New Orleans. A spotlight was on him, considering the expense of a first-round draft pick and the way his rookie year went. By all accounts, he played well. "Kadish Tackles First Big Chance," a *Miami News* headline read.

The next day, he was traded to Buffalo. He went on to have the kind of career he envisioned for himself. He moved to a more comfortable 275 pounds in Buffalo. He started eight years on the defensive line. He was named the team's Most Valuable Player in 1977.

The concussions didn't stop, though. He suffered fifteen in all playing football. Six were serious enough to hospitalize him. "Getting your bell rung" was the catchphrase used. Only slowly, over time, did an awareness come that it wasn't a bell. It was a brain. The severe health risks of concussions began to offer themselves only later in the degenerating lives of retired players who became touchstones to this trouble. John Mackey was reduced from a Hall of Fame tight end and players' union leader to a stoop-shouldered, blank-faced man who couldn't talk in the years before his death. George Visger had such little memory recall that he wrote what he did each day in a yellow notebook to have an accounting the following day. Dave Duerson's trauma-induced brain disease resulted in his committing suicide at age fifty.

Kadish typically was helped to the sideline after concussions to answer a doctor's questions such as, "How many fingers am I holding up?" Or "What's your name?" Or "Where are you?"

"A lot of times, if you weren't knocked out, you went right back in," he once said.

Upon retiring in 1982, all seemed normal until he returned to an annual Buffalo golf outing in 1994. A couple of former teammates who hadn't seen him in years noticed something wrong with his speech. Kadish began to note that his balance was off, too. He was diagnosed with postconcussion syndrome, a mild form of Parkinson's disease that, over time, would mushroom into the full-blown, life-threatening disease. He organized his life accordingly. With his wife and three children, he moved from Columbus, Ohio, close to his hometown in Grand Rapids, Michigan. He quit his job. He helped raised his children, coaching them in football. And he waited for the onslaught of the disease.

Just to move the muscles involved in speech, he took pills. But as he took years of them, a tolerance built up. He had to take more. The disease continued its assault on him. His life closed, day by day, like shutters on a home. Occasionally, for motivation, he slipped on the Perfect Season's Super Bowl ring. Sometimes it was for his sons' high school teams. Sometimes it was just for himself. As a reminder of what was real, what was accomplished.

Still, there was a schizophrenic quality to his achievement: the game that gave him such joy and personal achievement became the very thing that destroyed his life.

In this climate, at this point in his life, recovering from a bout of pneumonia for the sixth game of the season against Buffalo seemed like dandruff on the shoulder to Manny Fernandez. He was like most of this team, a blend of intelligence and recklessness. He hunted alligators in the Everglades and bear in his native California. He accelerated a motorcycle until the speedometer hit the 120-mile-per-hour limit. He once lost control of his bike on the Nimitz Freeway in Oakland and smashed into a roadside sign, breaking his jaw in two places, losing seven teeth, breaking his nose, and splitting his lip.

Soon, up ahead, he would pay for his devotion to football. In 1974 he played with a broken ankle, deep thigh bruise, pulled stomach muscles, knee problems, and a busted shoulder. By 1975 his body gave out, and his career was finished.

Later in life, Fernandez talked a tightrope between loving those days and living with their residue, between saying he would do his career all over again but quietly wishing, deep down, that there was some other way to achieve such glory than giving his body to football. He has bone spurs and no rotator cuffs in both shoulders, no cartilage in either knee, a torn-up ankle, and a back that needs two metal rods and a handful of screws even to begin repairing. He already has had one six-hour back surgery. He does forty minutes of nightly stretching and a few hundred stomach crunches to strengthen his stomach, take pressure off his back, and chase away more surgery a little longer. For arthritis, he takes ibuprofen and Celebrex. To loosen his elbow joints enough to bend them, he takes glucosamine.

This was his price for being a dominant presence in games. He was called a defensive tackle, but later generations of football labeled him as the nose tackle in a three-man line. The jobs were the same: hold your ground. Occupy two blockers. Do the grunt work. Free up line-backers to make the play. And only then, if possible, were you free to find the play.

In that context, Fernandez was remarkable. He made a staggering number of tackles. His career high in a game was 21, against San Francisco in 1971. In this sixth game in 1972, against Buffalo, he had 20 tackles. He was awesome. He ruined whatever concept of a running game Buffalo wanted to mount behind O. J. Simpson. I stood on the sideline, leaning on crutches, and marveled at what Fernandez was doing.

That feeling of invincibility on such days was why Fernandez navigated all the pain, he later decided. Even the pneumonia helped in one way. It meant that his legs were fresh by not practicing all week. Never was that more evident than in the third quarter of this uncomfortably close game against the Bills. To that point we had played wretched football. The offense lost three fumbles in the first half. They were well on the way to a season-high 11 penalties, including one by Shula for grabbing a linesman after a Buffalo lateral was ruled a fumble.

The defense held Simpson to 13 yards rushing in the first half but we still trailed 13–7. The fact that this was the first game without me hung heavily over the Orange Bowl.

With Buffalo facing a second down and 12 yards to go in the third quarter, Fernandez guessed that the Bills would pass. That was confirmed when he noticed Buffalo guard Dick Hart leaning ever so slightly back in his stance, weight on his heels, ready to pass-block. Fernandez decided not to occupy two blockers that play, as his role demanded. He would shoot the gap, beat Hart, and sack quarterback Dennis Shaw. At the snap, Fernandez sprang forward with a first step that came with its trademark quickness. He prepared to muscle Hart out of the way. But as he did so, as he braced for the collision, he was met by a surprise.

Hart was gone.

The play wasn't a pass. It was a run. Hart was leaning back to become the pulling guard on a trap play. So as Fernandez ran through the hole, the only problem he faced wasn't with Hart or pneumonia. It was his eyesight. He couldn't read the large "E" on an eye chart. His right eye had 20/200 vision. His left eye was worse: 20/300. He didn't wear contact lenses. Everything was a blur to him on a football field. In night games, especially, if the opposing team wore dark jerseys, he had difficulty seeing where the ball was going.

That was the problem now. The play was out of focus. He saw the blurred form of Shaw turning, his back to Fernandez. He saw the blurred form of fullback Jim Braxton moving as if to take a handoff. He just couldn't see the ball. What he did see clearly was opportunity. Fernandez moved to the spot of the handoff so quickly he beat Braxton there. He took the handoff from Shaw like a pickpocket on a busy street. Shocked, Shaw grabbed Fernandez as he took the football and kept moving toward the goal line. The quarterback rode Fernandez to the ground at the Bills' 10-yard line.

The Dolphin offense took it from there, and the day tilted back to normal there. That continued a run of what would be 19 straight

Dolphin wins over Buffalo across the 1970s. If these wins became standard for the Miami players, their effect was better understood on the other side. Joe DeLamielleure began to carry a $100 bill to Dolphin games. He didn't know how much beer that would buy, but he intended to find out in the hours after Buffalo broke that dismal stretch. If it ever did.

After his play sealed the win, after given a game ball in the locker room, after reporters swarmed him for details, Fernandez noticed a problem. He was sick again. The doctors looked at him again. They told him to return to the hospital.

Fernandez did so at midnight.

7

The Architect

GAME SEVEN
—at—
Baltimore Colts
October 29, 1972

A bad season had turned ugly for Joe Thomas, the new general manager of the Baltimore Colts, when we saw him in our seventh game. His inherited team represented the final, fading embers of a previous football era and had lost five of six games. That didn't surprise Thomas. On taking the job, he debated about how to rebuild the roster. Initially he tried in the traditional manner, slowly, like a spring cleaning, one room at a time.

But after five sloppy games, Thomas ordered the entire house torn down. That began the ugliness. He had released Earl Morrall and John Mackey in the off-season. Now he demanded the benching of the franchise's thirty-nine-year-old legend, quarterback John Unitas. When coach John McCafferty refused, Thomas fired the man who had won a Super Bowl just two years earlier. Overnight, Thomas graduated from a notably undiplomatic and slightly unpopular figure in a close-knit town to the Most Hated Man in Baltimore.

Fans criticized Thomas. Reporters questioned him. All that made for a bad week. What made it infinitely worse was this game, a 23–0 Dolphins win in which we—here's that formula again—ran the ball 52 times and passed just 16. Thomas had to watch the damage done by players he drafted, the havoc caused by players he traded for—the misery spread across Baltimore that Sunday by the team he assembled.

Not the Colts.

The Dolphins.

Thomas built the Miami roster from expansion dust in 1966. Nearly three quarters of the Dolphins, most of our starters, and five of our future six Hall of Fame players—Larry Csonka, Paul Warfield, Larry Little, Nick Buoniconti, and myself—were on the roster because of Thomas's shrewd work.

I first met Thomas in the Purdue locker room after the Rose Bowl, the final game of my college career. I talked with some reporters about being happy with the win but disappointed in my performance. I missed some passes. I didn't help the team enough.

As we finished talking, a middle-aged man wearing a suit and tie stepped forward, looking like any other reporter.

"Hi, I'm Joe Thomas, with the Miami Dolphins," he said.

I was surprised. "What're you doing here?"

Over a few minutes of conversation, Thomas was struck by my demeanor after such a big victory. He found me "wide-eyed and alert and interested in what we talked about," as he later told reporters.

Maybe so. But the conversation was so quick and casual in a celebratory locker room I only know it happened because Thomas later mentioned that it was important in drafting me.

Thomas made the trip to the Rose Bowl because he had a rule about trying to see every top draft pick. That involved considerable planning and travel. The NFL was years from organizing the draft so players met in one city for scouts to test, measure, interview, and compare against one another. Scouts were left to their own methods in the 1960s. Thomas went to the Rose Bowl to meet me because he had a heavy decision to make.

With the American Football League's second overall pick the year before, Thomas followed his architectural blueprint and selected the best-rated quarterback, Rick Norton of Kentucky. Nagging injury and immediate disappointment defined Norton, even as a rookie. Decades later his professional legacy was reduced to a question in the board game Trivial Pursuit: "Who was the first Miami Dolphin player?"

Thomas admitted his mistake. "I told our owners that we had to have a quarterback above all others, even if it took our five top draft picks in the first five years," he said.

The question entering draft day in 1967 was which quarterback to pick. Me, or the player I finished second to in the Heisman Trophy voting, Steve Spurrier. (Years later, as a network TV analyst, I'd needle Spurrier, then a college coach, over the manner in which southern voters lined up behind a favorite son. "My momma is asking if you're taking good care of my Heisman," I'd say.) Spurrier was a Florida star, too. That would be a bonus for a second-year team like the Dolphins, teetering over financial problems. He could sell tickets.

Thomas drove to Gainesville that winter to talk with Spurrier at his lawyer's home. "Actually, the lawyer and I talked," Thomas said. "Spurrier sat there playing solitaire the whole time. I had to interrupt to get his attention."

That cemented the decision by Thomas. He sweated its fallout on draft day, though. Picking me would strain him so much, Thomas knew. The target on him would increase. There would be added pressure on me. Robbie and the other owners would question him because of the ticket factor. And there was the very real question to consider: What if he was wrong? What if Spurrier was the better choice?

He had one hope: Atlanta, picking third and before the Dolphins, would take me or Spurrier. That would absolve him of blame. He'd take whoever was left. But Atlanta traded the pick to San Francisco, which had veteran quarterbacks John Brodie and George Mira. Thomas figured that both Spurrier and I would be available.

"I broke out into a cold sweat," he said.

Commissioner Pete Rozelle then announced in New York to the assembled media and teams via telephone, "San Francisco selects Steve Spurrier, quarterback, University of Florida."

That's how I ended up with the Dolphins.

Thomas had an uncanny ability not just to detect talent in the manner of a good scout, but also to mine the draft, the phone, and other teams for good value in the manner of a great executive. Within a fifteen-year span, Thomas found enough players for Miami to win two Super Bowls, Minnesota to have a foundation to reach four Super Bowls, and Baltimore to advance to the AFC championship game, blocked only by the great Pittsburgh dynasty of the late 1970s.

"Some people can't pick talent," he said. "You either have it or you don't."

He was blunt, gruff, and arrogant. When he did release Unitas, at the end of that season, *Baltimore American-Statesman* columnist John Steadman said, "Joe, you can't put John Unitas on waivers."

"Why not?" Thomas said. "He was there before, wasn't he?"

His lack of diplomacy was how he became a scout in the first place. He coached the defense for a rebuilding Baltimore team in 1955. The offense was awful, the defense respectable. In the final game of a bad season, Thomas's defense even had seven interceptions.

The night before the 1955 draft, Colts owner Carroll Rosenbloom assembled staff and friends in a New York hotel suite. The Baltimore columnist Steadman asked who the number-one pick would be in an era when the name wasn't a state secret. Coach Weeb Ewbank said it probably would be Georgia Tech linebacker Larry Morris.

Thomas, sitting in the back of the room, blurted out, "Mr. Rosenbloom, I've been reading about how we're going all-out to win in Baltimore. How we're going to get the 'best available chattel.' Those are the words I've been reading. And 'money is no object.' If we go for

Morris, we're admitting that money *is* the object. The best football player available is Alan Ameche."

An uncomfortable silence followed. Thomas wasn't proposing just to ditch Morris. Plan B for the Colts at the time was Maryland fullback Dick Bielski, a local favorite who could sell tickets. "They looked at me like I'd just jumped off the bench to make a tackle," Thomas said. "It was none of my business—I was the defensive coach. But I had to say it. We had not established a running game. We needed a big, tough back."

"Well," Rosenbloom said that night, "we want the best football players and we'll go for the best."

"That's Ameche," Ewbank said.

When Ameche was selected the next day and the back story went public, Thomas found himself at the center of a draft-related storm. The knock on Ameche was his big size and slow speed. Some thought him better suited for an NFL guard. Ameche soon made his statement. He ran for a 79-yard touchdown on his first NFL carry, 179 yards in his first game, and was named Rookie of the Year that season. Thomas, a Los Angeles Rams assistant by then, circled Ameche's stats in the newspaper each week and pinned them to a bulletin board for everyone to see.

"From that time on, I was fascinated with the idea that getting the material was half the battle—more than half," Thomas said.

This was an NFL era still rooted in a belief that scouting was a subculture of amateur football minds and coaches who found a soft landing spot before retiring. Ray Byrne, who ran his family's funeral home and kept statistics, was Pittsburgh's first personnel chief. Gil Brandt didn't play football beyond high school and was photographing babies in Milwaukee when his creative draft lists caught the eye of Dallas. The head of the New York Giants' personnel department, Jim Lee Howell, was their coach from 1954 to 1960.

"They used to say in the pros that scouting was a waste of money," Thomas once told *Sports Illustrated*. "With me, they didn't have to waste money. I was single. I was a loner. I was always going somewhere on my own, attending a clinic, a coaches' convention. I visited practices. I did a lot of hanging around."

Thomas's break came in 1960 when NFL commissioner Pete Rozelle recommended him as personnel manager for the Minnesota expansion team. Thomas visited ninety-two colleges his first spring with Minnesota. He immediately was questioned by coach Norm Van Brocklin by picking Tulane fullback Tommy Mason in the first round. Mason starred for Minnesota and played more than a decade in the NFL. That wouldn't be the last time he sparred with Van Brocklin, nor the last time Thomas would prove correct. It was a third-round choice by Thomas that put him square in the sights of doubters. He picked a scrawny, scrambling quarterback from Georgia named Fran Tarkenton, whose skill set ran counter to the drop-back, stay-in-the-pocket NFL game. He fought daily about Tarkenton with Van Brocklin, an old-school, drop-back quarterback himself.

"With Tarkenton," Van Brocklin said sourly, "a coach has to come up with a good third-and-40 offense."

Thomas was sold on Tarkenton's mobility.

"Trends," Thomas said, "usually are started by one man. Jackie Robinson, for instance."

Plus, in a theme that carried to the Dolphins, Thomas said, "No matter what kind of football team you're building, the first thing you need is a quarterback, and if you are an expansion club, you better have a quarterback who can move, because with the blocking you'll get there won't be a pocket fit to live in very often."

It was Thomas's nature to think differently and question accepted beliefs. He was as tough as the land that formed him. He grew up on a farm outside Warren, Ohio. He was thirteen months old when his father died. When he was three, his mother married a steel-mill worker from Youngstown. Starting at age ten, he worked all day in the summer sun beside grown men on farms. The next, scheduled step after high school was to follow his stepfather and older brother to the steel mills.

"That kind of background can either make you or break you," Thomas said. "Either you can give up and say to yourself, 'Aw, what's the use, I'm going to end up in the mills anyhow?' Or you can bear down and get yourself an education and be something. Discipline. That's the answer. My parents didn't discipline me. I disciplined myself. I knew I had to if I wanted to be anything. I worked in school."

He went to Ohio Northern University on a football scholarship. He earned a master's degree at Indiana University, where he also began coaching, and then worked toward his doctorate. Two brothers ended up in the mills, and a sister married a mill worker, but when two younger brothers began down that path after high school, Thomas gave them a dose of his discipline, too. He called the president of Ohio Northern, who admitted one brother. That brother became a teacher. The other brother "I practically took by the neck to Ohio State," Thomas said. He became a veterinarian.

After the 1965 season, Van Brocklin blamed a losing record on the players Thomas selected. "A bunch of stiffs," Van Brocklin called them. Thomas was livid. Even with Van Brocklin soon running Tarkenton out of town, these stiffs Thomas selected represented the core of the team that got Minnesota to four Super Bowls: Alan Page, Carl Eller, Jim Marshall, Roy Winston, Mick Tinglehoff, and Bill Brown. Management sided with Van Brocklin.

As Minnesota wavered on his worth, Thomas received a call from a Viking season-ticket holder who recognized the scout's eye for talent from the twentieth row at games. Joe Robbie also recognized charitable timing. He needed someone to assemble his expansion football team and offered Thomas a $10,000 raise to do so. After a secretary, Thomas became Robbie's first hire for the franchise, and it became a significant one for their future greatness. It was not without early trials. Thomas's first draft pick, Jim Grabowski, signed with NFL rival Green Bay, and his next two selections, Rick Norton and Frank Emmanuel, had no lasting impact. There were border wars inside the franchise early on, too. Coach George Wilson convinced Robbie to trade a third- and a fifth-round draft pick for veteran running back Cookie Gilchrist, over Thomas's objections.

"Cookie was trouble," Thomas said. "It stood out like a neon sign. He was over the hill and he still wanted credit cards, a Cadillac, all kinds of junk."

At that point, Thomas demanded that the personnel decisions be his complete kingdom. He didn't want to make decisions by committee or have another Gilchrist stuck on the roster because a coach remembered a good game he played. A one-person department fit his personality and Robbie's budget. Thomas traveled 150 days a year. He refused to fraternize, or usually even hold conversations, with other scouts. He was so thorough about players' details, personalities, and idiosyncrasies that he was once standing in the Syracuse locker room checking players' prepractice weights on a clipboard when a player came out of the shower.

"Wasn't that Jim Nance?" he asked a coach about the star fullback.

"Yeah, that's Nance," the coach said.

"But he just took a shower before practice."

"Yeah, he always does."

He scratched Nance off his list in much the same manner he did Spurrier for playing solitaire in his lawyer's office. He didn't want players whose personality tics stood out. He wanted good, big, strong football players, not pets or projects. And draft pick by draft pick, trade by trade, player by player, Thomas's shrewd moves toward the coming Dolphin dynasty were made with what he called the "artichoke method."

"You build from the inside," he said. "At the core is the heart of the team, the tender young rookies, the ones you get in the draft. You build under the veterans and then you keep peeling them off, like the leaves of an artichoke, until you're down to the heart, to the guys who are really going to help you once they're ready. Don't let anybody kid you. You don't get much to start with in an expansion draft. Depth is an illusory thing. Not many teams really have depth. The players the other teams are forced to put up for grabs aren't going to be of the highest caliber. By the fourth year at Minnesota, we had only one player left from the original expansion draft."

At Miami, only right tackle Norm Evans survived from the expansion draft into our years. In the place of the Gilchrists, Wahoo McDaniel, and Joe Auers came Thomas's draft picks, like leaves of an artichoke. Maybe any fan could pick Larry Csonka with the eighth overall pick in 1968. But Thomas also watched Jim Kiick for three years, spending two days at a Wyoming practice just to study him.

"Van Brocklin said he was too fat and too slow when Kiick was in the All-Star camp," Thomas said. "But my answer for that is: Can the guy run the damn football?"

He picked Kiick in the fifth round. He traded backup quarterback John Stofa to Cincinnati for a first-round draft pick that yielded tackle Doug Crusan. He sifted through three hundred letters from football wannabes and called in placekicker Garo Yepremian for a tryout. He traded Green Bay a young receiver named Jack Clancy, who played one year with the Packers, for veteran tight end Marv Fleming. He demanded an exception to Robbie's rule of not signing free agents west of the Mississippi—travel expenses were prohibitive, Robbie said—and signed defensive tackle Manny Fernandez from Utah. He traded quarterback Jon Brittenum, an eighth-round pick, to San Diego for a third-round pick that he used on safety Dick Anderson. He picked Bear Bryant's mind when Robbie was recruiting him to be the Dolphins coach, and drafted Alabama linebacker Mike Kolen with a twelfth-round-round pick.

He pulled off moves that I'm dumbfounded by today. We all are. When Thomas wanted to trade for Nick Buoniconti, he sent New England a selectively edited film of third-string Dolphin quarterback Kim Hammond, who threw 26 passes as a rookie in 1968. New England wanted receiver Howard Twilley thrown into the deal, too. Thomas got them to take linebacker John Bramlett. By 1972, Buoniconti was the Dolphins' defensive captain, Hammond a lawyer, and Bramlett a year into retirement.

Thomas's former boss in Los Angeles, Sid Gillman, wanted Dolphins cornerback Mack Lamb and called with the name of a San Diego player to trade.

"Sid, I want Larry Little," Thomas said.

Little wasn't a star and only occasionally a starter at the time. Gillman called later with another player he would trade for Lamb. Thomas repeated he wanted Little. Gillman called again, naming someone else.

"Sid, don't call again unless you say one word: Little," Thomas said.

Gillman called with that one word, and then announced the trade to San Diego writers as a "nothing for nothing" deal. Lamb didn't make the Chargers team. Little made the Hall of Fame. At Little's induction in Canton, Gillman approached him and said, "Trading you was the worst trade I ever made."

Thomas had little pretense and no time for chitchat. The day before the 1969 draft, Georgia defensive end Bill Stanfill received a phone call at his sister's home in Cairo, Georgia. After introducing himself, Thomas said, "I've got one question: What's your draft status?"

"I'm married with children," Stanfill said, meaning he wouldn't be drafted into the Vietnam War.

Click.

End of conversation. No thank you. No good-bye. Stanfill was left holding the receiver and wondering how Thomas tracked him down at his sister's home. The next day, Thomas selected Stanfill with the eleventh overall pick. Stanfill went on to hold the franchise's career and season sack records for more than three decades.

The coup by Thomas, the gem, the cherry on top of his acquisitions, came just before Shula arrived early in 1970. We needed a downfield threat to stretch the field. I knew that more than anyone. Thomas dangled the third-overall draft pick to teams. He asked Gillman about Lance Alworth. Gillman offered a running back named Dickie Post.

"You've got to be kidding," Thomas said.

He called fifteen teams who had receivers he might accept in a trade. Cleveland owner Art Modell, he thought, showed the most interest. That made Thomas realize, as he said later, "I don't want a downfield threat. I want *the* downfield threat."

Cleveland needed a quarterback. Louisiana Tech's Terry Bradshaw and Purdue's Mike Phipps were the only ones worth a high pick. Green Bay, picking second, indicated privately it was drafting Notre Dame defensive tackle Mike McCoy, so the Dolphins' third pick had value to Cleveland. It was certain to get one of the quarterbacks, probably Phipps.

"There's only one player I'm interested in," Thomas told Modell.

"Who, Warfield?" Modell asked.

"Yeah," Thomas said.

Modell laughed. He said no. He didn't stop calling Thomas, though, offering a different Cleveland player to trade for the draft pick each time. Thomas asked for Warfield each time. As Pittsburgh closed in on Bradshaw, Thomas also played a public game of telling writers that Phipps would be his number-one pick.

"Phipps is six-feet-three, strong, a great arm, a natural pro," Thomas said.

Four days before the draft, Thomas made his stand to Modell: it was either Warfield or no deal. And if the deal was off, Thomas said, he'd pick Phipps and trade him to the highest bidder.

As time slowed to a crawl that weekend, Thomas remained hopeful. Gillman called again for the pick, offering Post again.

"Can't do it, Sid, but I might have something going on," he said.

"Who?" Gillman asked.

"Can't say."

"C'mon, this is your old coach."

"Okay, but you've got to keep it under your hat. Warfield."

"Wow."

The day before the draft, Modell called Thomas and said, "The trade is on." Warfield was a Dolphin. The football world was stunned. Thomas, who rarely drank, went to his favorite restaurant that night and kept drinking wine in celebration until he was happily drunk.

"I can't recall ever being more satisfied with myself," Thomas, who usually was satisfied with himself, said.

The next day, he stood by the list of available names on the Dolphins' draft board. Warfield's name was on top of the list.

"Look at that board," he told reporters. "That's our number one up there, and you can bet you won't see a name close to it today or tomorrow, either."

He then proceeded to select Jim Mandich, Tim Foley, Curtis Johnson, Jake Scott, Hubert Ginn, and Kolen that draft to stock the roster with six more players for the Super Bowl runs.

"The greatest judge of talent I've ever seen," Buoniconti called Thomas.

That's how I felt, too. It was part of Thomas's makeup to heartily agree with such statements. "It's embarrassing, but I guess I never made a bad trade," he said.

Thomas's hard-driving style came with a price. One, he thought, was a lifestyle that caused him to remain single until age forty-eight, when he married a flight attendant, Judi, in a nine-hundred-year-old Italian cathedral. The other price was life-threatening. He needed open-heart surgery in 1971. He cut back on some duties while recovering.

If our players appreciated the collective talent Thomas gathered, most thoughts were colored by the other part of Thomas's job: he negotiated their contracts. I didn't deal with him much in that regard. Joe Robbie did my deal as a rookie, and it stretched beyond Thomas's time. But in an era when there was little negotiation and with a franchise where the owner collected pennies, Thomas's gruff personality stood out in the negotiating room to my teammates.

"We're paying you $20,000 this year," Thomas told cornerback Tim Foley in his second year, in 1971.

"Okay, where do I sign?" Foley asked.

That was the common negotiation. When a player expressed disappointment about the offer, Thomas had a favorite line: "There's a bus leaving every hour." He had all the leverage, and he wielded it like a hammer. Any movement off the offered price was minimal and strategic, most players felt, as if to give management the illusion of generosity. When Bob Kuechenberg arrived as a free agent in 1970, Thomas offered a $15,000 contract. Kuechenberg summoned all his courage and said other teams offered more. The Oakland Raiders, he said, proposed $17,500. Thomas grumbled for a while but eventually raised the offer to $17,500, which Kuechenberg figured was the price all along.

"This is the most we've ever given a free agent," Thomas told him.

That was another line players often heard.

When Thomas offered Little $18,000 in 1970, Little became upset. He was a three-year veteran. He wanted $20,000. Thomas pointed out his twenty-fourth-floor office window.

"If I give you that, I'll jump out this window," Thomas said.

"You'd better get some wings, Joe," Little answered.

Little got his raise, but Thomas again assured that it held to the small increments of the era. He was tough, hard, and brusque with players, who could treat him the same way. In the 1970 training camp, he sat in the dorm room of a defensive lineman named John Richardson and refused to meet the player's demands. And he kept refusing. Finally, Stanfill, who was Richardson's roommate, went to a box where he kept a pet native to the backwoods of Georgia. Stanfill walked over to Thomas with a four-foot, white oak snake wrapped around his arm. He held it six inches from Thomas's face.

"Give John what he wants," Stanfill said.

Thomas ran out the door. A few minutes later, Shula called the room. That snake was the first cut in the 1970 training camp.

The hint of a new age for players arrived in 1971, when Larry Csonka and Jim Kiick got an agent, Ed Keating, and copied the negotiating strategy of Los Angeles Dodger pitchers Sandy Koufax and Don Drysdale by holding out together. Thomas tried all the traditional means to separate them. Once, he went to a hotel suite where they waited out training camp and pulled Csonka into a room to talk privately. When Csonka returned to the room, he told Kiick everything.

"You can't do that," Thomas said.

They not only did it, but they also negotiated matching three-year deals worth a staggering total of $60,000 a season each. The time of more money was coming, the players felt. The rising television contracts with the NFL and ticket sales across the league demonstrated that. Thomas soothed many of them by saying their next contract would be better.

By the 1971 season, however, Thomas was attempting to negotiate something for himself: the title of general manager. Shula's arrival with full control of the football side undercut not only Thomas's work but also threatened his power. There was some friction there. Monte Clark remembers that the coaching staff grew so tired of Thomas's know-it-all attitude that they invented the name of a college player, put it on the draft board, and asked Thomas about him.

"He said he knew all about the player and proceeded to tell us," Clark said. "No one said anything. We just let him talk."

Thomas approached Joe Robbie and demanded the general manager title to reflect his contribution. Robbie wanted control of business operations himself and, having guaranteed Shula full control of the football side, refused Thomas. Robbie attempted to frame it as a philosophical issue in public.

"I don't believe in general managers," Robbie said. "Football isn't that kind of business, in my opinion. There are only two kinds of decisions to be made—business and football—and Shula has the final word if it has anything to do with football, from scouting to when to take the plane to Buffalo."

In place of a title, Robbie offered Thomas a raise to $40,000 a year to continue as its scouting department. Thomas declined. By the end of the 1971 season, Thomas said he would complete his obligations with the Dolphins' draft and then resign. He moved his wife and young child out of their Coral Gables home to an apartment. He refused to listen to Robbie's discussion of more money.

True to his threat, Thomas resigned a few days after the draft and waited for the phone to ring. Carroll Rosenbloom, the Colts' owner and an enemy of Robbie, became one of the first to call. He offered sympathy and help in any way possible. The ensuing conversation began one of the stranger chapters involving franchise ownership in NFL history and showed Thomas's array of talents. Through their conversations, Thomas discovered that Rosenbloom wanted to buy the Los Angeles Rams, whose owner, Dan Reeves, had died. Rosenbloom just needed an owner to take his place in Baltimore. Thomas initially presented Willard Keland as a candidate. Negotiations moved well until Keland, who two years earlier had lost a power struggle with Robbie for the Dolphins franchise, couldn't raise the necessary $19 million. Thomas then presented a second candidate courtesy of his heart surgeon, Richard Elias, and his brother, George Elias. They knew Robert Irsay, a multimillionaire through a Chicago-based heating and air-conditioning company. The deal involved Irsay buying the Rams, then swapping franchises with Rosenbloom in Baltimore.

Thomas got a new team, the general-manager title he coveted, and an owner who conceivably owed him dearly. Irsay was a Thomas creation, most people in the league thought. Thomas shared that opinion, as an exchange with Baltimore writers in a New York restaurant on the night before his second game with the Colts showed.

"Where's Mr. Irsay tonight?" a reporter asked. "If I were he, picking up the tab for this wonderful dinner, I'd want to be here to enjoy it."

"Forget him," Thomas said. "You guys are still living in the Carroll Rosenbloom era, where the owner took you by the hand. The owner counts for nothing. Just don't worry about him."

"Well, he hired you, so he counts for something," the reporter said.

"Get this straight," Thomas said. "He didn't hire me. I hired him. I could have had six guys for that job, and I picked him. He's in the league because I brought him in."

In the coming years, Thomas discovered that neither the arrangement nor Irsay was what he expected. In 1973, Irsay blew into the Colts' locker room after one loss and began berating quarterback Marty Domres in front of the team. Players thought it was a joke initially. Irsay kept yelling, though, until Thomas escorted him away. That was mere prologue to the next season, when Irsay marched down the sideline during a 30–10 loss to Philadelphia and up to Howard Schnellenberger, who was the coach by then. Irsay demanded that Schnellenberger replace Domres with rookie Bert Jones. Irsay and Schnellenberger began cursing each other. In the locker room after the game, Irsay fired Schnellenberger before the team and named Thomas the coach. Thomas, who wasn't yet in the locker room, found out as he passed Irsay leaving it.

"You're the coach," Irsay said with a snarl, "as of right now."

Thomas continued to work magic on the personnel side for the next few years after that. Baltimore quickly became a playoff team and Super Bowl contender. But by 1977, his relationship with Irsay and Baltimore coaches deteriorated to the point where he was fired. A year later, he replayed the formula. He found Edward DeBartolo, a multimillionaire in Thomas's hometown of Warren, to buy the San Francisco 49ers. Thomas became their general manager. In the process, he reduced the role of Monte Clark, the former Dolphins assistant who had a job with Shula-like powers in San Francisco. His job diminished to head coach, Clark quit on principle, just as he had threatened to do years earlier to Shula over the starting center position.

"A lot of bad things were said about him over the years," Clark said of Thomas, "but not nearly enough."

It took two years in San Francisco for Thomas to exhaust his welcome. In 1981, Robbie hired him back to the Dolphins with the publicly stated idea of negotiating contracts. But his return was lost in tragedy when he had a heart attack in the middle of the night after that first season.

•   •   •

That seventh week of the 1972 season, Thomas watched his Miami team destroy his Baltimore team. Csonka scored two touchdowns. Yepremian kicked a field goal. Warfield ran 26 yards on an end-around. Buoniconti led a shutout. All his guys.

During the week of the Super Bowl that year, a *Washington Post* reporter saw Thomas and commented how he had the "Midas touch" with the Dophins' roster. Another man might have shrugged his shoulders or mentioned that he was with a different team now. Thomas, however, felt that his good work never received the acclaim it deserved.

"Don't let anyone tell you otherwise," he told that reporter. "I put together 99 percent of that football team, and I'm very proud of it."

As he should have been.

8

The Names behind the
No-Name Defense

Over the years, whenever basketball star Kareem Abdul-Jabbar was asked what opposing center gave him the most trouble, he responded with the same player.

"Swen Nater," he said.

His backup at UCLA. His teammate for four years. That answer wasn't the one people expected, but I knew exactly what he meant. Of all the defenses I faced, our No-Name Defense presented me with the most challenges each week in practice. They were smart, disciplined, talented, and confounding to compete against.

Throw deep on Jake Scott? Try to outwit Nick Buoniconti? And it started with the man who packaged that defense, Bill Arnsparger. As I sat on the sideline for the first time, watching just how he thought and organized, I gained an even greater appreciation for the work he did.

115

Before the eighth game of the season, Arnsparger wrote his customary twelve-page defensive game plan on an upcoming opponent, in this case Buffalo. He condensed it as the week progressed, then condensed it further. By week's end, it consisted of the four or five paragraphs he gave to players before each game. What did Mark Twain say about writing a letter to a friend? He was sorry it was so long but he didn't have more time?

That was Arnsparger's philosophy about coaching. It took days of involved thinking to simplify things to a fundamental core. And simplicity was key to his system. When Buoniconti was handed defensive game plans in 1969 under George Wilson's staff, he became infuriated at how many pages there were. "What do you expect the guys to do with this?" he asked coaches. "They already have toilet paper at home."

With Arnsparger, Buoniconti sat at the breakfast table on game days and settled on the half dozen defensive sets to use that particular day. If they worked as Arnsparger planned, no more were needed. They usually did, too. In Arnsparger's eleven Dolphins seasons with Don Shula, the Dolphins' defense ranked first or second in the league nine times. The players just didn't respect Bill Arnsparger; they revered him. To a man, they considered him the smartest defensive mind they had met. They talked in terms, as Dick Anderson did, of it being "a blessing" in their careers to play for him. "The best," Jake Scott said.

"Every bit as close to a genius in his field as Einstein was in his," Buoniconti added.

They all felt that way, all the way down the unconventional defensive roster. Defensive end Bill Stanfill was the only 1972 starter drafted in the first round by the Dolphins. Ninth-round draft pick Vern Den Herder, undrafted Manny Fernandez, and second-round pick Bob Heinz rounded out the defensive line. The starting outside linebackers, Mike Kolen and Doug Swift, were a twelfth-round pick and an undrafted free agent via Canada, respectively. Buoniconti, a thirteenth-round pick by the Patriots, was traded to the Dolphins for two players out of the league by 1972. No defensive back was selected earlier than the third round.

Do you get the picture? After Super Bowl VI, Dallas head coach Tom Landry was asked about the Dolphins' defense. "I couldn't go down the line and name one of the guys in the front four," he said. "I don't recall any of their names."

That quote was tacked to our locker-room bulletin board in 1972 and circled in red ink. Radio shows and newspaper reporters tried to nickname the defense for the previous year and floated various offerings. Ragin' Rejects. Don's Demons. Florida's Fugitives. Landry's quote delivered the winner: the No-Name Defense.

The players loved the name, feeling that it encapsulated teamwork, sacrifice, humility. It quickly became their identity. Posters were made with players in uniform and wearing half masks like the Lone Ranger. They reveled in telling reporters stories about their anonymity. The week of this Buffalo game, Vern Den Herder and Bob Heinz flagged down a cab outside the Biltmore Hotel in Coral Gables. The driver, noting their size, asked which Dolphins they were.

"I'm Vern Den Herder."

"Vern Who?" the driver asked.

They were the rare collection of talent that looked better together on the field than individually on paper. And everyone knew it. After the previous week's shutout against New England, the No-Names were the first unit to be named the NFL's Player of the Week. You don't think they were deservedly proud of that?

Still, if any game showed who they were and how they won, it was this eighth week's matchup against Buffalo and its star running back, O. J. Simpson. Arnsparger had one overriding rule for Simpson: Don't let him turn the corner. Simpson's ability to accelerate and his sheer physicality became dangerous if he got around the end. He could bust big gains straight downfield. He could slash back across the defense.

Buffalo put him in plays to do this, too. One favorite was to send both receivers wide to one side and take much of the coverage with them. Simpson then would take the ball around the other end, at a cornerback. The Dolphins had big cornerbacks—we actually had no cornerbacks and four safeties, many felt—and on that play 195-pound Tim Foley or 194-pound Curtis Johnson had to cut off Simpson before he got to the edge of the line and turned the corner. They typically did. In the seven games Simpson played against the No-Names between 1970 and 1973, he gained a moderate 484 yards, an average of 69 yards a game. (In his nine years at Buffalo, Simpson averaged 90.2 yards.)

"The best defense I ever see," Simpson said after the Bills' first game against the Dolphins in 1973, when he was held to 55 yards on 14 carries.

Their second meeting that 1973 season still resonated to the Dolphins decades later. It was the only game Simpson ran for more than 100 yards on them—120 yards on 20 carries, to be exact. But the method was madness, we felt. Down 17–0 in the fourth quarter, Buffalo kept handing the ball to Simpson. And handing it to him. Coach Lou Saban wasn't trying to win. He was committing the team sin of lifting one player's goals above the day's mission statement of winning. The Bills, after all, discussed openly the hope of Simpson breaking the NFL's single-season rushing record. He would that season, too. He gained 2,003 yards. But at what expense?

"You assholes!" Buoniconti yelled across the line.

When Simpson crossed the 100-yard barrier, the Bills actually began to celebrate on the field.

"You stupid bastard," Fernandez shouted to guard Reggie McKenzie. "Look at the scoreboard!"

That second meeting in 1972 was more representative of the matchup. Simpson turned into a nonfactor. He ran 13 times for 45 yards. He made little impact. After the Dolphins' win, Arnsparger was asked what he did to contain Simpson.

"Me? I stood on the sidelines," he said, jerking a thumb to the players' locker room and delivering what constituted a long speech for him. "They're the ones who did it."

If Arnsparger had an unusual coaching mind, he also came with an equally unusual football background. His high school coach in Paris, Kentucky, was Blanton Collier, who went on to be an NFL coach, as well as Arnsparger's boss and best man at his wedding. Arnsparger had three head coaches in his three years at Miami (Ohio) University. Two of them were Sid Gillman, who entered the NFL Hall of Fame, and Woody Hayes, who became a legend at Ohio State. They were only part of the coaching education he received in college. His Miami team-mates included Ara Parseghian, Bo Schembechler, John Pont, and Carmen Cozza—all of whom went on to have such successful coaching years that Miami became known as the "Cradle of Coaches."

Arnsparger's connections helped him early in his career. His first job was at Ohio State, with Hayes. He moved a few years later to Kentucky under Collier, where he was on a staff with Don Shula and Chuck Knox and coached a lineman named Howard Schnellenberger. "Fifty Times" the Kentucky players nicknamed Arnsparger, because if they made a mistake he sent them to the blackboard to write the correct play fifty times. "My role on 36 Trap is to block the inside gap."

Arnsparger was fired with Collier's staff in 1961 (Shula had left the previous year). For the first time in his career, Arnsparger wondered about the coaching path. He studied real estate. He considered making that his livelihood. He discussed it with the former Kentucky assistants, who met at the soda fountain of a Lexington drugstore each day, since they weren't allowed in the school offices. "The Untouchables," they called themselves. For years afterward, they held a reunion, celebrating a dismissal that ultimately made each come to terms with his career and ultimately pushed them toward something better.

As Arnsparger considered what to do with his life, Tulane coach Tommy O'Boyle called him early in 1962. They had met a few months earlier at a coaches' convention about an opening.

"What have you done?" O'Boyle said.

"Nothing," Arnsparger said. "What have you done?"

"Nothing," O'Boyle said.

Arnsparger joined O'Boyle's staff. Within a year, he was Tulane's defensive coordinator. In what became a signature of Arnsparger's defenses, the opponents' points reduced from 293 the previous season to 191 in his first year as defensive coordinator. When Don Shula became the Baltimore Colts coach in 1964, he hired Arnsparger as his defensive coordinator, a relationship that lasted for more than two decades and carried each through the most successful days of their careers.

In Baltimore, there was a staff of six coaches all squeezed into the same room. When Shula got a phone call, they vacated the room. When the offensive coaches wanted to watch a tape of the opposing defense, Arnsparger and other defensive assistant, Charley Winner, watched with them. It worked the other way, too, the offensive coaches offering suggestions to the defensive coaches. Arnsparger felt that this free exchange of ideas among a small staff was better than a common practice in coming years among teams in the NFL when staff with four times as many coaches occupied entire floors and rarely worked together. In 1968, Arnsparger's defense kept the Colts' opponents to fewer than 10 points in half their games and finished with a league-low 144 points allowed. For the first time, his star went up.

When Shula moved to Miami in 1970, Arnsparger accompanied him. Schnellenberger, too, reunited with his former coach on the Dolphins' staff and noticed that nothing had changed in him. By then, coaches called him "One More Reel," for his penchant to watch one more reel of film before taking a break. Arnsparger had a quiet way about him. His round glasses, occasionally mismatched clothing, and brilliant schemes lent a professorial air to him. Anyone who mistook him for anything but a football coach became sadly mistaken. Several years later, a All-America safety from Oklahoma, Zac Henderson, took a look at Arnsparger's outfit at a Dolphin meeting and joked, "Nice clothes." He was cut the next day.

His standard was simple: either the job was done or it wasn't. That training camp, rookie safety Charlie Baab filled a large hole with a ferocious hit on Larry Csonka at the goal line of an intrasquad exhibition game. Csonka, who outweighed Baab by 55 pounds, barely crossed the goal line. Baab was especially proud of the hit and, watching the film, waited for some word of praise.

"The object of the game is to keep them on the other side of the line" was all Arnsparger said as the play flickered across the screen.

With Arnsparger, there was little joking and less conversation. Schnellenberger carpooled with him to work. Sometimes, Schnellenberger said, Arnsparger offered a "Good morning" in greeting. Sometimes his mind was already so deep in solving the next offense that he didn't even muster that much on the ride. His clipped responses as he clicked the rewind button to review a play, again and again, stuck with players years later.

"What were you thinking there?" he'd say.

Click. Rewind.

"What was going on?"

Click. Rewind.

"Why'd that happen?"

Players passed time by counting how many times Arnsparger rewound an offending play. Seventy-two was the record. It all came with the idea of education, because Arnsparger believed in his developed system. He also believed that the team that made fewer mistakes won. His defense took a test each week on the opposing offense. Each player had to know his job in the called defense and every teammate's role as well. By seeing the bigger picture, Arnsparger thought, each player understood his defined role better.

This was a smart team, too. Buoniconti said it made five mental errors all year. Others rolled their eyes at that number, but the idea behind it held. These guys were smart. Just look at what they did after football. Dick Anderson became a state senator before running, among other companies, his insurance company. Doug Swift took his medical board test on the Saturday before a Dolphin game in New England in 1975, retired the next year, and is an anesthesiologist in Philadelphia. Mike Kolen became a top real estate broker in Alabama.

Buoniconti? He became a players' agent for the likes of baseball stars Andre Dawson and Mickey Rivers before shifting business gears and rising to become CEO of the *Fortune* 500 company U.S. Tobacco. When tragedy struck his son, Marc, he cofounded The Miami Project to Cure Paralysis and has raised more than $200 million toward funding it.

Tim Foley, who made more money than all of us after becoming one of the top producers in Amway history, also was a college football TV analyst after his playing career. He often asked coaches what they planned against a difficult matchup—a speedy receiver against a slower cornerback, for instance. The coach often said nothing was planned. His player just had to win that matchup. Conversations like that made Foley appreciate the way Arnsparger created defensive schemes with players' strengths and weaknesses in mind. Foley was that cornerback without speed. He ran the timed 40-yard sprint once in his career for coaches. After that, he claimed a nagging injury prevented him from running. The truth was he didn't want to remind them of his weakness.

Arnsparger, Foley knew, took his speed and every other player's issues into account each week. The defensive statistics showed the results. When Arnsparger's defense started five rookies in his first Dolphin season, in 1970, it allowed 228 points. That was 104 points fewer than in the previous season. Over the next three Super Bowl seasons, the defense ranked among the league's top three in fewest points allowed, decreasing each year from 174 to 171 to 150.

Underscoring Arnsparger's talent, the players felt, was what happened when he left to become head coach of the New York Giants in 1974. The defense allowed 216 points that season under new defensive coordinator Vince Costello. The players had no faith in his thinking. It was like "going from Nirvana to hell," Buoniconti said. At one legendary practice, Jake Scott became so upset at Costello he screamed, "I don't like you and I don't like your fucking defense!" Costello was replaced after that one season.

Nothing demonstrated Arnsparger's shrewd ability to move chess pieces more than the 1972 season. That training camp dripped with misfortune. Heinz fractured a vertebra in his back during an exhibition game. A few days later, Jim Riley, a four-year starter at defensive end, tore knee ligaments. Shula and Arnsparger already knew the line was an area of concern. They used their number-one draft pick on defensive tackle Mike Kadish, who reported overweight and overmatched and who was not used that season at all.

Suddenly Arnsparger was down to five defensive linemen in training camp. He had two healthy defensive ends. One of them, Den Herder, was a second-year man who hadn't started. Each afternoon, Arnsparger scanned the waiver wire for help. He found none. Each night, he and Shula studied other teams' rosters and debated possible trades. They made none.

Each day, too, Arnsparger studied his own roster and contemplated how to best use it by doodling on a yellow legal pad. One day a glimmer of an idea struck him.

"What do you think of this?" he said.

The key to his doodlings was Bob Matheson, a six-four, 235-pound veteran who had alternated between linebacker and defensive end in an undistinguished five years. Matheson told friends he was "in the twilight of a mediocre career" when he was pulled from a Cleveland team meeting during the 1971 exhibition season and traded to Miami for a second-round pick. He hadn't found a way to harness his unusual talent in the NFL. He had played running back at Duke during his first two years there and linebacker in his final two. He competed on the track team, fast enough to run the 100-yard sprint and strong enough to compete in the shot put and discus. At 235 pounds he wasn't quite big enough to be an NFL lineman. But he was considered too big to be an every-down linebacker.

The Dolphins had limited plans for him in making that trade. Buoniconti had broken his wrist. Matheson became an insurance policy in case Buoniconti couldn't play. For the entire 1971 and 1972 seasons, Buoniconti played with a cast over the wrist. Matheson made 57 tackles in a back-up role during his first year with the Dolphins. As far as lasting legacies, that wouldn't be the most important item from his 1971 season. That happened when he arrived at the Dolphins and found that the number 56 jersey he wore in Cleveland wasn't available.

He switched to number 53.

That became the name of the defense Arnsparger created out of desperation in the 1972 training camp. In the team's third preseason game, against Cincinnati, Matheson played the first half as an end and the second half as a linebacker. That's where Arnsparger got the idea on his legal pad. Why not have him switch positions, not from half to half, but from play to play? In one scheme, Matheson lined up as a defensive end and rushed the quarterback. In another, he played linebacker and dropped into pass coverage. In yet another, he played a linebacker, and one of the other three linebackers blitzed the passer.

Arnsparger tried that approach in the following exhibition game and liked it so much he didn't use it in the final two exhibition games. The players practiced it, but wondered if Arnsparger had lost faith in it for games. The truth was, he wanted to surprise opponents with the "53" defense. It embodied every defensive concept he believed, he found. He didn't ascribe to an attacking defense. He typically played a soft zone in the secondary. An all-out blitz left too many holes. But if the offense didn't know where the pressure was coming from, that element of surprise allowed a safer way to attack. Arnsparger's developed scheme became so advanced in use of angles and technical thought that years later, Pittsburgh defensive coordinator Dick LeBeau used it as a philosophical launching pad for the "zone blitz" defenses.

The "53" defense was a work in progress, especially early in that 1972 season. There were times just before the ball was snapped when Matheson called over to Swift on the other side, "Doug! You're blitzing! You're blitzing!"

Reviewing the win against Buffalo in the eighth game, Arnsparger knew it caused problems for opponents. There, on film, Buffalo linemen came to the line of scrimmage each time and pointed at Matheson. They talked among themselves. They were so locked on what "53" was doing that all of us understood it unlocked doors for a very good defense to turn the corner to greatness.

9

The Man Who Fired Flipper—and Built a Dynasty

After beating New England, 52–0, in the ninth regular-season game, after becoming the youngest coach to achieve one hundred career wins, after refusing the game ball presented in the locker room by Larry Little—"There's only one game ball I want," he said—after a few postgame pictures, after some smiles, some softball questions and snappy answers, Don Shula then confronted the day's toughest issue.

Mike Rathet, the Dolphins' public relations director, asked him to allow the Dolphins to celebrate his accomplishment later that week. Congratulations. Trophy. Photographs. News conference. The whole bit.

Then came the kicker.

"And Joe [Robbie] wants to host it," Rathet said.

Shula grew silent for a beat.

"Boy," he said.

On my first trip to Miami after the 1967 draft, I drove along streets lined with palm trees, over the sparkling Intracoastal Waterway, along the ocean beaches, and by all the picture-postcard scenes of the semitropics. The Indiana kid in me couldn't help but inhale the scene. With me was a family friend and business adviser, Ferris Traylor, and we were going to the renowned Jockey Club to meet another semitropical fascination.

Joe Robbie.

"Great to meet you!" the Dolphins' owner said as we sat down in a suite.

And Robbie had a drink.

"How was your trip?" Robbie said.

And he had another drink.

"Let's get down to business," Robbie said.

And he had another drink. And, well, another. I'd never seen anyone throw down so much alcohol so fast in my life. In our forty-five-minute meeting, Robbie put down so many drinks I lost count. And I was trying to count, too. All the while Robbie was talking dollars and terms that made my sober head spin.

I deferred to Traylor on the financial issues. Traylor wasn't an agent—few players had agents at that time—but he was a successful businessman whom my mother worked for. Sitting there and observing the scene, I figured we'd have to repeat the entire meeting because Robbie was half in the bag.

Did he have a tape recorder going somewhere? Should I start taking notes for him?

I left the meeting equally dazed by dollar signs being thrown around and the idea that my new boss might not even remember tossing them around.

Who is this Joe Robbie? I wondered.

The next time we met, I got another surprise that indicated who the Dolphin owner was: Robbie remembered every bit of conversation from that initial meeting right down to the exact dollars, stipulated conditions—even the exact words used in the conversation. He also kept repeating the same phrases from the first meeting whenever Taylor asked for a better deal.

"That's too much," Robbie said.

When Traylor made a counteroffer, Robbie chuckled, shook his head, and said, "I can't pay that."

As it turned out, there was no negotiating. Such ideals were several years away. There was just accepting the deal Robbie offered. It was more money than I had ever thought of earning. I received a $100,000 signing bonus and a four-year contract that began at $20,000 and increased by $1,000 each year.

I also asked for one special clause in the contract. I wanted the Dolphins to pay for the Purdue education of my brother Bill and sister Joyce. Bill was working for a railroad then. Joyce was a year out of high school. They didn't have any money for college. Robbie, liking what this said about his new quarterback and, perhaps, of himself as well, immediately agreed to the deal.

And so by the end of my first dealing with Robbie, I saw an array of personal flaws and professional complexity that everyone agreed marked the Dolphins' owner as genuine and unique, for better and worse.

Most owners bought into the fledgling American Football League for the normal reason why anyone bought a sports franchise at any time. Ego. Civic duty. Hobbyist hopes. To realize a sports fan's ultimate dream.

The common denominator was that most of these owners smelled of new money, old money, or money dipped in oil. Baron Hilton, of Hilton Hotels fame, was the original owner of the San Diego Chargers. Lamar Hunt, the son of a Texas oil tycoon, started the Kansas City

Chiefs. Bud Adams, who made his fortune in oil, founded the Houston Oilers. Get the idea?

Theirs were the kinds of wallets AFL commissioner Joe Foss recruited. Add powerful, famous, and with roots deep into their team's community and you'd have the checklist of the dream American sports owner.

And everything Joe Robbie wasn't.

He was a Minneapolis lawyer on a business trip to Miami in 1964, enjoying the morning sun on his hotel roof, when he struck up a conversation with a multimillionaire from Philadelphia. At some point as their talk wandered, Robbie mentioned AFL commissioner Joe Foss.

"Do you know Joe Foss?" the man asked.

Know him? Robbie and Foss had opposed each other in the South Dakota gubernatorial race in 1950. Foss, a former World War II pilot, won the election. But Robbie came out with something, as this new client now was proving. Robbie was hired to take the man's bankable credentials to Foss and pitch the idea of an AFL team for Philadelphia. Which Robbie did. Foss said the new league didn't want an expansion franchise to go toe-to-toe against the NFL's established Philadelphia Eagles. He did float an untapped market, though.

"If you want a franchise," Foss said, "go to Miami."

The football interests of Robbie's client stopped at the Philadelphia city borders.

But the more Robbie considered the idea, the more appealing it sounded to own a sports franchise himself. The involved problems might have deterred a different man, considering that (a) Robbie earned only $27,000 a year, (b) he had eleven children to support, (c) he lived two thousand miles away, (d) he knew no one in the Miami business community, and (e) his toehold into football consisted of being a season-ticket holder of the Minnesota Vikings.

Robbie checked his Rolodex for an ally. He found one in the actor and television producer Danny Thomas, who like Robbie was of Lebanese descent and a board member of St. Jude's Hospital. But unlike Robbie, he was famous.

"Doesn't every Lebanese boy who grew up in Toledo want to own a professional team?" Thomas said at the news conference announcing the Miami franchise.

"I'm just the hired help," Robbie said.

Actually, Robbie's title of general managing partner was a tip-off that something unusual was afoot. He formed the Dolphins with a structure called a limited partnership. On one level were limited partners who had no personal liability beyond their investment but who could tap into some bountiful tax benefits through items such as player depreciation. On another level were the general managing partners, Robbie and Thomas, who had to cover costs if the Dolphins failed.

That was the concept, anyhow.

The reality was different. Thomas supplied that famous name to the franchise as the producer behind multimillion-dollar shows such as the *Andy Griffith Show* and the *Dick Van Dyke Show*. He made a dozen speeches to market the team, though he often neglected football while discussing his wedding, family, furniture, and television sponsor. Robbie stood in the back of the hall making desperate passing and kicking motions.

"We have spoken today of family, philosophy, religion, and charity," Thomas said to close one speech. "My partner reminds me we are here to sell football tickets. Remember, thou shalt love thy neighbor as thyself. And I am your neighbor."

Thomas continued his role by becoming the public picture of joy in the inaugural game in 1966. As Joe Auer returned the franchise's opening kickoff for a touchdown, Thomas, cigar in mouth, sprinted down the sideline with him.

That's about all Thomas offered. He put up only $25,000 through a shell corporation called Danny Thomas Sports Ltd., which protected himself from further liability.

Robbie forked over the bulk of his savings—all of $100,000—and signed over everything else he owned as collateral. His house, for instance. Of course, "if he mortgaged his house in Minneapolis, he might have as much as $25,000 in cash," a 1972 Dolphins game program said.

If the Dolphins failed, the limited partners walked away and Robbie was bankrupt. The league was vulnerable. Al Davis saw that after replacing Foss as the AFL commissioner. He saw the books for the first time, translated the business arrangement, and said later, "We had a big problem with Miami."

Robbie split time between Miami and his Minneapolis law practice. His Dolphin headquarters became a tiny, two-room office in downtown Miami's Dupont Plaza Hotel—rent-free, of course—and consisted of a phone bank, an operator to answer the calls, and Robbie himself. Robbie had two stated goals shimmering off in the distance: to break even on the field and to break even at the gate. He achieved neither in the Dolphins' first four years. They didn't win more than five games a season to that point and suffered losses totaling $3 million.

He needed to find limited partners to stop the flow of money. It's hard to say who he worked more at games, those potential investors or the worried bank creditors. ("They've just come to inspect the collateral," he once told a reporter about the bank officers.)

"I am where I am now for one reason," Robbie said years later. "That's because nobody wants to put their own money up. They want something for nothing. They don't want to take risks. That's why I have the club. I took the risk."

If he had little money, he spent accordingly. He counted towels in the locker room. He demanded that coaches log their phone calls and examined each one. He signed every check for the Dolphins in the opening years, even one for a pencil sharpener.

"When I was there, he even had his nose in the paper clips," Marsha Bierman, who was the coaches' secretary until Robbie fired her, once told *Sports Illustrated*.

She wasn't alone on that list. Robbie had the innate ability to alienate those who worked closest to him. He went through four business managers the first four years, staring with Chuck Burr, who fronted $11,000 of his own money so the Dolphins could travel to a game and who eventually sued Robbie. Raleigh Tozer assembled the Dolphins' radio network. When Bob Lundy, the team's first trainer, commented that the showers were dirty, he found a mop in his office the next day. When George Wilson cut players one training camp, he had to open his wallet to pay for the players' expenses home. When players got paychecks, Larry Seiple remembers, a weekly race to the bank would follow, for fear that they all wouldn't cash. When Robbie refused after the first season to pay for the transportation costs of the most famous Dolphin—Flipper—he became the Scrooge of sports.

"The Man Who Fired Flipper," read the front-cover headline of *Sports Illustrated* in a 1969 article that described Robbie as "tough as a wharf rat and as charming as a rent collector."

"He runs a $2 million business like a fruit stand," Houston Oilers owner Bud Adams said.

Even with the towel counting and phone monitoring, the Dolphins lost $300,000 that first year. Questions of their future abounded. Newspaper stories did, too. Amid conversation that the team was sinking, Robbie struggled mightily but met the franchise's first December payments of $600,000 for payroll and $1 million to the league.

"We'll never have another December like that," Robbie said.

Little improved during the next couple of seasons. When ice stopped being delivered to practice because the company wasn't paid, Bill Braucher of the *Miami Herald* began focusing on the Dolphins' financial problems. Robbie eventually sent a letter to Braucher's editor complaining about the reporter's "morbid fascination with the club's finances." The editor was so impressed that Braucher received the biggest raise of his sportswriting career.

Beyond their methods ("These pack rats that are trying to gnaw on my bones!" he said.), Robbie's frustration with the media was that they didn't appreciate his achievement. He occasionally laughed at his closed-wallet policy.

"The last of the bootstrap operations in pro football," he called the Dolphins.

He said it with pride, though. Didn't the writers understand? Couldn't they look above the methods to see his accomplishment? Anyone could build a franchise with Daddy's money or a corporate credit card. His success was making something grand out of nothing at all.

"Once people sympathized with the guy who could climb up the ladder, the Horatio Alger thing, you know," he once said. "But I think in this affluent society, where lots of people have lots of money, they resent a working stiff making it. That kind of thinking exists particularly in the glamorous area of professional sports, which has always been a rich man's plaything in the past. They're big business now and there's going to be more and more of my kind one day. I know how to fight. I came from a town called Hard Times."

Hard Times actually was Sisseton, South Dakota (population, 3,218). His father immigrated there in 1900 at age fourteen to escape the military draft in his native Lebanon and to meet up with two great-uncles who had settled in Sisseston after peddling across the United States. The family name was "Arabi," but the immigration officer heard "Robbie," and that was that.

Joe was born in 1916. Hard Times? Hard work, too. At fourteen, he was sports editor of the *Sisseton Journal Press*. At fifteen, he temporarily dropped out of high school to earn $30 a week in the Civilian Conservation Corps, sending $25 of it back home to help during the Depression. He returned for his high school degree and worked through Northern State College in a haberdashery, as a radio announcer, and "mixing grasshopper poison," he once said. He became student body president at Northern and, later, a debate champion at South Dakota State, where he earned his law degree. To help pay his tuition, folks in Sisseton passed a hat in the pool hall his father owned.

On the day after Pearl Harbor, he joined the navy. He served in five invasions in the Pacific, earned a Bronze Star, and entered politics upon returning to Mitchell, South Dakota. He was an odd fit: a Democratic,

Lebanese lawyer in a Republican state with little ethnic diversity. Robbie became a state representative and quickly was a known commodity. He befriended George McGovern and Hubert Humphrey, both South Dakota natives who became national names in politics. Robbie lost the state's governor's election to Foss, moved to Minneapolis, and set up a law practice.

By 1969, Hard Times for Robbie was the inner sanctum of the Dolphins' offices.

The team was losing money it didn't have, and the infighting with Robbie was reaching beyond business managers. He booted one limited partner, John O'Neil, out of the owner's suite at home games and banned him from riding on the team plane. O'Neil filed a lawsuit claiming that Robbie "embarked on a calculated, systematic, malicious and unlawful scheme and plan to embarrass, humiliate and annoy the plaintiff and deprive him of his rights as partner."

Robbie had a more significant concern than O'Neil's words. This one was with Willard Keland, a Wisconsin developer and cattleman. When Danny Thomas's lawyers demanded that he sell his stake in the Dolphins because of the team's financial state, Keland and Robbie agreed to become general partners. A problem arose.

"Joe didn't come up with the money, so I figured I was in control," Keland said.

Being in control, Keland had ideas of moving the team to Seattle. Robbie's dream was on the brink, and he applied all his creative scheming and bare-knuckle personality to solving the problem. He called banks, brokers, businessmen—any possible lifelines that could help his cause. One morning a relative newcomer to Miami named Harper Sibley left his home at the Jockey Club—one of the luxury condominium complexes he had developed—and was met outside by the president of Hertz Rent-A-Car, Earl Smalley. They knew each other well. Smalley lived at the Jockey Club and often threw parties on his boat that carried the name of the slogan he constantly shouted: "What a Way to Go!"

Smalley didn't bother with a greeting that morning.

"You've got to buy the Dolphins," he told Sibley. "No one else can pull it off. And if you don't, they're moving to Seattle."

"What are you talking about?" Sibley asked.

Sibley began to shift his life from Rochester, New York, to Miami at about the same time Robbie arrived with the Dolphins. That was about all they had in common. Sibley was the great-grandson of the Western Union founder and served on that company's board of directors. He raised hogs in upstate New York and hybrid cattle on a Colorado ranch. He developed the Boca Grande Club on Gasparilla Island, the Mountain Queen Condominiums in Aspen, the Jockey Club and the Ocean Reef Club in South Florida, and affordable housing in the Bronx. He hunted with Humphrey, the current vice president.

Sibley was worth millions and, as such, was the best hope to keep the Dolphins in town. Robbie set up the plan. First National Bank would lend $3.5 million to Sibley. That would give him 80 percent of the team. A handful of civic-minded millionaires would then enter and split up the shares among themselves as limited partners. Robbie would remain as managing general partner. The Dolphins wouldn't go anywhere. Everyone would be happy, right?

"No one else is qualified to do this but you," Smalley told Sibley.

Sibley didn't think very long. And what he thought had less to do with football than establishing himself in his new community. There also was a sense of adventure to it all.

"I did it as a lark," he said. "I signed the papers that day."

On the brink of losing everything, Robbie won again. He escaped not only with the team, but also with the financial support that had eluded him during the first three seasons. He was joined now with the biggest movers and shakers in Miami's business community. What's more, the financial clouds were clearing ahead. His television payments jumped from the contracted half share of $500,000 the first four years to a full share of $1 million. The AFL's merger with the NFL immediately bumped it to $1.25 million.

The 1972 Miami Dolphins were called the "smartest team I ever coached," Don Shula said.

The first significant hire by Joe Robbie (left) when starting the Dolphins was Joe Thomas (right), the director of player personnel who drafted or traded for five of the six future Hall of Fame players on the 1972 Dolphins.

I was shocked the Dolphins could trade for Paul Warfield in 1970, and learned valuable insight into the passing game by working with him after practice.

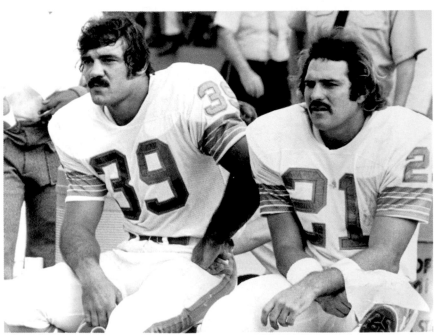

Larry Csonka (39) and Jim Kiick (21)—"You can't spell them," as one AFC coach said, "and you can't stop them."

I knew from the second
I met Don Shula he was
exactly what this team
needed. He never changed
my mind on that idea.

Don Shula knew Mercury
Morris provided a necessary
element of speed to the
Dolphins offense and so
instituted a platoon system
to much controversy.

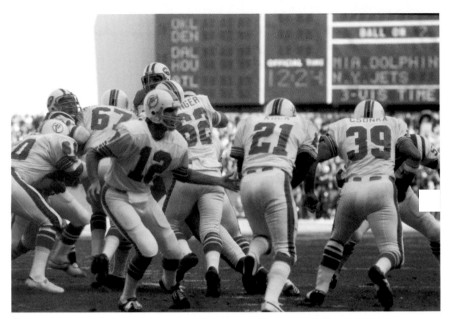

The media called me the "Thinking Man"s Quarterback" but I didn't have to think too hard about the way our running game punished teams like the Jets.

I returned from my injury for the second half of the AFC Championship game at Pittsburgh and we were as physical as ever in the win.

In the fifth game, I broke my fibula, dislocated my right ankle and figured my season was done.

Earl Morrall wasn't just a fill-in at quarterback after I got hurt. He played well enough to be named the AFC offensive player of the year.

Guard Larry Little came
from San Diego in a trade
that was so lopsided the
Chargers' Sid Gillman said
at Larry's Hall of Fame
induction it was the worst
move he ever made. And, by
extension, as good as move
as the Dolphins ever have.

Linebacker Nick Buoniconti
was the heart of the No-Name
Defense, the first player
offensives drew up game
plans to neutralize.

Bill Stanfill was called
"Stretch" by teammates
because of the 6-7 frame
he used to menace
quarterbacks.

Defensive tackle Manny Fernandez was said to be signed by
the Dolphins to market the team to Miami's growing Cuban
population, but he often said he couldn't say, "Adios," in Spanish.

Jim Kiick was a nimble inside runner as he shows here in scoring against Washington in the Super Bowl.

Jake Scott had two interceptions and was named the Super Bowl MVP despite a serious shoulder injury.

After hiring Shula, Robbie's dream materialized completely. The team began winning. The finances began working. Near the end of that 1970 season, Robbie announced that the Dolphins had turned a profit for the first time. Owners typically didn't announce such things. But Robbie wanted a headline of this achievement after so many years of financial questions.

When the Dolphins went to the Super Bowl in 1971, Robbie probably had the best balance sheet in pro football, with a $2 million profit, according to Jim Steeg, who became a Dolphins accountant, rose to become Robbie's top lieutenant, and then moved to an executive job in the NFL.

While revenues rose even more in 1972, Robbie remained true to his managerial style of upsetting those closest to him. He refused to pay dividends on those profits to those limited partners who helped save his franchise. To anyone who complained, he had a pat answer.

"I'll buy you out," he said.

That upset some partners even more. But as his friend and lawyer William Frates often said, "Joe is difficult in adversity and impossible with success."

Those on the football side saw a schizophrenic quality to Robbie. He didn't meddle in personnel decisions, like some of his peers during that decade—George Steinbrenner, Ted Turner, Al Davis, and Robert Irsay. In his entire ownership, Robbie made one player decision: he demanded that George Wilson cut his son, George, and keep Larry Seiple in 1967 when the coach planned to do the opposite.

Nor did Robbie turn down Shula's major requests. When Shula laid out to Robbie why Earl Morrall should be signed, he admitted there was "just one problem with Earl."

"What's that?" Robbie asked.

"He makes $75,000," Shula said.

That made him one of the most expensive players on the team, they both knew. Robbie shrugged. Sign him, he told Shula.

This made another of Robbie's decisions strange. When Shula asked to buy a $68 kicking net for Garo Yepremian on the sideline, Robbie refused. When Bobby Beathard wanted a raise for scouts just once in four years, Robbie refused. It took Beathard six months just to get Super Bowl rings for his scouts, who also were allowed to call home just once a week on the road. When Shula asked to hire a cleaning lady so coaches wouldn't have to keep cleaning their offices, Robbie hemmed and hawed and eventually allowed a cleaning lady twice a week.

One Robbie fixation became the high cost of practice footballs. How could so much be spent on them? One day Beathard walked by an office to see Joe's son, Mike, pumping up department-store footballs.

"What are those?" Beathard asked.

"We're going to use these at practice," Mike said.

They were cheaper. But they weren't game quality. They weren't even game size. Beathard threw up his arms at how a NFL team could operate like this and moved down the hall to tell Shula. The department store balls never made it to practice.

If Robbie hated the miserly tag while poor, he saw some benefit to perpetuating it. For the 1972 season yearbook, public relations assistant Arthur Mickelson wrote Robbie's bio to include $100,000 in charitable contributions that year. Robbie deleted the line. Mickelson was stunned. He figured it was good public relations for a man needing some and asked Robbie why he wouldn't allow it.

"When I sit across from Csonka or his agent, I want them to think I'm the meanest sonuvabitch in town," Robbie said.

Nor was there mention that he gave $800,000 to a Notre Dame charity in the wake of his son, David, a Notre Dame graduate, jumping off the Golden Gate Bridge to his death in 1971.

"It's not charity if you talk about it," he once told the *Miami Herald*.

Robbie's other private habit didn't stay private. As I saw in our first meeting, Robbie was more than a living, breathing, working version of the American Dream. He was a drinking one, too. He enjoyed drinking contests with Native Americans growing up in South Dakota, he once said, and nothing changed as an adult.

"Irish heart disease," Robbie called his drinking habit.

Twice while living in Minnesota, Robbie was arrested for driving under the influence. In 1959, he admitted to drinking three martinis and a highball and was found to have a blood alcohol level of .159. The legal limit was .150 at that time. The lawyer in Robbie immediately demanded a jury trial and questioned the accuracy of the reading. Wesley Paulus, the Minnesota officer who arrested Robbie, was struck by the emotion with which the lawyer pled his case and how the jury let him off. It became the only one of the officer's 150 drunk-driving arrests that was overturned.

In 1960, Robbie was arrested for drunk driving, operating on the wrong side of the street, and running a stop sign after a poker party with a Minneapolis Supreme Court judge, a federal judge, and two labor leaders. He represented himself again. He was found guilty only of running a stop sign.

"A floating cocktail party," linebacker Nick Buoniconti called the first-class section of the Dolphins' flights when Wilson was coach. Shula buttoned up behavior, banning drinking on the way to games even by the owners and kicking off all the women but Robbie's wife, Elizabeth.

Once the ownership group reached the ground, the party began. On game days, Bloody Marys were mixed in Robbie's suite starting at 9:30 a.m. His preferred gin martinis started soon thereafter. Players often visited these suites after games to find Robbie in a regular position.

"How'd you like the game, Joe?" Manny Fernandez would ask.

Robbie would be unconscious on a table after a full day of drinking.

"Yeah, I thought it was pretty good, too," Fernandez would say.

Beathard refused to deal with Robbie after midafternoon, fearing he would be drunk by then. Sibley tells how in meetings of the

Non-Group, a collection of Miami insiders, Robbie often passed out. Charlie Nobles of the *Miami News* once interviewed Elizabeth Robbie about her husband's drinking. She recounted how a limousine driver once wondered what to do with his slumped body in the backseat. "Mrs. Robbie, what should I do when I get where we're going, dump him on the sidewalk?"

Each year for Catholic Lent, Robbie quit drinking.

"It's the greatest sacrifice I can make," he told friends, "and proves to me I'm not an alcoholic."

Through the years, sloppy stories followed him like empty bottles tied to his legend. One such story came after the preseason opener in 1972. The team buses were loaded. The Dolphins started to roll to the airport. That's when one of the team officials noticed something wrong.

"Where's Joe?" he said.

No one knew. The other buses were checked. No Joe. They went to the locker room. No Joe. They dispatched a search party up to the owner's suite and only by opening a closet was Robbie found, slumped on the floor and passed out, in the darkness. He was helped to the buses and the trip home. The next Monday, when public relations director Mike Rathet entered the office, he was met with a bellow.

"Get in here!" Robbie yelled.

Rathet, a former sportswriter, was in his first season working inside the Dolphins and still growing accustomed to the multilayered personality of the owner.

"You're responsible for making sure I'm taken care of!" Robbie said.

Rathet solved that problem by assigning Jim Johnson, the club's sales director, to chaperone Robbie at games thereafter.

That left one problem. It was no one's doing, either. As the Dolphins won, Shula was put on a pedestal. That's natural in any sport. What did Teddy Roosevelt say about the man in the arena counting most? The coach talked to the media every day, too. He made headlines. He developed a persona. And so when Shula shaped these Dolphins into a winner, he became celebrated, as coaches of championship teams are everywhere.

And Robbie? No one talked of him in terms of a shrewd business-man who scraped together $100,000 and created a highly profitable franchise by 1972. Nor did anyone talk about the mind behind turning an expansion team into a champion in that short time.

"I'm the idiot who hired all the geniuses," Robbie said.

As the years moved on, as the Dolphins won more, as Shula drew more praise, Robbie became jealous that he didn't receive his share of acclaim. And resentful. Rathet tried inventive things to soothe that. He invited New York writers to dinner with Robbie as a means of broadening his national image. He had fruit baskets and champagne waiting in Robbie's hotel rooms, as if sent by the hotel's management as a token of his esteem. But in the 1973 season Robbie crossed a line. He wrote a scathing, seven-page memo to Shula, condemning him for everything from the ban of women on the team plane (except Robbie's wife, Elizabeth) to his general sideline conduct. It wasn't made public. But the secretary who typed it up knew. People in the office knew. And Rathet knew it was a matter of time before lava flowed.

It happened in the most public of places. At the 1973 team banquet celebrating a second Super Bowl title, Shula waited outside the Fountainebleau Hotel for his wife, Dorothy. Robbie, anxious for the evening to begin, came for him.

"We've got a thousand people waiting for you," Robbie said loudly to Shula in front of a group of people. "Let's get up there."

"Yell at me again, and I'll knock you on your ass!" Shula said.

"Go ahead and knock me on my ass!" Robbie said back.

"You ever raise your voice at me in public again, and I'll knock you on your ass," Shula said.

The exchange stunned Nick Buoniconti, who was among the witnesses. Soon it was in all the Miami papers. The night wasn't finished, either. Washington columnist Morris Siegel, who served as emcee for the banquet, later related how Robbie asked if he was speaking before or after Shula.

"Before Don," Siegel answered.

"Why?" Robbie asked.

"I don't know," Siegel answered.

"I'm speaking last," Robbie said.

"It's your dinner," Siegel said.

Shula then approached and asked what Robbie wanted. When told, Shula said, "I'm speaking last."

Robbie set himself up as the final speaker. But after a highlight of Super Bowl VIII was shown, Shula returned to the dais and said a few final words.

"Why did you let him speak?" Robbie asked Siegel.

"How was I to stop him?"

The next morning, Shula called Robbie, who didn't return the call. Shula called him again the next day. And the next. Finally he told Robbie's secretary to take a message every day that he called. Meanwhile, their clash went public when *New York Times* columnist Dave Anderson recounted the banquet scene and the blow-by-blow involving Siegel. It became the hottest story in sports, the two-time Super Bowl champion owner and coach feuding to the point of fighting. Shula said what? And Robbie did what?

After nineteen days of silence between Miami's two most public Catholics, Coleman F. Carroll, the archbishop of Miami, called each to broker peace. He had lunch with them. Both men acted contrite. Shula issued a statement afterward, saying, "If we have not been behaving like champions, I regret it."

But apologize to each other? Neither man did that. And the media played in the mud.

"*The Exorcist*," the *Miami News* front-page headline ran after the lunch with the archbishop, referring to the just-released movie. The subheadline read "Archbishop Ousts Devil in Dolphins Leaders."

Over the next couple of decades, their relationship was as distant as the thirteen-mile gap between their respective offices. Perhaps Bob Kuechenberg framed it best, saying that Shula and Robbie were "two bulls in the same pasture." Both driven. Both strong personalities. Neither willing to back down to anyone.

All that was ahead of Shula and Robbie during the public celebration of Shula's hundredth victory at the Miami Lakes Inn and Country Club. Players came. Media came. Robbie handed a trophy that included the game ball to Shula. Robbie read a message from President Nixon: "This new milestone is convincing proof of your coaching ability."

Robbie got what he wanted out of this: his share of the spotlight. He smiled with Shula for the photos. He beamed that this landmark came in this great season. And perhaps everyone even remembered he was the person who brought Shula to town.

10

Too Small, Too Short, Too Much

GAME TEN

———

New York Jets
November 19, 1972

Years later, when they met at a friend's house for a dinner party in the Hamptons, Nick Buoniconti crossed his feet at his ankles in front of Joe Namath and put on a middle linebacker's full glare.

"Remember this?" he asked Namath.

Buoniconti then crossed his arms over his chest and resumed the glare.

"And then this?"

The memory and a smile came to Namath. In the Dolphins' tenth game that season, in the fourth quarter at the Orange Bowl, on a New York Jets drive inside the Dolphins' 10-yard line, Namath twice brought his offense to the line. Twice he backed away because of the crowd's noise and huddled up again. The Dolphins led, 28–24, in the kind of frantic game we rarely had that season. Namath's offense reeled off

145

17 unanswered points at one point. Dick Anderson's interception then set up one touchdown, and his fumble recovery another. The Dolphins took the lead. Now the Jets came back.

A third time, Namath came to the line, and now Buoniconti took a step closer to him to be heard.

"Run the fucking play!" Buoniconti yelled across the line.

I knew what it was like to compete mentally against Buoniconti. I'd call a play in practice, come to the line, and hear him yell, "It's gonna be a run left!" I'd think: How'd he know that? What's tipping it off? That made me work harder to conceal plays and work overtime on fake checkoffs. We had to use them in games. Buoniconti made us practice them, too.

"Set!" I'd yell.

"Run left!" he'd yell.

"Two-forty-eight!" I'd yell.

"Watch forty-eight!" he'd yell.

I'd smile inside then. That's when I had him. It was always fun matching wits with someone that good. And he was so good at reading our plays, offensive tackle Norm Evans would become so frustrated he'd ask Buoniconti, "Are we giving it away? Are we doing something you see?"

We weren't. It was just that he was sharp. And now here he was, yelling at Namath, in a game that was emotional beyond words for both sides. Namath refused to shake hands with Earl Morrall during the pregame coin toss at midfield. Morrall chuckled it away. Their battle was rooted in the 1969 Super Bowl, Namath's best moment and Morrall's toughest. Namath guaranteed a win and launched into fame off it. He became football's top pitch man, using his good looks and Broadway Joe personality to sell Ovaltine, Arrow shirts, Franklin jerseys, and Buttertop Poppers. And it was Namath who sat in a chair that 1972 season while an unknown Farrah Fawcett asked, "Ladies, want to see Joe Namath get creamed?" before slathering shaving cream on his face.

That was Namath. I got along with him fine. But we were opposite personalities. He was loud and brash and enjoyed fame. I was quiet and reserved and enjoyed my family. When the rest of my teammates went out for a beer after practice, I raced home to see my wife and boys. And if I was different from Namath, Morrall was from a different generation, too.

"I don't respect him, his lifestyle, his actions," Morrall said that week of the Jets game. "I wouldn't want to follow in his footsteps. I don't want to be like him. And I hope my kids and the younger generation don't grow up to be like him."

That headline earned Morrall a trip to Shula's office. And a non-handshake from Namath. Morrall pushed his thirty-eight-year-old legs on the longest Dolphin run of the year—31 yards for a touchdown—and now stood on the sideline as Namath tried to win the game.

"Run the fucking play!" Buoniconti yelled again.

From his film work, from the Jets' formation, from the time left and their place on the field, Buoniconti figured there were four plays Namath might select on this third down. Buoniconti was ready for the one called, a crossing pattern over the middle. He broke on the ball just as Namath released it. He cut in front of the intended receiver, running back John Riggins, and intercepted the pass to seal the win, the division title, and a playoff berth.

Buoniconti didn't exude the animalism of Dick Butkus. He didn't have the strength of Willie Lanier. But no one had to tell me about Nick's talent. I saw it daily in practice. For years, he was told how he was too small, too slow, too weak, which made his son, Marc, conclude upon introducing him to the Hall of Fame years later that he had one other deficiency.

"You don't listen very well," Marc said.

Buoniconti grew up in the South End of Springfield, Massachusetts, an Italian section where he remembered everyone was his aunt or uncle and the smell of spaghetti sauce came from every home. He lived in a duplex beside his grandfather Henry Mercolino, who emigrated from Naples and started a bakery in 1918. When his wife became pregnant, he repainted the bakery's sign to read "Mercolino &

Son's." After his wife gave birth to a daughter, he changed the sign back to "Mercolino's." He repainted the sign all thirteen times his wife was pregnant. She gave birth to thirteen daughters, including Nick's mother. The entire family worked the bakery, which Nick's brother, Peter, later ran.

Buoniconti's formative years were dotted with annual crises. At two, he nearly drowned off the Connecticut shore. At three, he fell out of a moving car. At six, he was hit by a truck. At eight, he developed scarlet fever. At nine, Buoniconti first donned shoulder pads and helmet, then ran out of his home and down the street for a game. He tripped. He broke his arm. He also told his mother not to try to prevent him from playing football for fear of injury.

Thus began a football career full of surprise turns. At Springfield's Cathedral High, a Catholic school, he suffered a knee injury as a junior and had most of the cartilage taken out. He nonetheless starred enough as a senior to get several letters a week through the school from college football recruiters. But when one came from Notre Dame, and was followed by a scholarship offer, he received no more letters.

After a few weeks went by, he asked his coach why other colleges weren't writing anymore. He was told to ask the principal.

"Didn't you get an offer from Notre Dame?" the principal asked.

"Yes," Buoniconti said.

"I've been throwing all the other letters in the wastebasket."

He indeed chose Notre Dame, where he had the misfortune of falling into an empty coaching era between those of Frank Leahy and Ara Parseghian. Buoniconti's years aligned with Joe Kuharich, a former professional coach who never grasped the college ways. When Buoniconti was a junior, a spring practice called Black Saturday was held to toughen up the team. It consisted of a 45-minute scrimmage centered around the offense, a 30-minute scrimmage for the defense, 20 minutes of calisthenics and, finally, a mile sprint. All in 100-degree heat. Buoniconti, who did everything all-out, dropped from a 200-pound linebacker that day to a 182-pound hospital patient.

Kuharich never had a winning season at Notre Dame and became the first losing coach at the school. The only lesson Buoniconti received from losing is that he didn't like it much. He enjoyed what came next even less. Buoniconti was named All-America his senior season, but Kuharich told pro scouts he was too small.

"I can't in good conscience recommend you," the coach told Buoniconti before the 1962 draft.

A pattern developed even outside football. Upon entering Notre Dame with low test scores, he was informed by a counselor that as an athlete of questionable academics he was flagged as someone who probably wouldn't make it academically. He graduated in four years and was accepted into Notre Dame's graduate school of economics. Later, in downtown Boston, he mentioned his hope of becoming a lawyer to an established attorney. The man laughed that a linebacker could attend law school. Buoniconti studied at night for four years, passed the Massachusetts bar, and became an assistant prosecutor. He later passed the Florida bar and took a job with Greenberg and Bonde, a business law firm, where he dealt with business contracts and real estate deals. He then became a sports attorney, negotiating million-dollar deals for the likes of baseball stars Andre Dawson and Tim Raines, before becoming the CEO of U.S. Tobacco.

Kuharich's doubts presented a trickier problem. He played briefly and coached for more than a decade in the pros before Notre Dame and so had a known voice among the decision-makers. No NFL team drafted Buoniconti. The Boston Patriots of the AFL selected him in the thirteenth round. He felt it was a decision made as much for his local status as a scouting report that Joe McArdle, a former Notre Dame line coach, sent to Patriot coach Mike Holovak.

For the first time, Buoniconti's lack of size hindered him. He couldn't believe it. All he wanted was a chance in the pros, and now he feared he wouldn't get that. The Patriots didn't even call after taking him. A month after the draft, Patriot owner Billy Sullivan brushed into Kuharich in New York. Kuharich was returning from watching film clips of linemen on the All-America team as part a coaching conference. He asked Sullivan if the Patriots had signed Buoniconti. Sullivan said they didn't, because there was no rush since the NFL didn't draft him.

"Sign him," Kuharich said. "I don't care who your middle linebacker is, Nick will take the job from him."

Suddenly and belatedly, Kuharich realized he had graded Buoniconti as if he were a grown, professional product. Boston signed Buoniconti to a $10,000 deal with a $1,000 signing bonus. He immediately called a friend at Notre Dame who had a beer distributorship and ordered $1,000 worth of beer. A beer truck pulled up outside his cottage in South Bend. The party lasted two days. The police came by eight times. Weeks later, they were still finding beer cans in bushes in the neighborhood.

Hoping to drum up publicity, Boston announced Buoniconti's signing with a press conference. During it, Nick's father mentioned to publicity director Gerry Moore to warn the Patriot players about his son. "He can get just as worked up in practice as he does in a game," his dad said.

Five minutes into his first practice, Buoniconti was in a fistfight with veteran tight end Tony Romeo. Nick didn't talk to any teammate through the three weeks of training camp and six weeks of exhibition games. On the final day of cuts, he figured that either he or Syracuse linebacker Bob Stem would be the final cut. He watched Holovak come slowly up a long flight of stairs at the Patriots facility at Boston University, walk past him in the locker room, and tap Stem on the shoulder. That's how Buoniconti knew he made the team. By the second game of the year, he was in the starting lineup. He didn't come out of one until he retired fourteen years later. In Boston, the defensive line coach, Marion Campbell, taught Buoniconti to read the center and guards to decipher what play was coming. The running backs might crisscross or be decoys. The quarterback might mask his intentions. But the triangle in the middle of the line formed by the blocking schemes of the center and two guards told a linebacker everything if he knew what to spot.

During that first season, Buoniconti freelanced in the Patriots' system, typically blitzing seven out of ten plays to compensate for a bad Patriots secondary. The criticism became that he was a one-dimensional linebacker. That changed as the Patriots' secondary improved, and Buoniconti's role took on more dimensions in line with that of a dominant middle linebacker. His competitiveness knew no boundaries. Patriot coaches often took him out of practice because he was constantly getting into fights or hitting too hard.

"The game becomes my whole being," he said at the time. "Every play is like life and death, whether it's practice or a real game. I can't think of anything except the play that is occurring at that moment."

After his rookie year, he was named to the All-AFL team five straight seasons. He became the defense's leader. It was a good, rich, hectic time in his life. He had three children with his wife, Terry. He attended Suffolk Law School and passed the bar. After some practices, a couple dozen players met at the Red Boot in nearby Taunton for beers and sandwiches. Every Tuesday was Guys' Night Out, when the defense met at the Bola Lounge near Fenway Park.

One day he signed a lease to open a small law practice in Chestnut Hill. The Patriots had just hired a new general manager, Clive Rush, whom he hadn't met when he received a call from the Dolphins' personnel director, Joe Thomas.

"We've just acquired you in a trade," Thomas said.

Buoniconti, for one of the few times in his life, was speechless. And heartbroken. Slowly, over time, Buoniconti pieced together what be believed happened. He was making a healthy $40,000, and Rush evidently didn't believe in paying linebackers big money. He also had a knee injury in 1968, the same one the cartilage was taken from in high school. His play dropped as a result. He didn't make the All-AFL team for the first time in six seasons. Doctors also wondered if the knee was a chronic issue. Finally, some assistants feared he had jumped the line from leader to clubhouse lawyer. Rush, in his first moments as boss, wanted to show who was in control.

Buoniconti reacted to the trade by announcing his retirement, even filing his retirement papers with the league. Miami? He didn't see it as anything beyond an expansion team and certainly didn't want to move there. The Dolphins asked him to visit. He demanded a guaranteed three-year contract paying $42,000, $44,000, and $49,000, respectively. Thomas asked him to visit Miami. He met Thomas and Joe Robbie at the Jockey Club. Robbie, true to form, drank so heavily that he had to be taken to bed that night by both Thomas and Buoniconti. The contract wasn't agreed on, either. Buoniconti said he was returning to Boston. Thomas said he was sorry it didn't work out.

The next morning, Robbie met Buoniconti and said, "You're awfully stubborn." He had Buoniconti's three-year contract in hand. Buoniconti learned the lesson of leverage in that deal: When you have it, use it.

Miami was exactly what he expected in 1969, a loosely disciplined team under George Wilson that didn't know how to win and, more to the point, didn't care in some respects. It was a party atmosphere in a party town. When Namath's Jets went up 35–7 on the Dolphins in 1969, he walked over to the head coach, Weeb Ewbank, and said, "Weeb, do me a favor and take me out. I'm feeling sorry for those guys." Babe Parilli replaced Namath. He threw a touchdown pass.

When Shula instituted four-a-day practices in his first move as Dolphin coach after the 1970 players' strike, he first went to Buoniconti. As the Dolphins' player representative, Buoniconti was due five days off as part of the agreement. He took none. He backed Shula's move. That helped a new coach begin with the full backing of a team leader.

In Bill Arnsparger's regimented defensive system, Buoniconti's freelance days ended. He found himself as one man in an eleven-man defense, asked to perform specific tasks and fill exact roles. He remained the defense's central force. The only starter more than thirty years old, Buoniconti led this defense in name and action. He was the player the other defensive players looked at to shift a game when the moment demanded, Manny Fernandez thought. Arnsparger was impressed enough with Buoniconti to allow a player to partner with him on calling the defenses, for the first time in his coaching career. Arnsparger called the secondary's scheme each play. Buoniconti called the alignment of the front seven. The more Buoniconti was involved with a game, Arnsparger came to realize, the better he played and the more responsible he seemed for what happened.

Buoniconti had such an ability to decipher a play, he regularly disrupted practices. "I just sense it," he would say.

Film work helped against opponents. Nick brought a lawyer's mind to analyze the offense each week and then calibrated its formations for options. For instance, against San Diego, Buoniconti saw a formation and reduced it to one of five plays. He noticed the spacing of a lineman several inches wider than usual and guessed the play. He began running before the ball was snapped. Quarterback John Hadl took the center snap and immediately pitched the ball to Mike Garrett, who began running around the end to the sideline. Buoniconti beat him there, knocking him for a yard loss.

O. J. Simpson claimed that Buoniconti gave him more problems than any other defender. The linebacker was waiting so regularly in the designed hole, Simpson said, he purposely began running into the wrong holes against the Dolphins. "A lot of backs like me who cut back, we improvise against Buoniconti," Simpson said.

Years later, Namath still was running a play in his mind. He came to the line, saw the center of the field open, and checked into a play for tight end Rich Caster to attack that open area. As the ball was snapped, Buoniconti turned and began running. Namath threw the ball to Caster, but Buoniconti intercepted it. "I've never been able to figure out how he did it," Namath said.

The keys to Buoniconti's game were quickness and agility. "I am not big and I am not fast," he said during the 1972 season. "In a 40-yard dash, I wouldn't finish in the top 20 on the team. But I have the quickness to start before those fast backs start. And I have the agility to evade those big linemen so they'll get no more than a hand on me."

In Super Bowl VI, Dallas coach Tom Landry built his offensive game plan against Buoniconti. "Do-dad blocking," Vince Lombardi called it, to free Jim Taylor and Paul Hornung. "Slip-wedge blocking," the more sophisticated Cowboys called it. The center was responsible for blocking Buoniconti, but often had Fernandez over him. That freed Buoniconti many times. Dallas decided that center Dave Manders and All-Pro guard John Niland would both hit Fernandez, then one would slip off and continue to push Buoniconti in the direction he was going—in effect, using the linebacker's quickness against him. The running backs were key, Niland said, for setting up a fake, "to take Buoniconti a step or two in that direction, then cut back over the middle."

"He's 5-10 and 210—what we call a reject in the Cowboys' system," Manders said in the *Breakthrough 'Boys*, a book by Jaime Aron written after that Super Bowl.

O. J. Simpson considered Buoniconti something else. "The best linebacker I face all year," he said.

In the locker room after this Jets game, Larry Csonka sat with a bloodied towel against his nose.

"I'm sure it's broken," he said. "I've had this feeling before."

Don Shula stopped to check on him. Shula said he had broken his nose four times as a player—twice in college, twice in the pros. Csonka said this was the eighth or ninth time he had broken his. He'd stopped counting exactly.

"It's the one individual stat I excel in," he said.

In the Jets' locker room another Csonka statistic was being tabulated. Dr. James Nicholas told reporters that Csonka "put three of our men out of the game. The guy is unbelievable."

Csonka ran over safety Gus Hollomon, who was knocked out and taken off the field on a stretcher. He had a concussion. Safety Chris Faraspolous suffered a bruised kidney from his collision with Csonka. Linebacker Bill Zapalac had a thigh contusion.

It was an exceptionally physical game. Eight Jets left the game for various other injuries: sprained ankles, sprained neck, kneecap injuries. Dolphin punter Larry Seiple left the day in a cast after being hit after a punt.

"It was a great game for the fans," Riggins said. "But there were some people out there almost giving up their lives."

Csonka broke his nose this time when he landed on his head at the end of a run. The bridge of his helmet came down and smacked it.

"Come on, Larry, you going to the party?" Morrall asked on his way out of the locker room.

"I'm going home and put ice on my nose," Csonka said. "Alcohol gives me a nosebleed."

Shula slapped Csonka on the back.

"The next time I break it," Csonka said to him, "you might say something more sympathetic than 'Go back in there.'"

11

Howard and Us

GAME ELEVEN

———

St. Louis Cardinals
November 27, 1972

For six weeks on crutches, I did any small part to help us win and keep my mind sharp. Watched film. Attended meetings. Sat through practice. Took notes and offered whatever scrap of insight that might help Earl Morrall.

Finally, before our eleventh game, the cast came off the ankle. I felt free again. I could start to exercise. The Dolphins' trainer, Bob Lundy, began having me do a series of small exercises, such as going up on my toes, to strengthen the ankle.

Shula came over to watch. "How you doing?" he asked.

"Fine," I said.

A couple of days later he asked, "Are you running yet?"

"No, Lundy says not yet."

A couple of more days and Shula stood beside me again as I worked.

"Maybe you should start running," he said. "Let me see you jog down to the line there and back."

"When Lundy tells me it's ready," I answered.

No one was more anxious than I was to get back. If I could get back. If the body could mend and I could compete at the necessary level. I started throwing lightly. I dedicated myself to therapy. In the coming weeks, I began to jog lightly, then run around a series of orange cones and, finally, run with the team and join practices.

But from the time the cast came off, the questions began. And not just from Shula. That eleventh week, against St. Louis, the Dolphins' game was on *Monday Night Football*. And I knew what that meant.

"How you coming along, slugger?" Howard Cosell asked.

He was a trip. One of a kind. And in their third season together, Cosell and *Monday Night Football* were lifting each other to record ratings in 1972. ABC was paying a rights fee of $8.5 million to the NFL that year and bringing in $20 million in ad revenue. *Variety* magazine reported that movie attendance had dropped sharply on Monday night since football had started being televised then, bowling leagues rescheduled the night, and restaurants reported a 25 percent drop-off in business on Mondays.

Cosell's entrance into Miami showed just how big an event *Monday Night Football* had become by just its third season. Cosell was a phenomenon. He was the centerpiece of the show. When ABC hired him, Cosell's public persona was primarily for being a defender of and having a whimsical relationship with Muhammad Ali. Most of the hate mail he received early on, as he wrote in his autobiography, referred to him being "a nigger-loving Jew."

By 1972 he didn't just have the Monday night game. He also had a Sunday night show called *Speaking of Everything*, carried by two hundred ABC affiliates. He did twenty-two radio commentaries a week. He appeared in Woody Allen's movie *Bananas* and Disney's movie *The World's Greatest Athlete* and made cameos on TV series such as *Love, American Style* and *Nanny and the Professor*.

In just three years, he became such a part of the national fabric that he was part of comedians' monologues. Bob Hope: "He's great for football, because his is a voice that leaves cleat marks in your ears." Buddy Hackett: "There have always been mixed emotions about Howard Cosell. Some people hate him like poison and some people just hate him regular." Bill Cosby imitated the nasally staccato delivery of Cosell in a mock newscast: "Flash floods in Iowa [pause] killed three hundred people yesterday [pause]. They all [pause] deserved it."

He was a phenomenon. Just ask him.

"Isn't it absolutely incredible what wondrous verbiage flows from my mouth?" Cosell asked in a *Newsweek* cover story that appeared that week he arrived in Miami.

Nothing showed the lofty status achieved by Cosell and *Monday Night Football* than the utter outrage over him in Miami. And over what? A slight he made about Don Shula? About the Dolphins? About Miami in general?

Nothing like that.

In place of the normal fare of halftime bands that carried the intermission, ABC executive producer Roone Arledge had a different idea: a highlight show of Sunday's games. In an age before ESPN and ESPN-2, before cable and DirecTV, before Internet and cell phones that carried games, these several minutes of Cosell narrating halftime highlights were the only national outlet for fans to watch the previous day's fare. They took on a life of their own, especially in the manner Cosell delivered them.

"That man, right there," Cosell would punch out to introduce a star from the previous day. "The Juice!" he'd shout when Buffalo running back O. J. Simpson appeared on a highlight run. Cincinnati quarterback Ken Anderson was from "tiny Augustana College."

To have made Cosell's highlight reel was like getting your name in lights for a player. It meant you'd made it. It told America you were a star.

Or, in some cases, you were a nobody.

The Pennsylvania legislature censured Cosell for omitting Pittsburgh games from a highlight show (Cosell said he didn't pick the games). Washington fans wrote en masse once when their team wasn't shown (Cosell said again he didn't pick the games).

Then there were Miami fans.

As a player, I was often isolated from the greater drama playing out. I didn't know of the civic insult people felt because our games weren't put on the *Monday Night Football* halftime show. To be honest, I didn't even know they weren't on the halftime show.

But they weren't.

"Suddenly, out of nowhere, I began getting vile mail," Cosell wrote in his autobiography. "The letters this time mounted into the thousands. 'What did I have against Miami? ABC should take action against me.' The same drivel that had occurred with Washington was taking place—only a new twist was added: The mail took a threatening tone."

A year later, a Buffalo fan would be arrested when postal authorities noticed a postcard that read: "Howard Cosell—the Mouth. Why don't you drop dead you Homo-Fag Big Mouth." That didn't alert officials. What did was the final line: "There's a bomb in Rich Stadium. It will blow you up."

Before the Dolphin game against St. Louis, Cosell got a letter that read, "Better not come to Miami, Howie, you'll not make it home again."

The FBI was called in. Security was increased. It turned out that the letter writer was "a young lady who was simply a rabid fan," Cosell wrote. "I was told she apologized and invited me to visit her when I came down for the Miami-St. Louis game. Fat chance."

"The fans in Miami have a lot of growing up to do," Cosell told the *Fort Lauderdale News*. "Did they expect to see highlights of a 52–0 beating of the Patriots?"

That was just the appetizer. Cosell did an interview with local ABC affiliate sportscaster Joe Croghan from the Sonesta Beach Hotel on Key Biscayne that was the main meal. Cosell or commentator Don Meredith did this in every city as a means to market their product and help the corporate family. That only added to the strain, though. What began under the pretense of Cosell's thoughts on the game and the city quickly disintegrated into "I do have better command of the language and nuances and inflections than you!" Cosell said. "Otherwise, you'd be in New York. But what's your next question?

"Would you like to move to Miami, Howard?" Croghan asked.

"No."

"I don't think the town could stomach you. But to get back to [director] Chet Forte—"

"To get back to *you* that's a rude and insulting remark and—"

"What was yours before that, Howard?"

For several minutes they slung names, mud, and accented reputations at each other. At the center of their argument was Miami fans' anger at Cosell for not showing highlights. And Croghan egged on that anger.

"You stirred them up," Cosell said.

"Stirred them up to what? I said, 'Don't get me on the phone. Call or write ABC.' Not you, by the way, Bunky. A-B-C."

"That's the end of this interview," Cosell said.

The strange thing is, I had a fine relationship with Cosell. Csonka had a great relationship with him. Cosell even came to our 1973 training camp and did a two-part special on the Dolphins. He put on a Dolphins uniform and played quarterback at one point. Not very well. But it made for good TV.

That *Monday Night Football* game in the Orange Bowl against St. Louis was something else. A police escort surrounded Cosell on his way into the stadium and stationed itself outside the ABC booth. That was a first in the show's history.

"I'm not going to blame South Florida just because there are a couple of kooks around," Cosell told reporters.

Stadium officials tried to enforce a no-banner rule, too. "Will Rogers never met Howard Cosell!" one read. "Dolfans can't believe ABC is showing the whole thing," read another.

"Roses are blue, violets are read, not all Dolfans want to see bad Howard dead," yet another read.

If anything, the game proved why our highlights should be part of *Monday Night Football.* Jim Kiick capped off a long drive for an early touchdown. Lloyd Mumphord returned an interception for a second one.

Once, Morrall went to pass as St. Louis safety Larry Wilson blitzed.

"Zo-o-onk!" Morrall yelled as he backpedaled.

Csonka took down Wilson. Morrall threw 31 yards to Otto Stowe. Touchdown.

"Don't worry, I saw him," Csonka said as they went off the field.

"I just wanted to remind you," Morrall said.

Cosell talked up the Dolphins. Why wouldn't he? We were on the way to 11–0. He said the Dolphins and Washington were the best two teams—"one-two, either way," he said. He called Don Shula one of the three best football coaches since World War II—"along with George Allen and Vince Lombardi."

On Shula and the defense, Cosell said, "Don Shula's genius lies in his coordination of these people, the cohesion he's created. Their secondary is ubiquitous."

"They are pretty good, too, Howard," Meredith said as announcer Frank Gifford laughed.

By the time *Monday Night Football* signed off, we had a 31–10 win against St. Louis. We were 11–0. And slowly but surely my body was mending.

12

Shula: A Study in Character

GAME TWELVE
—at—
New England Patriots
December 3, 1972

In our twelfth regular-season game, against New England, we clinched the AFC East. We proved we were among the NFL's elite. And the only story left until the playoffs was the one none of us had thought much about. A reporter even asked if Shula would rather have the Dolphins lose a game to relieve the pressure of remaining undefeated or keep winning and have the pressure build.

"Before I throw you out of the press conference," Shula said, "can you tell me why we have to feel pressure at all?"

No player made going undefeated a goal. None of us had even thought about it until now. That was the strange part of all the history to come. It became an almost accidental companion to our primary goal of a Super Bowl championship.

And by this twelfth week, in small groups and almost in whispers, players began to ask, "Who's going to beat us?" Tim Foley asked the question in the training room and immediately wondered if it was like jinxing a no-hitter in baseball. Nick Buoniconti asked it at his locker and pulled out a schedule to see who was left.

"Okay, we know someone will beat us, right?" Bob Kuechenberg said one afternoon to Jim Langer as they lifted weights in the team's weight room—a converted bathroom with a multipurpose Universal Weights set.

"Right, we've got to lose one," Langer said.

"Which game are we going to lose?" Kuechenberg asked.

"Well, not to the Patriots this week," Langer said.

"No, and not to the Giants the next week."

"Then we play the Colts in the last game."

"They won't beat us."

If the players slowly were coming to this thought now, Shula was ahead of them. He had felt the national spotlight turning on them for a while. That week, *Time* magazine came out with him on its cover under the headline "Building for the Super Bowl."

Years later, as Shula's legend took root, as he became the gold standard of football coaching, as he won his Super Bowls, won in different decades, won with different rosters, and won more games than any NFL coach ever, it became difficult for a sports world to understand the pressure he felt in this 1972 season.

Before he won a championship.

Before his name stood for something good.

"Any Joe Doakes could've taken this team to the Super Bowl," the Dolphins' former coach, George Wilson, said of Shula's work the previous season.

"How's he done in the big games?" Shula's former boss in Baltimore, Carroll Rosenbloom, asked.

As the cameras followed Shula off the Super Bowl field that previous season, the televised sentence shouted for all America to hear said, "Don

Shula is a brilliant coach who now twice has brought a team to the Super Bowl—once, the veteran Baltimore Colts, who lost to the New York Jets, and now the young Miami Dolphins, who have lost to Dallas."

Throw in the NFL title game he lost in 1965 to Vince Lombardi's Packers—the one they extended the goalpost uprights for after Green Bay's controversial field goal—and he was a three-time loser in championship games.

That's what drove him. That's why he pushed us. New England in our twelfth week was a speed bump, a game where we nearly doubled them in yardage, led 30–7 after three quarters, and coasted at the end to a 37–21 win.

And Shula was fuming. Irate. He pointed to our three turnovers. He couldn't believe we had a season-high eleven penalties. And giving up four sacks to a team like the Patriots?

He played and replayed those in film sessions the next week, yelling and cursing to the point when Csonka left the room saying, "I thought we won that game."

This was Shula at his best. The last thing he wanted was a great team to relax just as the playoffs game into view. If the opponent couldn't motivate us, he would. He never lost sight of the goal.

From the first moment he took over in 1970, I thought, This is it. This is exactly how football should be coached. His first training camp was a new world for those of us accustomed to George Wilson. Under Shula, there were assigned parking places. There were assigned seats on the bench. There had been a players' strike that cut into training camp, so when we returned he held four-a-day practices. Who had ever heard of such a thing?

"Csonka!" he yelled in that camp. "What the hell are you doing?"

Csonka, lining up for a play, froze. What was wrong?

"You're a step too wide!" Shula shouted.

Everyone looked and saw Csonka indeed lined up a step wide.

"If a linebacker was coming, you'd have been too wide to block him!" Shula shouted.

That was Shula. Smart. Strong. Detail-oriented. He was, as he said upon being introduced as the Dolphins' coach, "as subtle as a punch in the face." Organized? This was a man who proposed to his wife by writing a letter. Focused? He had Dorothy backpedal on their honeymoon to see what kind of football genes she'd pass on to their kids. His mind was always on X's and O's, such that when media relations aide Arthur Mickelson once asked Shula to sign a book "to my father-in-law, Jack," Shula wrote, "To my father-in-law, Jack. Best wishes, Don Shula." Nor was this unusual. In his parents' home, a framed photo of him was signed, "To Mom and Dad, Best wishes, Don Shula." Everything in his world was ordered. He was told that a stranger standing with team owner Joe Robbie that 1972 season after beating the New York Jets was the writer James Michener.

"A writer!" Shula said, then loudly booted Michener from the locker room, no doubt scrapping some homework for Michener's upcoming book *Sports in America*.

As demanding as Shula was, as loud as he could be, nothing shows the relationship he had with players better than a prank pulled against him. Each Monday during the season, a hunting guide in the Everglades refused to take on any clients, knowing that Manny Fernandez, Bill Stanfill, and friends would join him. One day, they came back with a four-foot alligator. The question was how to get the most mileage out of it. While Csonka talked with Shula's secretary, Fernandez put the alligator in Shula's shower stall. Bill Arnsparger walked in to take a shower, saw the alligator, and turned around, saying nothing. When Shula opened the door to take his shower, he screamed. He came into the locker room, saw Jim Kiick, and went up to him for an explanation.

"You should feel fortunate," Kiick said.

"Why?"

"We had a vote whether to tape the mouth shut. It passed by one vote."

• • •

Shula's father emigrated from Hungary at age six, with the family name Sule, to northeastern Ohio. He worked in a nursery in Grand River (population 500) and got Don, his oldest child, a job there. Don immediately killed all the plants under his care. When the Shulas moved to nearby Painesville (population 18,000) and the elder Shula took a job as a fisherman on Lake Erie, he'd take his son along. Don always got seasick. What Don excelled at were sports and directness. He was all-league in four sports in high school, starred at John Carroll University in football, and, upon going undrafted by the NFL, called the Cleveland Browns' legendary coach Paul Brown and asked, "Aren't you going to sign me?"

Brown became the biggest influence in Shula's career. As a Cleveland defensive back for four years, Shula wasn't introduced to just the NFL. Brown's novel use of the classroom made an impression on Shula. Players took notes. They carried notebooks. They were tested on assignments. Brown even taught Shula other useful lessons that came in handy later. He taught Shula what it felt like to be benched by a coach with no explanation. He taught Shula how it felt to be traded by an organization he bled for. Ultimately, in Baltimore, Weeb Ewbank taught Shula the final lesson of how it felt to be cut as a player. After seven years, Shula's playing career ended in 1957. He wore sunglasses after Ewbank broke the news so no teammate could see his eyes, and he then drove aimlessly around Baltimore for hours.

Then he became Coach Shula. If his talent was obvious, his career also was blessed. In his first three jobs as an assistant—Virginia, Kentucky, and the Detroit Lions—he left the season before the staff was fired. It wasn't like he was the difference, as he later joked. The Virginia team he was part of went 1–10. In Detroit, where he became defensive coordinator, he remembered the first defense he ever called giving up a length-of-the-field touchdown pass.

His ideas, his teaching, his mere presence had impact. In 1963, Rosenbloom asked veteran Gino Marchetti who should replace the fired Weeb Ewbank. "There's only one guy for the job—Don Shula," Marchetti said.

At thirty-three, Shula became the youngest coach in the NFL. He inherited John Unitas at quarterback, starting a run of Hall of Fame quarterback partnerships for him: Unitas, me, and Dan Marino. Baltimore's problem initially was one of mistiming. It had a very good team at the same time Green Bay had a great one. Then the Colts went 13–1 in 1968 and famously were upset by the New York Jets in the Super Bowl, the first old-line NFL team to lose to an AFL team. Shula was crushed. Rosenbloom was livid and loud, saying, "When you're a three-touchdown favorite and you lose, it's coaching."

By the next season, a general manager was installed above Shula, who had the title of vice president. When asked what the titles meant, Rosenbloom's son, Steve, the team president, told reporters, "You know how we throw titles around." He then allowed that Shula was given the title because the Colts "needed somebody to sign checks."

"I've never been big on coaches," Rosenbloom said after the Colts went 8–5–1 in 1969.

At the same time Shula was having an owner problem, Joe Robbie was having a coaching problem. He couldn't find a successor to the fired George Wilson. He first tried Ara Parseghian of Notre Dame. He next tried Bear Bryant of Alabama. He had the Bear agree to terms until the governor of Alabama landed a private plane in Miami, scooped up Bryant, and whisked him away. That was the end of that.

Robbie had no third candidate. It tells how stumped he was that he asked the advice of *Miami Herald* sportswriters Edwin Pope and Bill Braucher.

"Why don't you go right to the top and get the best there is?" Pope asked. "Hire Don Shula."

"Do you think he'd be interested?" Robbie asked.

"Have Braucher call him—they went to college together," Pope said.

This was a patient era in newspapers when reporters didn't turn every conversation into a headline. And Robbie's end run technically avoided NFL rules on tampering with another team's coach. This would factor into the questions NFL commissioner Pete Rozelle would ask later. But as things worked the next day when Braucher called, the changing destiny of two franchises had to wait a few hours.

"Hi, Don, this is Bill Braucher and—"

"I can't talk now," Shula interrupted.

Click.

Two of Shula's Baltimore assistants were in a fistfight on his front lawn. Shula hung up the receiver, rushed out the front door, and separated them. When Braucher called back later that day and told about Robbie and the Dolphin coaching job, Shula again broke off the conversation.

"Tell Robbie I'll call him in the morning," Shula said. "I want to hear the offer from him."

With Baltimore owner Carroll Rosenbloom in Asia, Shula informed his son and team president, Steve, of the Dolphins' interest. Shula had read in the sports pages all about the Dolphins' attempt to hire Bryant and considered inquiring about the job himself after two years of a deteriorating relationship with Rosenbloom.

Shula immediately heard how serious Robbie was about hiring him. The offer bordered on revolutionary: a five-year contract at $75,000 annually plus 2 percent of the team. Shula did the math. Two percent of a team worth, conservatively, $10 million? That was $200,000. He'd never seen that kind of money in his life. This from an owner who people said counted towels and paper clips?

And it wasn't just some dream.

"Let me come up and meet you," Robbie said.

A few days later, Robbie and Shula met in a Washington hotel with their lawyers. Robbie and Shula discussed ideas and philosophies to see if they could work together. Their lawyers discussed responsibilities and limits.

"Don has to have total control of the football side," Shula's lawyer, David Gordon, kept saying.

"Joe doesn't want control of the football side," Robbie's lawyer, Peter Fay, kept answering.

Robbie closed the deal on Shula, later calling it "the easiest transaction of management that I have ever made in my life." It soon came with an additional cost, as NFL commissioner Pete Rozelle ruled. Since Carroll Rosenbloom wasn't directly contacted for permission, the Dolphins were penalized a first-round pick for tampering. Robbie and Shula disagreed. It became the Dolphins' best first-round investment anyhow.

"The Dolphins bought themselves into contention," Al Davis said.

By this third season, in 1972, Shula had the machine so oiled that even an acquired veteran such as Howard Kindig was struck by the team's uniqueness. The Dolphins talked Kindig out of retirement that season to provide them depth on the offensive line. He had spent the previous seven years losing in Buffalo, including a recent 1–13 season. He immediately discovered football the way he thought it should be played. A sound system was in place. The players were talented and, as important, acted professionally. They showed up on time. They practiced hard. They respected the coaches, who, in turn, were demanding without acting dictatorial. When Kindig moved to Washington the following year, Redskin coach George Allen debriefed him on the Dolphins and couldn't believe that they practiced only an hour and forty-five minutes each day. It was the same reaction Oakland coach John Madden had for Jim Langer at the Pro Bowl.

"You can't have that type of execution practicing that little," Madden said.

Shula took a page from his mentor Brown in that regard. He actually took the entire notebook. The Dolphins' use of classroom time allowed practices to move crisply. This opened the football mind of another newcomer, Bobby Beathard, who joined the Dolphins in the personnel department that season. He had watched the previous Super Bowl as an Atlanta Falcon employee and was thoroughly unimpressed by the Dolphins. No speed. No size. Not enough elite talent. As he stepped behind the curtain that first season in Miami, however, he rethought everything. The schemes were simple yet flexible. The coaching was innovative. And the players? They provided Beathard with a lesson he would take in building Super Bowl teams in Washington and San Diego later in his career. Never before had he weighed the intangible of intelligence as a major factor in football. But as he saw this team work, as he understood the decisions made, all that changed for him.

Shula understood just what an intelligent team he had, Beathard decided.

13

A Partnership
of Opposites

GAME THIRTEEN
—at—
New York Giants
December 10, 1972

Before our thirteenth game of the season, I came out of the locker room a couple of hours from kickoff, looked around the stadium, and remembered something I hadn't in years.

I remembered being a kid in Evansville.

Our game was against the New York Giants in Yankee Stadium and, growing up in Indiana, this was the mecca I never saw. Baseball was my game. The Yankees were my team. I'd go out in the backyard with my brother and play Wiffle ball as all my favorites in Yankee Stadium. I'd be Mickey Mantle one game. I'd be Yogi Berra the next.

Now here I was, jogging around the field, looking at the Yankee monuments, and reflecting on how far I'd come since my youth.

And how far there was to go. Shula called over to me. Him again.

"You doing okay?" Shula asked.

With that question again.

"Getting close," I said.

It's true, I was. And getting anxious. But Shula had more pressing injury questions that day. Punter Larry Seiple was hurt. And there, practicing his punts on the pregame field, was the most versatile athlete on our team: Dick Anderson.

Before Anderson came to Miami as a rookie in 1968, he traded in his old Willys Jeep and run-down Chevy station wagon for the only new car he bought for the rest of his life: a Pontiac station wagon. Anderson worked that summer at a Pontiac dealership in Boulder, Colorado, where he attended college. He got a good deal on the car, for $3,500. He and his wife loaded all their earthly goods in it and made the long drive from Colorado.

That was Anderson. Smart. Sensible. Financially savvy.

When Jake Scott came to Miami in 1970, he arrived in a new, shiny, red Corvette.

That was Jake. Fast. Flashy. Rebellious.

At first glance, they were so different. Anderson, married. Scott, single. Anderson, business-minded. Scott, fun-minded. Anderson, so goal-oriented he sold credit life insurance in college and, upon realizing that the company had no presence in Florida, worked the entire state as his sales territory between playing football. Scott, so defiant that after a falling-out with his college coach, Georgia's Vince Dooley, he negotiated a deal with the Canadian Football League and left school early.

Yet Anderson and Scott shared traits that trumped any surface differences with rare smarts, uncommon athleticism, and matching wills to win. I saw it every day in practice. Anderson would be working on techniques and with his side of the defense, assuring everything was in order. Scott did the same. He then would do something in practice, freelance to make a play when he was supposed to be running the upcoming opponent's defense.

"Jake! What're you doing?" I'd have to yell.

He laughed. He knew what he was doing. Scott had the highest test scores of any Georgia athlete the year he entered and was considered by Dooley the best athlete he ever coached. Anderson, too, had a natural athleticism, as shown when ABC started a *Superstars* show after the 1973 season that involved athletes from different sports in competition on Key Biscayne. He was skiing in Colorado when the show's organizers called saying they needed a replacement. He listened to the events, such as running, swimming, cycling, tennis, and an obstacle course. They were the things he did all day as a kid, he thought. Without one day's notice, he beat the likes of O. J. Simpson and finished second overall in the competition to pole vaulter Bob Seagren.

Here, in Yankee Stadium, Anderson showed off that athleticism. He punted three times for a 37-yard average. At safety, he and Scott locked down the middle of the field and anchored the defense that caused four turnovers in our 23–13 win. They were so supremely talented that Don Shula considers them the best safety tandem ever in football. The Elias Sports Bureau ranked both among the top three hundred NFL players ever. More than thirty years after retiring, Scott and Anderson rank first and second in interceptions in franchise history, with 35 and 34, respectively. And tough? For six years during this Dolphins glory run, they started every game beside each other despite various broken bones and twisted body parts. The only time they weren't on the field together during those years was for a stretch in a game against Buffalo. Scott suffered a concussion. Anderson told the coaches not to play him.

They became, as with the best of partnerships, a small team within the bigger team. They invented hand signals to communicate. They advanced the other's skills and covered for weaknesses. Scott, for instance, was quicker and often took receivers in goal-line defenses that normally were Anderson's responsibility. They also were the two punt returners. Scott took the deeper position and had more returns.

Anderson, as the short man, took his responsibility seriously to block and spring Scott free.

Scott and Anderson grew so close that after the 1971 season they took their playoff shares and bought a 130-acre ranch together in Colorado. A few years later, they sold the ranch and Scott bought 60 acres of land 9,800 feet up a Colorado mountain. He built an A-frame house. He laid electrical wire himself. His closest neighbor was two miles away. He saw the ski runs of Aspen, 40 miles away to one side of the house, and those of Vail, 60 miles away to the other side. The driveway to the home was a minimally kept, 5-mile road. Don Shula once visited in the winter and had to ride in 2 miles on a half-track due to the snow. That home served as Scott's base until he bought a geographical alter ego in Kauai, Hawaii, after his career, often waking up to decide if he wanted to golf, drink, or fish the day away.

In a world where few people live original lives, Jake Scott certainly achieved that. He didn't just meander down the path of life. He took a machete and made his own path. As life moved on, he once drove to Alaska to "piss in the Arctic," he said. He rode a helicopter to remote fishing spots in Australia. He drove his Harley-Davidson motorcycle to Mexico with a friend and was getting run off the road by a strange driver, hard, when his friend pulled out a gun and began shooting at the driver. Did he hit anyone? Scott didn't know. The driver quit trying to run them off the road, though.

The stories teammates told about Scott, off in the corners, and that only they understood, gave him a near-mythic status. He drank forty-three beers in a setting. Joe Namath once visited Scott, noticed all the women flocking around, and said, "And I thought I had women in New York." A Colorado mountain man, hearing Scott was a pro football player, once picked a fight with him, saying, "I'm the toughest guy in here." Scott knocked him out with one punch, then said, "No one's tougher here than him?" He told a heavyweight in a bar to quit throwing out comments when he and Jim Mandich were playing a game of Pong. When the guy didn't, Scott walked over and punched him so hard he was still in a neck brace when they met in court weeks later. Self-defense, the decision came. Scott, it seemed, had friends everywhere.

Jacob E. Scott III grew up in the segregated town of Athens, Georgia, in the 1950s. He never accepted societal boundaries, then or later, and made the friends he wanted, lived the life he wanted. As a youth, he often went to the black part of town to play. As a young teen, he teamed with black youth in pickup football games against University of Georgia fraternity boys.

While in high school, his mother, Mary, took an executive job with the National Education Association outside Washington, D.C. Jake attended Washington-Lee High School, where athletic director John Youngblood called him "the most courageous football player we ever saw."

He earned other superlatives there, too. Biggest handful? Most rebellious student? After his senior football season, Scott skipped classes to hang out at a local pool hall. He learned to play the game while racking balls deep into the night for famed hustlers such as Luther Lassiter and Bill Staton. He became a hustler himself, visiting various pool halls where he often was not just the lone white but also the youngest, skinniest kid, too.

"You're not even good enough to beat the white boy over there," one of his friends would say to the mark.

A game was struck. Bets were made. Scott typically won, then hustled out of the hall with the winnings before anyone connected the dots. He became the schoolboy champ in Washington. He once ran in fifty-four straight balls on a table. He visited school just to take tests, skipping fifty days after the football season ended. School officials didn't care that, in a testament to his intelligence, he still had As in his classes. They said he couldn't graduate, which ended his decision on which of the dozens of college football offers to take. The next fall Scott attended Bullis Prep, a small preparatory school for the U.S. Naval Academy. Many of his classmates used it as a one-year stop before attending the academy. Classes were designed to help the first-year cadet. Scott had no intention of joining the service. His dream already was to play pro football, and he saw how the navy's mandatory service rule clipped the career of Roger Staubach.

Scott applied himself to his studies that year at Bullis, and his rare combination of grades and athletic talent had college football coaches from across the country writing him, wooing him, wanting him. He had his choice of America's most prestigious schools. Stanford. Harvard. He was leaning toward Duke when Georgia coach Vince Dooley made an intriguing recruiting proposal. Dooley promised to change from a traditional, ground-oriented offense to a pro-style passing attack. Scott would become his star receiver, Dooley said. Another talented recruit, Rick Arrington, would be his star quarterback. NFL star and Georgia alum Fran Tarkenton called Scott and said he was returning in the off-season to help install the offense. Tarkenton, an Athens native, had coached Scott in Pony League. Georgia always had a place in Scott's heart as his hometown team, and this kind of talk decided it for him.

He signed with Georgia.

The offense never changed.

Arrington eventually transferred to Tulsa, and developed enough as a quarterback there to play a few years with the Philadelphia Eagles. Scott was put at defensive back and remained there through his Georgia career. He also was roomed with a defensive lineman from Albany, Georgia, named Bill Stanfill. Scott had the highest entrance-exam grades of any Georgia athlete. Stanfill showed little interest in schoolwork. The Georgia coaches hoped Scott would rub off on Stanfill. And he did. It just wasn't always in the way the coaches planned.

"They didn't know what a screwup I was," Scott said.

Scott took Stanfill to bars he knew as a hometown kid. They hung out with Scott's boyhood friends in town. They'd go to after-hour clubs where they were the only white people. They studied just enough to play football. Stanfill showed Scott some of his interests, too.

Like hunting. One night, Stanfill stood over a large buck he shot in a field, deer blood all over him, when a police car pulled up. It wasn't deer season. Stanfill went to jail. Scott bailed him out.

They became such lifelong friends and standout football players that their names eventually went up on the Dolphins' Ring of Honor together. From their first days together, Stanfill noticed that Scott's class grades were either As or Fs. Nothing in between. That represented Scott's personality, Stanfill observed. He excelled at anything that interested him. He completely tuned out anything that bored or didn't suit him. One semester Scott was put on academic probation. The next, he made the All-SEC academic team. All or nothing.

The legend of Jake began at Georgia. In one incident that became part of campus lore, he rode a motorcycle up the concrete supports and over the top of the Georgia basketball arena. "Come on!" he yelled back to teammate Brad Johnson, who was on another motorcycle. Johnson stopped and watched, becoming a witness to a story repeated through the years. Barriers that remain today were immediately placed around the columns.

Football benefited from the unbridled recklessness and the unmatched smarts of Scott. He was named the Southeastern Conference's most valuable player as a junior in 1968. He was voted to the All-America team. "He could have won the Heisman that year, really," Dooley said. "He did everything. Interceptions. Punt returns. He ran a 90-yard punt back against Tennessee in which every Tennessee player touched him."

Jake was Jake, too. After suspending him "two or three" times for various misdeeds, Dooley said he became so exasperated by something Scott did in the 1968 season that he called a team meeting and had players vote on whether to keep him on the team. The vote was unanimous. The players wanted Scott like they wanted to win. Didn't the two go hand in hand?

Before a climactic game against Auburn, Scott detected a flaw in the Auburn offense while watching film. He sat with defensive coordinator Erk Russell each week and looked for "tells," or clues, to what the offense did. Russell taught him how to read defenses in those sessions. Auburn, Scott noticed, sent its fullback to block on whatever side it planned to pass. It proved to be vital information, especially with a national debate over Georgia's bowl decision before that game. Georgia could take a lesser Sugar Bowl game or risk missing that by waiting to see if it beat Auburn to secure a national title matchup against Kansas in the Orange Bowl. Dooley said he would let the players decide. Scott had two interceptions in the defeat of Auburn. After the game, his teammates sent Scott into Dooley's office holding oranges as an indication of their decision. The celebration quickly ended. Dooley, in a move he regretted later in life, had committed Georgia to the Sugar Bowl before the game.

Burned previously by Dooley in recruiting and now by this bowl decision, Scott's principled fire turned on the coach forever. This second time was more than about football, too. It was about trust, loyalty. It was about the team. Isn't that what the coach asked players to put above all else? The team? Scott had the capacity to "love, love, deep and hate, hate, deep," his mother, Mary, said. He believed deeply in these teammates, a fact that bore out as their lives lengthened. He risked fines and suspensions in his opening Dolphins practices to drive to Georgia to give blood to Brad Johnson, who was suffering from stomach cancer. Scott later flew halfway around the world from his Hawaii home to Georgia to say good-bye to his dying teammate Dick Young, only to arrive too late.

Dooley, however, never was a part of his life after that Auburn game. Scott refused to attend the banquet to pick up his conference MVP award (his mother went instead). He debated whether he could play a senior year with Dooley and decided he couldn't. One night early in 1969, Johnson received a phone call from the general manger of the British Columbia team in the Canadian Football League. He was an All-SEC fullback and, by then, Scott's roommate. Johnson, a senior, was offered a healthy contract.

"Let me talk to him, too," Scott said.

By the end of the conversation, Scott was playing for British Columbia, too. Scott and Johnson took their signing bonuses, bought new Corvettes, and drove to Canada. Dooley was irate that a Canadian team signed an underclassman. Scott didn't care. He was done with Dooley. Years later, an aging Dooley tried to make amends by offering to lobby for Scott's entrance into the College Football Hall of Fame. He made one stipulation: that Scott promise to appear at the induction. Dooley used Stanfill as an intermediary, since Scott still wasn't talking to him. Scott declined the offer. Nearly four decades after leaving Georgia, and after Dooley officially had left the school as athletic director, Scott returned to Georgia as an honorary captain before a game. (A few years after that, when Dolphin teammate Jim Mandich asked him to join the College Hall of Fame, Scott relented. He attended the induction, too.)

In Canada, Scott finally played receiver. He was coached by Jimmy Orr, the veteran Baltimore receiver who coached in Canada because of the two leagues' staggered seasons. That provided an unusual element a year later, when Scott moved to the Dolphins' secondary and played against Orr in the NFL. Playing receiver, Scott found, helped his defensive-back skills in a way he didn't anticipate. He better understood how receivers thought, the moves they had to make, and, perhaps most of all, the need to attack the thrown ball. For the rest of his career, Scott's mind-set shifted from a previously passive one of defending the ball in the air to a more aggressive one of thinking that any ball in the air was his.

He was a standout from the start in British Colombia, and a fan favorite for the reckless manner in which he played. But his heart was in the NFL. Isn't that what he grew up watching? Wasn't it the gold standard for football? That off-season, he visited Stanfill, who played in Miami as the Dolphins' first-round pick in 1969. Scott grilled one night with Stanfill and Manny Fernandez and told them about his NFL desire. He told everyone about it, really. British Columbia feared his departure and traded him to Montreal, which took a different tack to keep him. It put a three-year deal worth $100,000 on the table before him. That was more money than Stanfill received as the NFL's eleventh overall pick. Scott declined it. He was afraid of his dream passing him by.

And for what?

Money?

He never tied himself to that. As the draft came into view, NFL teams began expressing some interest. Gil Brandt, the Dallas Cowboys' personnel head, told Scott he would take him with one of the team's two third-round picks. Washington's Vince Lombardi looked into Scott, but like a lot of NFL types didn't do his homework properly. He thought Scott was locked up in the Montreal contract. The Dolphins' Joe Thomas began considering Scott only after a conversation with Stanfill clarified Scott's situation.

"I thought he signed a three-year contract with Montreal," Thomas said.

"No, he never signed it," Stanfill said.

"You sure?"

"Positive."

"I'll look into it," Thomas said.

What do they say about small moments yielding big dividends? Thomas still wasn't convinced about Scott being available. Montreal had him under contract for one more season, after all. Who knows what would happen after that? On draft day, Dallas passed on Scott. On the second day, sensing a bargain, Thomas rolled the dice and took Scott in the seventh round. What the heck, his talent was worth that small gamble, right? Even if the Dolphins couldn't get him for the upcoming season, they could wait a year at that price. All-America players didn't just tumble out of trees onto rosters.

Scott kept telling Montreal's management that he preferred to play in the NFL. Montreal's officials reminded Scott he was under contract with them for that season. They tried to appease him. They put him on the cover of the media guide. See? He'd be their star. But as past events showed, Scott couldn't be appeased once his mind was set. When Montreal hadn't released him by the start of training camp in June, Scott took matters into his own hands as only he could.

"Let's put it this way: I didn't make curfew very often," he said.

Eventually Montreal's management had enough and, as Scott heard it, agreed to free him to the Dolphins for $10,000. Thomas, in turn, agreed to bring Scott to the NFL if he took a pay cut of $10,000. Thomas had to answer to Joe Robbie's budget, after all.

So Scott took a pay cut to play in the NFL. By late July, he was in Miami, where the only question was where to play him. Thomas considered him a cornerback. Shula, however, put him at safety. After a few days of practice, they saw it probably didn't matter. He could star anywhere on the field. Thomas framed the addition in a manner he so often did.

"I got a first-round player for seventh-round money," he said.

They got more than that. They got a player who changed the entire defensive mind-set just by showing up. He was smart, motivated, reckless. And tough? Pick a story. When other 1970 draft picks were forced to sing their college fight song as part of their rookie hazing, no veteran asked Scott to sing. "He's the one guy no one messed with," Manny Fernandez said.

He played a game against the Jets as a rookie with a separated shoulder (and intercepted a pass). He played most of the Longest Game with five bones in his right hand that were shattered on Kansas City fullback Jim Otis's helmet. He then broke his left wrist during the Super Bowl against Dallas and, despite the two injuries, didn't miss a down, even fielding punts. When he reached the Pro Bowl the following week, they refused to shoot him up with a numbing agent to let him play. He had casts on both hands. "Now I find out who my real friends are when I go to the bathroom," he said.

Scott made more Pro Bowls (five) in the Dolphins' run of glory than four Hall of Fame teammates. He remains the franchise's all-time leader in interceptions (35), one ahead of Anderson. But the moments that defined Scott came as much off the field. One involved a contract negotiation that Jim Mandich called "the greatest display of chutzpah I've ever seen."

This was in the days after Larry Csonka, Jim Kiick, and Paul Warfield signed with the fledgling World Football League after the 1973 season. Scott told Dolphins owner Joe Robbie that he had received a $500,000 offer over three years from the Hawaiian entry in the World Football League.

"That's for starters," he told the media.

It was a very good offer. It was a very unusual offer. It was entirely false, too. Scott invented all of it. Mandich, taking Scott's lead, claimed the Birmingham team offered him $200,000 with the additional bonus of a red Thunderbird with the license plate "Maddog." Five days after they went public with this news, Scott and Mandich each signed new deals with the Dolphins. Scott became the first six-figure defensive back in the league, signing a three-year contract running from $105,000 to $120,000.

The gold rush was on for other teammates. After an all-night party, Manny Fernandez and Bill Stanfill told their agent, Ed Keating, to call Robbie and say the players were offered five-year deals for $750,000.

"You're nuts," Keating said. "I can't do that."

"Okay, you're fired," Fernandez said.

Five minutes later, Keating called Robbie, and "every expletive that's ever been said comes out of Joe's mouth," Fernandez said. Fifteen minutes later, they became the NFL's first defensive linemen to have six-figure contracts.

No incident defined Scott's defiant pride and principles like a private feud with Shula that lasted decades. If Dooley drew Scott's wrath for deceiving him, Shula's transgression was different and more personal in Scott's mind. The two had a good relationship early on, when Shula visited him in Colorado. They ate lunch in Vail. Shula's son David idolized Scott enough to wear his number 13 in high school.

That quickly unraveled in ways big and small. Scott was a contract holdout one training camp. That didn't sit well with Shula. Then, when Bill Arnsparger took the New York Giants head coaching job in 1974, Vince Costello became the Dolphins' defensive coordinator. Like many teammates, Scott didn't respect Costello's tactics. Scott yelled at Costello one practice. Shula came across the field to ask what was wrong. "I wasn't fucking talking to you," Scott said.

And so it began. After that season, Shula said in a team meeting that players' attendance was mandatory at a postseason banquet.

"I won't be there," Scott said.

"Everyone will be there or they'll be fined $500," Shula said.

Scott didn't go. He was fined. Scott said he was simply being consistent after turning down speaking engagements for upward of $20,000 following his Super Bowl MVP award. But a test of will between two proud and principled men ratcheted up. Scott asked to be traded. Shula said he couldn't find a buyer. Scott demanded it. Shula told him to call around and find a team.

Scott didn't practice much in the 1975 preseason due to a bum shoulder. Doctors couldn't find the problem. Shula wanted him to play in an exhibition game, regardless. The injury was such that Scott needed to take a painful, long-needed shot up through his armpit to numb the spot in his shoulder. He refused. Hadn't he proven his toughness through the years? Never missing a real game despite broken limbs, shattered bones, and ripped shoulders?

Now his reputation was based on a meaningless exhibition game?

The truth was that the Dolphins wanted to showcase that he was healthy enough to play and complete a trade. After the rest of the team left for the field, Shula and Scott entered into a toxic shouting match in the locker room. That was it. The next day, Scott and a fourth-round pick were traded for Washington safety Bryant Salter. The deal wasn't Shula's finest moment. Salter played only that season with the Dolphins. Scott played three years, intercepted 14 passes for Washington, and divorced himself from the Dolphins.

He returned briefly for the Perfect Season's ten-year reunion and tried to resolve things with Shula. Scott didn't announce he was coming. He just showed up and found himself in an elevator with Shula. As Scott remembered, the conversation went like this:

Scott: "Don, we've got to meet next week and iron out this thing between us."

Shula: "Fuck you."

Shula doesn't recall the conversation, or even seeing Scott that day. Scott says he walked out of the elevator, returned to his home in Hawaii, and renewed his Dolphin divorce vows.

He resurfaced occasionally into the football world. He attended a Super Bowl MVP reunion during the Super Bowl in 1986 in a manner befitting his style. All the other MVPs wore a league-suggested jacket and tie as they were introduced on the field and to the national TV audience. Scott wore a golf shirt and jeans. His mother received dozens of ties in the mail after that.

He occasionally did a memorabilia show, too, such as one in 2001. Jim Langer greeted him, saying, "I see a ghost."

But his feelings for Shula, like those toward Dooley, didn't soften. Scott once was set up on a blind date with a model. She said to meet at Shula's Steak House. He canceled the date.

Other players had issues with Shula in the manner coaches and players often did. Mercury Morris was traded to San Diego, a deal he expressly asked Shula not to make. Morris eventually shrugged it off. Lloyd Mumphord was so upset at the events that led to him being released by Shula that in his first meeting against the Dolphins with his next team, Baltimore, he intercepted a pass and, after being tackled, rifled the ball at Shula.

"Hey, you almost hit me," Shula said.

"I was trying to fucking kill you," Mumphord said.

That off-season, Mumphord approached Shula at a golf tournament, but Shula wouldn't shake his hand. A while later, they met again. "My wife says I made a mistake in releasing you," Shula said. Mumphord figured it was a proud coach's way of apologizing. He accepted it. They moved on.

Scott didn't resolve his problems with Shula for nearly four decades. Teammates invited him to reunions.

"Ain't no way," he said to Jim Langer in 2001.

Finally, at a memorabilia show in 2010, Scott and Shula bridged their relationship. I couldn't have been happier to have witnessed it. Shula was eighty by then. Scott was sixty-five. Their faces loosened, and some of their ideas, too. Scott walked over to Shula.

"I've missed you so much," he said.

They hugged. Several of us got into a picture together. It was a warm moment for all of us. A time to remember. A time to forget. A time to smile, most of all.

14

The Mushrooms

GAME FOURTEEN

———

Baltimore Colts
December 16, 1972

I n the days before the final game of the regular season, against Baltimore, Monte Clark closed the door and turned off the lights in the
meeting room with his offensive linemen. He then did with them what
he did each week. He had them visualize plays in the game plan.

"Start in the huddle," he said to them softly. "Hear your breathing
. . . feel the sweat roll off you . . . see everyone lean in the huddle and
hear the play called, 'Ride-34, on two . . . on two.' . . . You jog to the
line."

Clark was the most unusual of football coaches. He wrote poetry.
He studied history. He loved music to the point where he took the
$8,000 winner's check from his 1964 NFL championship game in
Cleveland and bought a Hammond organ to play at home.

One day that 1972 training camp, he invited the linemen into his dorm room at Barry College. He was learning the bass fiddle during his free time and wanted to play something for them. He put on a record as accompaniment but had trouble keeping up with the beat.

"Aw, I know what's wrong," he said.

He lay down on the bed. He placed the fiddle on his stomach. That's how he practiced most afternoons, and immediately he began to play well again.

The curious passion he brought to other aspects of life percolated in his football thinking. He chastised players for "Lamaze blocking" of all pushing and shoving. He stared down players in the classroom who took "SWAGs"—"Scientific, Wild-Ass Guesses."

"Sympathy," he'd tell anyone making an excuse, "could be found in the dictionary between 'shit' and 'syphilis.'"

The visualization sessions using that week's play sheet were a staple of Clark's teaching. They stemmed from Maxwell Maltz's book *Psycho-Cybernetics*, which Clark gave to each lineman. One chapter told how two groups of basketball players shot a series of free throws. For a period of time, one group continued practicing free throws while the second group merely visualized shooting them in detail. Both groups improved at similar rates, the book reported.

More than in any other sport, football practices were limited by concerns of injury and physical fatigue. But an endless number of blocks could be performed in a player's mind, as Clark explained to his players. Bob Kuechenberg thought Maltz's book changed his career. Jim Langer could quote from it decades later. Doug Crusan began to visualize plays driving, sitting at home, anytime at all. At times Clark's psychological ideas didn't pan out. After winning the Super Bowl this 1972 season, he worried that there might be a letdown. He called the Psychology Department at the University of Miami, told a professor his concerns, and asked for suggestions.

"Maybe you should get them laid the night before every game," the professor said.

That ended that.

If such stories amused his players, they felt lucky to be coached by Clark. We all did. I reaped as many dividends from his curious passions and rich knowledge as anyone. When he arrived with Shula in 1970, Clark brought a cutting-edge idea from his Cleveland playing days called "Check with me." It became an integral part of our offense.

Here's how it worked: I called two plays in the huddle, studied the defense at the line, and decided which play to use. If the signals I called out at the line started with an even number, the play called to be run to the right was used. If it began with an odd number, the play to the left was used. The concept sounds so simple and effective it's a wonder it wasn't a staple of every offense by then, right? Well, by the end of the decade it would be. As it was, it was so unusual that Morrall related how when he played for Baltimore in 1971 linebacker Mike Curtis came cursing to the sideline, saying, "I know Griese's changing their plays, but I can't figure out what he's doing."

Cleveland used it for a few fundamental plays. Our Dolphin teams expanded it to a full arsenal of them. It became a great weapon for me. It allowed all my film work on the opposing defense and information-gathering through the work week to be used fully in games. We even added a twist to the system: by beginning my cadence with "Five," it erased both plays. If I saw something else to attack in the defense, an entirely new play would be called. The key was that we had a group of smart players and, again, this played to that strength.

Clark wasn't all novel ideas and musical notes. He could be a disciplinarian, if needed, but he was more a technical perfectionist and motivational leader. His goal, he told his linemen, was for offensive line coaches across the league to wait impatiently for the Dolphin game films to arrive in the mail each week to use them as textbook examples for their own players.

"I want those coaches to say, 'I want you to run the sweep like Larry Little does in Miami," he told Little in team meetings. He planted greatness in each of their minds. "I want them to look at a trap block by Bob Kuechenberg and tell their guards, 'Kuechenberg is the yardstick to measure how well you do it.'"

To that end, Clark used the phrase "Best in the business" for the Dolphins' line. He instilled it as a repeated mantra in their daily work. To start sprints at the end of practice, he didn't blow a whistle. "Best in the business," he said. At the end of drills, the players put their hands together and chanted "Best." He wrote it on blackboards. He used it in conversation.

By 1972, Clark's unit indeed was the best. Often it was the unheralded muscle to the franchise's success. It also represented a couple of years of nonstop work and professional trauma by Clark. In his first Dolphins practice in 1970, Clark marched a veteran group of linemen on the practice field, lined them up, and went from one end to the other working on individual stances. Lower your hips, he said. Adjust your head. Move your right foot back six inches. No, one more inch.

"Oh, brother, this is Pee Wee football," Norm Evans thought.

Evans wasn't alone, because many of these linemen had established careers at this point. Evans, Bob DeMarco, Maxie Williams, and Tom Goode had played at least five NFL seasons when Clark arrived. That was one of the problems, Clark thought. The bigger problem was what I discovered while being nicknamed the Scrambler: they weren't good enough. Clark watched the first practices and immediately wondered if he was up for a job whose primary assignment was finding several immediate replacements.

This was Clark's first coaching stop after an eleven-year pro career, the bulk of which was spent with great Cleveland teams. He planned on playing a twelfth year, in 1970, when fate intervened. Playing basketball that winter, Clark was poked in his eye and immediately suffered from double vision. The only way he could see normally was to tip his head and look out the top of his eyes, an idiosyncrasy players of his would imitate in coming years without knowing the backstory. When the double vision continued long after the injury, he knew his career was finished. He decided to coach and heard that Shula needed a line coach in Miami. Clark's only brush with Shula to that point was wishing he would stop screaming at Baltimore defensive end Bubba Smith during games, because Clark had to block Smith.

He called Shula and offered Blanton Collier as a reference, knowing the Cleveland head coach was one of Shula's mentors, too. The next morning Shula called back, offered the job for $18,500, and Clark began the formidable task of rebuilding this offensive line. Larry Little, he saw, was an immense talent. Doug Crusan, a first-round pick in 1968, was very good. Evans came to him after a couple weeks of practice and revealed his mind-set by apologizing to Clark for being petulant to that point.

"What do I need to do?" Evans asked.

"Work on your stance," Clark answered.

Clark also noticed a player cut by two teams the previous year who had never played in the NFL. He pointed the kid out to Shula, who didn't bother noticing. It was training camp. The kid was raw. Clark, as a first-year coach, was overly enthusiastic. Besides, Shula had more serious issues that first year than learning the unpronounceable name of some kid who couldn't help them immediately. But the more Clark observed Bob Kuechenberg, the more he understood what made the player tick, the more the coach liked what he saw.

"That's one," Clark told himself.

That was a start. Clark knew he needed to find more players to upgrade the talent. He watched films of other teams for possibilities. He talked with friends throughout the league. He scoured the waiver wire for rejected talent. One day, he watched a couple of preseason game films of his Cleveland buddies and noticed the play of a rookie who moved from linebacker in one game to guard in another. The kid had a ferocious manner about him. When he phoned his Cleveland pals, he asked them about this new player, Jim Langer. Gene Hickerson and Dick Schafrath raved about his play. Clark needed to know more. What about his work habits? His mind-set? Did he accept coaching?

Cleveland indeed had future plans for Langer, but put him on waivers in hopes that no team would notice this undrafted kid from South Dakota State. The plan was to re-sign him after he cleared waivers and deposit him on the taxi squad to develop. Clark saw his name on waivers and demanded that the Dolphins grab him.

"That's two," he said.

That same day, Clark saw a curious name among San Francisco's cuts: Solomon Moore. Clark knew the San Francisco players well, considering he trained with several in the off-season. At six-six, Clark often was matched in basketball games against a six-seven tackle the 49ers considered a grand project named Wayne Moore. Long and athletic, Moore played basketball in college and was a handful for Clark to play in these pickup games. The 49ers saw enough ability to get Moore an off-season job with the Redwood City Recreation Department and hoped to sculpt him into a football player. Clark called a friend with the 49ers and discovered that Wayne Moore's given name was Solomon. The 49ers waived him as "Solomon Moore" to minimize the risk of losing him. Like Cleveland, they wanted to re-sign him and place him on the taxi squad. Clark had the Dolphins claim him.

"That's three," Clark said.

Over that first training camp, Clark found the foundation for the future. The present was the problem. The first Dolphins game with that veteran-laden line reminded Clark how much work was needed. In the 1970 opener, against the Boston Patriots (they didn't become the New England Patriots until the following season), I was sacked eight times. So now Shula saw what I said about building me a pocket. Clark was so distraught he was hospitalized after the game. Doctors thought he was having a heart attack. He had a cardiogram, was given some medicine, and spent the night in a Boston hospital as the team flew back.

Over the first couple of seasons, the line improved to the point that by the 1972 training camp Clark had one final move to make. He wanted the unproven Langer to replace thirty-three-year-old veteran center Bob DeMarco. Clark felt Langer was better at this point. And hungrier. And more open to his teaching methods.

Langer played most of that exhibition season, the public idea being to rest DeMarco's body. But after each game Clark pointed out to Shula how well Langer played. After the final preseason game, two weeks before the opener, Clark saw that Oakland was on the verge of waiving guard Terry Mendenhall, who had started every game as a rookie the previous year. He proposed claiming Mendenhall, starting Langer, and releasing DeMarco.

"Dammit," Shula said, "we've been talking about this Langer thing every meeting."

"Let me put it this way," Clark said. "Either DeMarco goes or I go."

There it was on the table for Shula. He knew to take Clark seriously here. Several years later, as San Francisco's head coach, Clark was stripped of personnel decisions when the new owner, Eddie DeBartolo, brought in former Dolphins personnel chief Joe Thomas. Clark resigned. DeBartolo then proposed a raise. Clark didn't return.

Shula relented to Clark's conviction. It was a surprising move to the other assistants, and they feared that the release of DeMarco would have ramifications beyond the playing field. DeMarco was good friends with Larry Csonka and Nick Buoniconti. The media would become involved. Clark didn't care.

"Jim, you're the guy," he told Langer a week before the opening game, against Kansas City.

"What?" Langer asked.

"You're going to start," Clark said, walking away.

Langer was stunned. Shula traded DeMarco to Cleveland, where he indeed showed he had some good football left. He started for Cleveland for three seasons before finishing his career, at thirty-seven, in St. Louis. Langer started nine years for the Dolphins and made the Hall of Fame.

By this point in the 1972 season, the offensive line represented the emotional and tactical core of this team, the other players felt.

"The Mushrooms," Monte Clark began calling this rebuilt offensive line, because its players "sat in the dark and ate shit," as he said. It was a remarkable collection of similar-minded players with similarly strained backgrounds. None of them had been drafted prominently, if at all. Each was rejected by at least one other team. But as much as any group, they defined who we were on the field. The Mushrooms were a team within the team. Often Don Shula would begin to correct something in the line play during the team's film sessions, only to be interrupted by Clark.

"I'll take care of it, Don," he'd say.

By this point, this line was the perfect blend of age, experience, and unbending hunger, exactly as Clark envisioned. It was young enough to master their positions' physical demands but old enough to have seen everything the NFL could offer. Clark reminded them every once in a while to "Give the other team the business," which meant for Little to peek subtly to the outside as he came to the line if a running play was up the middle. Langer made blocking calls to the guards, but Kuechenberg might relay something else entirely to Wayne Moore, who understood it as an attempt to confuse the defense.

The idea was to wear on a defense mentally as well as smash it physically. "Your turn again, Bob," Kuechenberg said to Minnesota defensive tackle Bob Lurtsema as they lined up before one of the fifty-three rushing plays (against seven passes) we ran the following Super Bowl against Minnesota.

Often there wasn't much finesse to their game plan. "Hey, you guys aren't going to run the same play again, are you?" Cincinnati defensive tackle Mike Reid once said as the Dolphins came to the line.

After the Dolphins ran the same play at Baltimore linebacker Billy Ray "Rabbit" Smith all game in this final game of the regular season, Smith finally stopped one. He smiled at the bottom of the pile. "You shouldn't keep doing this to old Rabbit," he said. By then, the Mushrooms were, as Clark envisioned, the best in the business.

• • •

As the NFL draft began in 1967, Larry Little blocked the path to the communal phone in his dormitory at Bethune-Cookman. He expected it to ring at any minute. Houston wrote him a letter expressing their interest. Los Angeles and San Diego scouted him closely, too.

Little wasn't a top prospect, but he figured to get a celebratory phone call at some point in the day and didn't want another student using the only available line. So he waited by the phone. He shooed away anyone wanting to use it. He didn't eat all day. Only when the evening came and he realized that the final rounds were finished did he give up hope that he'd be drafted.

The next day San Diego's innovative coach, Sid Gillman, called him and delivered the best offer he'd receive: $750 in a signing bonus.

"I'll take it," he said.

When Dolphins general manager Joe Thomas called the following day, Little initially didn't tell him about the San Diego deal in hopes the Dolphins would dangle more money. Thomas offered $500, and wouldn't increase the figure even when Little mentioned San Diego's offer. Little figured even that small difference was something and packed up that summer for San Diego.

He packed everything he owned for the trip, too. That gave him no option but to make the team, he told himself. When he arrived in San Diego, he read in a newspaper that it wasn't just the rookies showing up a few days early to camp, as Gillman told him. It was thirty-five free agents, rookies, and veterans. Two or three would be lucky to make the team, the story said.

That upset Little. He asked for his release. Gillman persuaded him to stay. But what he heard when the free agents went around the room and introduced themselves by name and college upset him even more.

"Larry Little, Bethune-Cookman," he said.

"What's that, some kind of cooking school?" a player from Ohio State asked when Little mentioned Bethune-Cookman.

That day in one-on-one drills, Little put Mr. Ohio State down on his back and started punching him. If that opened coaches' eyes, so did his 40-yard run in full pads in 4.9 seconds. For a 280-pound man, that was telling. San Diego coaches moved him briefly to fullback and began touting him as the next Jim Nance, an acclaimed fullback in the league. But Joe Madro, the veteran Chargers' offensive line coach, put dibs on Little as a guard. Little was a better nose tackle at Bethune-Cookman, though as a two-way player for most of his college time he played at guard, too.

With his speed and athleticism, he made the San Diego roster, although for the next two seasons he started just four games. Little became known inside the team for his appetite as much as his football. As a child, he not only ate more than any of his five siblings, but often finished anything left on their plates. Nothing changed over the years. One night in San Diego, he ate two half chickens for a snack in front of a couple of teammates.

"Look at Chicken Little," one said. It was quickly reduced to "Chicken," which became Little's nickname for life.

By the end of his second year in San Diego, Little was more than 300 pounds. The coaching staff had seen enough. "I can't motivate the guy," Gillman said. And so before training camp opened in 1969, Little received a call saying he was a Dolphin.

"I finally got you," Joe Thomas told him.

Little started ten games for the Dolphins in 1969, but the weight remained a problem. At Don Shula's introductory news conference, he called Little over after all the formalities were finished.

"How much do you weigh?" he asked.

"About 285," Little answered, rounding down.

"I want you at 265 when you report," Shula said.

Little looked at his new coach to register his seriousness. Shula added that Little would be fined $10 a day for each pound he was over that. And so for the first time in his life, Little began to watch his diet. He went a full day without food before reporting to camp to hit that weight. But he did hit it. And the results were obvious. He moved better, quicker. He became the most polished lineman the Dolphins had and one of the most punishing in the league. In each of his first three seasons under Monte Clark's coaching, Little was voted the league's most outstanding lineman by his peers through the NFL Players Association. He ground defensive tackles on inside runs. But it was running outside, using his speed and agility in a manner people noticed, where Little made a name for himself. His signature play was "Ride 38," where he'd pull from his guard position and escort Mercury Morris around end. Often, Morris held onto Little's shirt for guidance. Little's combination of size, speed, and smashmouth physicality resonated throughout the league. Once, Chicago cornerback Charley Ford attempted to submarine the sweep. Little went down with him and punished him. "You can't get lower than me, Charley," he said on top of him.

"The Monday morning after Little got finished with us," New York Jet cornerback Earlie Thomas said in 1971, "our whole secondary was in the training room."

Pittsburgh defensive tackle Joe Greene said Little was "one of the best" in the league. Little, at the height of his powers, scoffed at that.

"The best," he said of himself.

Jim Langer was crushed when the Dolphins grabbed him off the waiver wire near the end of training camp in 1970. He knew the Browns intended to reclaim him and put him on the taxi squad, where he'd earn $500 a week. Langer never expected to survive to this point, much less make such good money. He expected that just being invited to Cleveland's camp would cap his football career. He was a better baseball player at South Dakota State, but his football coach knew a Cleveland scout and got him invited to the Browns' camp. He was so excited after ten weeks in training camp to hear that he had made the taxi squad that he called his wife back in Minnesota to say, "Pack up your stuff, get down here, and I'll get us an apartment."

The next day he walked into the locker room and was told that the Dolphins had signed him off waivers. A ticket to Miami was waiting for him at the Cleveland airport. He called his wife back and told her to hold off on the move. He didn't know exactly where Miami was. He knew no one on the Dolphins. And when he arrived, Joe Robbie said he'd get $350 as a taxi-squad member.

"Cleveland was going to pay me $500," Langer said.

"This isn't Cleveland," Robbie shot back.

Robbie, in a fit of sympathy, paid Langer $375 a week. That was the start of a rough transition. Langer was thrust into a new role as reserve center—the Dolphins needed one for their scout team. Two physical quirks came into play here, Langer said. The first was that he had limited vision without his glasses and he couldn't wear contacts. The lack of vision helped him at center, because he simply aimed his block for the middle of the blurry physique before him.

The second quirk became a career-making bonus: he was left-handed. Initially that was a problem. Quarterbacks, accustomed to right-handed centers, didn't appreciate the ball coming up from a different angle. That caused regular fumbles on the center exchange. Langer was told to learn to snap with his right hand.

After he mastered the new technique, this turned him into a force at center. As he snapped the ball with his right hand, he took a quick step and fired his left hand into the opposing defensive lineman—in effect punching him to neutralize his movement. That quick assault with his stronger hand often was the difference in earning a winning or losing grade in his personal battle.

Langer was athletic enough to pull from his center position and afford the offense a rare commodity in the NFL at the time. One of the first times Langer pulled, he surprised veteran Baltimore linebacker Mike Curtis. As he lay on the ground, he stared at Langer and said, as players did for the next decade, "Where the fuck did you come from?"

Years later, Bob Kuechenberg joked how the only signing bonus he got with the Dolphins was breakfast. There was good reason. He had never played in the NFL, was cut by two teams the previous summer, and spent the season playing for the semi-pro Chicago Owls. He fought such long odds to make the Dolphins that Don Shula didn't even watch him that first training camp in 1970 and, much to Kuechenberg's anger, released him.

"Coach wants to see you, and bring your playbook," were the tell-tale words a locker-room attendant told him near the end of that camp.

Kuechenberg cursed. He threw his gear in his locker. He grabbed his playbook and stomped out of the room, still cursing, when he bumped into Clark, who was purposely stationed in his way.

"I know you're mad, but here's what we're hoping happens," Clark said.

He laid out the plan: They had too many lineman and needed to release someone. Already having been released twice, Kuechenberg could pass through waivers, be reclaimed by the Dolphins, and put on the taxi squad. "That began one of the worst twenty-four hours of my life," Kuechenberg said.

Compounding the sadness, his older brother, Rudy, was released the same day after three years in the NFL. Bob's two heroes growing up were Rudy and his father, Rudolph, the toughest man he ever knew. Rudolph was a German immigrant and an Indiana steelworker when Bob grew up. Rudolph started out as a professional boxer, winning twenty-seven of thirty fights, and then converted into a rodeo man. While in Florida one winter, he made another career change that delivered a lifetime of stories: he became a human cannonball in a circus. Once a day and twice on Saturday, Rudolph was shot out of a cannon, over a couple of carnival rides, and into a net.

Rudolph was knocked unconscious upon being ejected from the cannon and came to his senses at the apex of the flight. The trick, he told his son, was not to panic, to stay relaxed rather than reach out for the net, because you then could land wrong and break something. One night he was sick, and his brother, Al, took his place. On his maiden voyage out of the cannon, Al evidently stayed relaxed. But he missed the net completely and landed headfirst in the seat of a Ferris wheel. His face was torn apart. Doctors grafted skin off his backside to sew his face together, creating a functional, if unseemly, look for him. That was the end of the Kuechenbergs in the cannonball business.

From the time he was a kid, Bob knew he wanted to play football. He was lucky that Rudy, four years older, smoothed the path for him with his parents, who didn't see sports leading to any future. He also was lucky that Rudy was a star who played in the North-South All-Star Game following the 1966 season in the Orange Bowl for the incoming Notre Dame coach, Ara Parseghian. Rudy had the game of his life, making tackles all over the field and intercepting a pass to win the game. When Parseghian congratulated him in the locker room, Rudy said he should recruit his younger brother.

"He's not big or fast, but he's got a lot of heart," Rudy said.

That winter, Bob took the train a hundred miles from his hometown of Hobart, Indiana, to South Bend. His suitcase was a brown paper bag. Parseghian offered him a scholarship. As a sophomore, Kuechenberg was the starting tackle, playing opposite Bubba Smith in a historic 1966 game against Michigan State. Philadelphia saw enough to take him in the fourth round. Kuechenberg found himself recently married, homesick, unhappy, and in the Eagles' Reading, Pennsylvania, training camp at the first of several crossroads.

"Why are you doing this?" he began asking himself in bed at night.

For the first time playing football, he was lost for an answer. He quit the Eagles, returned the next day, but was among the final roster cuts. Atlanta immediately signed him. Coach Norm Van Brocklin expressed his appreciation for Kuechenberg, and told him to collect his wife and belongings and move south. Kuechenberg did. He was cut a week later.

"Van Brocklin didn't have the decency to tell me himself," Kuechenberg said.

Later, after he became an accomplished player, Kuechenberg considered it fitting that the Dolphins' 42–7 win against Atlanta helped get Van Brocklin fired. This was in 1974, when the Dolphins were kings, and Kuechenberg insisted that they not let up one bit. "I wanted to run a sweep to their bench so I could put spike marks in [Van Brocklin's] neck," he said.

Kuechenberg's fate was different as he left Atlanta in 1969. Football wasn't part of his plans for the first time in his life. He took a job selling business forms in Chicago for $600 a month plus commissions he never reached. He was home by midafternoon most days, bored. The emotion moved to unhappiness watching football on the weekends. He wanted another chance but had no idea how to create one.

Then he heard of a semi-pro team composed of teachers, mechanics, and insurance salesmen called the Chicago Owls. They earned $150 a game, used some of their own equipment, and played a sandlot version of football in Soldier Field before a few thousand fans. Kuechenberg loved it. Football was fun again. Even when the team went bankrupt halfway through the season and stopped paying players, he kept playing. After home games, the players went out for pizza and beer and replayed the afternoon. For road trips, they bused together and received a box lunch with a sandwich, a banana, and a bag of pretzels.

That winter, Kuchenberg sat down with rosters from each NFL team and analyzed which presented him the best chance. It boiled down to two teams. Green Bay had aging guards Jerry Kramer and Fuzzy Thurston, who needed replacing soon. Miami had players he didn't know except for Ed Tuck, a reserve guard. Tuck played behind Kuechenberg at Notre Dame. If he couldn't beat out Tuck again, Kuechenberg figured, he didn't belong in the league.

The plan to release him that 1970 training camp worked just as Clark hoped. No team claimed him, the Dolphins signed him back, and by the ninth game he replaced veteran Maxie Williams as the starting left guard. Kuechenberg didn't leave the lineup for the next fifteen years. He started in four Super Bowls, made six Pro Bowls, and played in a team-record 196 games. Stories piled up about him. When injuries depleted the Dolphins' tackles, Kuechenberg moved there for the 1978 season and was named to the Pro Bowl. He named his boat *34 Trap* after his favorite play, one in which he knocked out Bubba Smith and in which Mike Reid said he got hit so hard, "I couldn't fall down." Before the Super Bowl against Minnesota in 1974, Kuechenberg noticed whenever defensive tackle Alan Page stunted to the inside, he put his left leg a few inches farther back to gain more leverage on the first step. A cardinal rule for guards was not to get beaten to the inside and allow an instant attack on the quarterback. Kuechenberg called Clark to look at the film. He didn't see it as clearly and told Kuechenberg not to adjust his game.

On the game's first play, Page put his left leg back those few inches. Kuechenberg didn't adjust, blocking straight ahead, as his assignment called. Page blasted inside, nearly took the handoff from me, and threw Jim Kiick for a 5-yard loss.

"Screw it, I'm doing what I know is right," Kuechenberg said.

That ended Page's afternoon. He wasn't involved in another tackle. He also was getting clubbed by Kuechenberg's steel-reinforced broken arm to the point where the cast was reduced to plaster particles by game's end. Page became so frustrated that near game's end he took a cheap shot at me and was thrown out of the game.

Norm Evans had no illusions about his natural talent. He understood his strengths and limitations better than any coach or critic, who often were one and the same. When the Houston Oilers drafted Evans in the fourteenth round in 1965, his college coach at Texas Christian, Abe Martin, said he didn't have enough talent to make the pros. Martin didn't say this harshly. He liked Evans enough to offer him a job on his staff in the same conversation. When Evans insisted on trying the NFL, Martin called Houston general manager Bud Martin upon hearing his former player's rookie contract terms.

"You ought to be ashamed of yourself for offering that kid that little amount of money," the coach said.

Evans's contract immediately rose, from $8,000 to $10,000. A signing bonus doubled, to $1,000.

Still, his college coach wouldn't believe that Evans had NFL talent. He drove to where the Oilers trained in San Antonio midway through preseason and told Evans that the coaching offer remained on the table until the following week. Then he'd have to find someone else. Evans immediately went to the Houston coach, Hugh Taylor.

"Coach, I need to know if there's any chance I'm going to make this team," he said.

Taylor stared at him a moment before saying, "Norm, you've started the last two games. What do you think?"

Evans remained insecure of his talents, too. He understood early on that most players were more gifted athletically than he was. Only by applying himself and wringing every ounce of talent from his body could he survive in the league.

Unfortunately, Houston's wayward situation didn't help. It had a staff of coaches who considered themselves the head coach. Offensive coordinator Sammy Baugh, a former Hall of Fame quarterback, actually was the Houston head coach the previous year. Baugh returned to the locker room after watching the opposing team warm up and drew up new plays. Evans, who had studied the game plan all week, took to retreating to a bathroom stall and ignoring the new schemes. He was nervous enough without having to relearn everything an hour before the game. He began taking medicine to calm his stomach.

That rookie year, Evans started every game in a dismal Houston season. Whenever a player made a mistake, teammates began singing "Moon over Miami," in reference to the upcoming expansion team. To his surprise and initial anger that off-season, Evans was exposed for the expansion draft and taken by the Dolphins. But the more he considered it, the more he liked the idea of leaving Houston. The Dolphins ended up with two other offensive linemen from Houston, Tom Goode and Maxie Williams, so everything wasn't completely new.

It was while staying at a St. Petersburg beach hotel in 1966 for the first Dolphins training camp that Evans had a life-altering experience. With his wife, Bobbi, Evans watched an evangelist on the hotel television. Then they went to see him in person and became born-again Christians. He went to Dolphins' coach George Wilson and asked about bringing a minister to a Sunday chapel.

"If anyone else is interested, okay," Wilson said.

It took much of Evans's strength to stand before the team and ask if anyone else was interested in having a Sunday chapel. Five other players raised their hands. They met with a minister before home games in a corner of the lobby in the Biscayne Hotel, where the team stayed. Only three other teams—Cleveland, Baltimore, and Green Bay—were doing similar things. One Sunday, a Boca Raton minister, Irsa Eshelnan, appeared and said he could organize chapel on the road for the Dolphins. Soon the idea caught on across the league.

Slowly, Evans began to feel assured about his place in football. After starting for two years, an appendectomy set him back on the edge of the 1968 training camp. He then suffered a knee injury and wore a cast from his ankle to his hip for four weeks. It was removed the week before the opener. He started every game again that 1968 season, after which general manager Joe Thomas began contract negotiations by saying, "You didn't have a very good year."

"Don't you ever talk to me that way again," Evans said, walking out of the room and slamming the door. He got the biggest raise of his career that season, from $17,000 to $25,000.

By 1972, he still was the only right tackle the team had known. And he still was undersized despite constantly drinking protein shakes and eating hamburgers in the middle of the night. Years later, when Evans returned to visit the Dolphins after retiring, Don Shula looked at him and asked, "What do you weigh these days?"

"About 250," Evans said.

"You're skinny," Shula said.

That was Evans's playing weight throughout his nine-year career.

• • •

I considered our offensive line the emotional and tactical core of this team. The numbers said as much. We set an NFL record with 2,960 yards rushing in 1972—more than 30 yards a game that season better than second-place Pittsburgh. We rushed the ball twice for every pass. We averaged 11 more plays a game than opponents. Our ball-control offense also kept the defense off the field and rested, helping it lead the league in fewest points allowed.

That final Sunday, against Baltimore, there was one final record to get. Despite linebacker Mike Curtis's pregame vow—"Merc, you're not getting no fucking record off me today!"—Mercury Morris gained 85 yards to reach 1,000 yards exactly. With Csonka's 1,117, the Dolphins became the first team to have two 1,000-yard rushers.

This final game was notable for another reason to me: I got back on the field. With the game won, with out offense going back on the field, Shula asked if I was ready midway through the fourth quarter.

"I'm ready," I said.

I started to run on the field, but he grabbed my arm.

"Wait a play."

It was a nice touch by Shula. He wanted me to run on the field, alone, and have the crowd recognize my return.

"You should be writing for the movies," I said.

As I came on the field, the crowd indeed noticed. Earl Morrall and I exchanged greetings. The crowd applauded for us. I ended up playing two series that day. We gained four first downs. I completed two of three passes for 19 yards. And in as important a play as any, Ted Hendricks grabbed my jersey and spun me to the ground for a sack.

Nothing hurt. I was fine. And so the questions began.

"Would you like to start next week?" a reporter asked after the game.

"I would like to start every week," I answered. "But I'm not completely healthy yet and Earl Morrall is."

"What if you get healthy?"

"I think the chances are that Earl starts no matter what."

"So you're resigned to it?"

"Yes."

No way I was playing that game. We were winning. Morrall was playing great. I felt good, but the next game was the playoffs. This wasn't a time to change the formula. I understood that. I understood the stakes. Everyone did. And if they forgot, there was Shula being handed the game ball after a 14–0 regular season.

"There's only one game ball I want," he said, as he had after the New England game.

Shula then called up Monte Clark. He noted the offensive line's play and talked of the rushing records set that season.

"This is for you," Shula said, handing over the ball.

Clark held it up in the air, then walked it over to the Mushrooms, who passed it among themselves.

15

The Next Season

GAME FIFTEEN
—AFC Divisional Playoff—
Cleveland Browns
December 24, 1972

Over the years, people have asked what made our team special, and I can't offer a secret or a magic pill or a motivational catchphrase. I return to the same themes: we had Hall of Fame talent and coaching, and we had forty players on the roster in proper roles, who accepted those roles and who made winning plays from those roles every week.

Clichés, right?

Well, in our first playoff game that year, against Cleveland, the clichés came to life. A player at the bottom of the roster, a rookie, a reserve, a special-teamer—a nobody in the national limelight at the time—made an early play to give us some life. Charlie Babb was exhausted by this point in the season, too. With linebacker Larry Ball, Babb was the only rookie on the active roster that year. Babb had played in six exhibition and then in fourteen regular-season games—more than double the college season he had been accustomed to. But midway through the first quarter he wasn't tired. He split through a crack in the Cleveland line, blocked a punt, stumbled after it, and fell on it. That would have been enough. But he was helped up by Maulty Moore and Curtis Johnson and half-pushed, half-carried the 5 yards to the end zone.

Touchdown.

We led 10–0 after the first quarter.

Simple win, right? We'd use the formula from there? Let our running game kick in, our defense take over, and we've got a fifteenth straight win? There was just one problem. The defense got dented just enough. And the running game? Well, Cleveland keyed on Csonka. He gained 32 yards all day. Cleveland's great defensive tackles, Walter Johnson and Gerry Sherk, made a pregame pact that "the big bastard wasn't going to beat us," as Sherk said.

Midway through the fourth quarter, Cleveland went ahead, 14–13. Anxious? Sure. I was on the sideline. I felt helpless. There were times in the second half when I wondered if Shula would ask me to warm up. We struggled across the offense most of the afternoon. We didn't look like the focused, confident team we'd been through so much of the regular season. Maybe it needed something. That's the mind-set I had to keep, in case I was needed.

We hadn't trailed in a fourth quarter since Minnesota in the third game of the year. Cleveland knew that. "We thought they'd choke at that point," Cleveland tight end Milt Morin said.

After Cleveland took the lead, I found Morrall on the sideline and told him there was plenty of time left. More than eight minutes. But to that point Morrall had completed just 4 passes for 38 yards on the day. And everyone knew the stakes here. As if to underline them in the huddle, in the silence, in the late afternoon at the Orange Bowl, an unusual voice was heard.

"Come on, let's get it together," Paul Warfield said. "We've got to score here."

Warfield, you have to understand, was the quietest superstar of them all. He never raised his voice. He was known for doing crossword puzzles at his locker, ignoring the louder world around him. He also was one of the most respected players on the team, because of the talent he had and the regal manner in which he carried himself.

So when he spoke like this in the huddle it was like Moses coming down the mountain. Everyone listened. Everyone took note. This changed the tone of the huddle and added to the importance of the moment.

It told everyone just how badly Warfield wanted to win this game. He had not caught a pass all day against the team he wanted to beat more than any other. Cleveland was his childhood team, the one he started with in the NFL and the one that traded him to the Dolphins a few years earlier for the right to draft quarterback Mike Phipps. For three seasons, the Browns tried to spin it as a successful move.

"I think it's one of the greatest trades the Browns have ever made," Cleveland coach Nick Skorich said that year after a win. He was a partisan minority, though. Phipps threw for a respectable 13 touchdowns that season against a still-learning 16 interceptions. He got the Browns in the playoffs. He also ran 5 yards for a third-quarter touchdown and threw 27 yards for the fourth-quarter touchdown that gave Cleveland the 14–13 lead. That had the chance to shift thinking about the trade. Everyone recognized the possible story line considering the players involved.

Warfield felt a great player's need to match the moment. A year after the trade, at an off-season golf tournament, Cleveland owner Art Modell walked over and put his arm around Warfield in a gesture to hope there were no hard feelings from the trade. And there weren't by then to Warfield. Business was business. He understood that. But Warfield's business mind also wanted to show in this high-stakes game just what the Dolphins got in the trade—and what Cleveland was missing.

He didn't sleep well that week, it was so on his mind. He actually woke up early the day of the game and had a panic attack that he'd overslept. His family had moved back to Cleveland that week for Christmas and taken much of their furniture. Warfield couldn't find a clock. He had to call the time and temperature service. Only then did he hear that it was 5:56 a.m. He wasn't late after all. Just ready.

And now, as Warfield spoke in the huddle, Morrall got the distinct idea where to go with the ball. Starting at the Dolphins' 20-yard line, Morrall threw a simple pattern over the middle that Warfield took for 15 yards. That breathed life into our offense. You could see it. Morris next gained 5 yards over Larry Little. Then 5 more. The gears were turning. The machine was moving. After a slow day, it was like everyone was reminded who they were and what they could do.

Morrall next called for Warfield to run a deep post pattern. Warfield immediately knew how to set it up. He had not used the maneuver called "the Weave" all afternoon. Warfield had perfected it in his Cleveland years with the help of veteran Ray Renfro and kept it in his repertoire. He came off the line and accelerated forward a few steps at a very slight angle to the right. He then took the next few steps at a similarly slight angle to the left. By now, if Warfield had made the moves properly, the defensive back was wondering where the route was going as he backpedaled. The irony here is that he was up against Cleveland's Ben Davis. They had practiced years together in Cleveland. They were good friends. They later became neighbors.

Warfield took a few more steps angled back to the left.

Then to the right again.

All this happened within 15 yards of the line of scrimmage with a clock ticking in Warfield's head. He had 2.9 seconds to become an available target before Earl Morrall's protection threatened to evaporate. By now, Warfield was nearing the crucial move of this route. Like all his moves, it hinged on his getting close enough to the defensive back.

"Close enough to shake his hand," Warfield liked to say.

At these close quarters, every small fake was magnified, any small defensive error fatal. And he now was that close to Davis. Warfield made a hard step to the left. At this distance, Davis had to honor the move. He made the cornerback's commitment of opening his hips in that direction. Warfield had him. He cut back hard to the right, accelerating into the open field like the world-class athlete he was. It was a thing of beauty to stand on the sideline and watch him separate from Davis in the open field. One yard of separation. Two yards.

Morrall saw it unfolding the entire way. As Warfield made his final cut, he threw the ball down the middle of the field. Warfield chased it. And chased it. And you could see, like in a bad dream, that that ball was going to be overthrown just a bit.

Warfield jumped. He tapped the ball in the air just enough to stumble under it and catch it as he fell to the ground.

"That's why he's Paul Warfield," Davis said later.

The pass went for 35 yards. The Dolphins were on the Browns' 20-yard line. The Orange Bowl was alive. The offense was in the moment. And Morrall did what a smart veteran quarterback does in that situation. He rode the hot hand.

Warfield again.

This pattern went to the sideline, and Warfield ran it so perfectly that he was open again in a tight window. Morrall threw right there. Cleveland linebacker Billy Andrews crashed into Warfield before the ball got there for a pass-interference penalty. We had first-and-goal at the 8-yard line.

On the next play, Kiick took the ball up through the middle, picking his way, finding the hole, and ending up in the end zone. After Yepremian's extra point, we were up 20–14.

The drama wasn't done. Phipps, as if to steal back the day, drove Cleveland to our 34-yard line. Less than a minute to go. Now it was time for our defense to meet this moment. When Phipps tried to find a seam in our zone, linebacker Doug Swift stepped in the lane and intercepted the pass. A test was passed, a drama played out.

At his locker, Warfield was asked about that last drive. His two catches accounted for 50 of the 88 passing yards all day. Throw in the penalty and he gained 62 of the 80 yards on the winning drive. He saved the season. He was the star everyone knew he was.

"I've got a plane to catch," he said.

It was Christmas Eve. He was flying home to Cleveland to be with his family for Christmas. The Browns were, too, with the lump of coal he gave them.

It was the tightest game of the year, considering the stakes.

It was the best thing that could have happened.

We were 15–0 and had a renewed confidence about how we could play with the season on the line.

16

Sweet Returns

I was walking into the locker room at halftime of the AFC Championship Game in Pittsburgh when Don Shula fell in step beside me.

"Are you ready?" he asked.

"I'm ready," I said.

He nodded. "Okay, you're in then."

"Okay."

Nothing more was said. Nothing had to be. Shula later called it the toughest decision of his career, pulling Earl Morrall out of this important game after all he'd done that season. But the offense needed something—a spark, a change, a dose of confidence, anything to shake it from the funk it was playing in for so much of the game against Cleveland and, again, this first half against Pittsburgh.

Shula watched me closely that week in practice. I worked mainly with the second team and was throwing the ball well. I had a good week. The eleven-week layoff wasn't something to wish on anyone, but it had some great benefits. My arm was fresh. My legs were fresh. My mind was fresh, too, from not having a long season of stress and scars.

As a teammate watching that first half, I wanted the offense to play like it had all year. As a competitor, I wanted to get the chance to lead it myself. As a rational observer, Shula's move didn't surprise me. I half expected it, considering the week of practice. I already was plotting what to do when Shula said it was my time.

It was lucky the game was 7–7 at the half. Pittsburgh used their first four plays to score their touchdown. It came with a cost, though. Quarterback Terry Bradshaw took a hit from Jake Scott, suffered a concussion, and fumbled the ball in the end zone, where guard Gerry Mullins recovered it for the touchdown. Bradshaw said he couldn't remember the offense until the fourth quarter. In the interim, he sat.

We tied it primarily because of a bold play by another player back from injury. Punter Larry Seiple wasn't even back from injury, not really, not if that meant he was healthy.

Just that morning, Seiple put his kicking leg down on the floor at the William Penn Hotel in downtown Pittsburgh and couldn't put any weight on the leg. It was clipped in the St. Louis game and suffered a tear in the medial collateral ligament. He missed the final three games of the regular season. For the playoff game against Cleveland, the knee was drained, wrapped, and shot up with what he considered to be Xylocaine. He didn't ask. He just went out with that numb leg and punted five times for a healthy 42-yard average.

He underwent the same treatment in Pittsburgh—drain, wrap, shot—but the other issue was that this game offered him a rare opportunity. That week, Tom Keane, the Dolphins' secondary and special-teams coach, noticed something telling about the Pittsburgh punt-return team. They just turned and ran if the punt-return game was on. No one faced the punting team. They just turned and ran downfield as fast as they could to set up the punt return.

"You're going to get a chance to run," Keane said to Seiple. "But don't do it on your own. Wait until we give you the okay."

That was no problem for Seiple. On his bum knee, it wasn't like he wanted to embrace risks. Shula didn't exactly let players freelance with such decisions. Seiple was more athletic than most punters; he started at tight end his first few seasons. In three years under George Wilson, Seiple also ran nine punt fakes, eight successfully. The Dolphins even became known for such plays. Under Shula, it was different.

"Larry and I have an understanding," Shula said. "If Larry can make the first down, he can run."

And if he didn't make it? Seiple knew who that would fall on. He ran just three fake punts in Shula's three seasons. Of course, most of that was because the Dolphins didn't need much trickery. They did just fine beating teams the conventional ways under Shula.

There was so much unusual about this AFC Championship, though, starting with the fact it was in Pittsburgh. By all rights and competitive standings, this game should have been in the Orange Bowl. But this was a time when the NFL rotated championship sites between divisions. It was the Central Division's turn to host the game. So here we were, on the road, having to play a team riding their own wave heading into this game. A desperate, last-second throw against Oakland by Terry Bradshaw was deflected, then scooped up at the shoelaces by rookie running back Franco Harris, who ran it in for the winning touchdown. "The Immaculate Reception," the catch was called.

Pittsburgh hadn't won a title in forty years, and the city acted the part heading into this championship game. Harris's fan club—Franco's Army—accepted two new members in the days before the game, with Arnold Palmer and Frank Sinatra. A press release from the club said, "A light aircraft, carrying two of the army's crack officers, dropped 2,000 leaflets" on the William Penn Hotel, where we stayed. The leaflets evidently read, "Surrender! This leaflet will guarantee safe passage out of town for any member of the Miami Dolphins if presented to a member of Franco's Army."

None of us saw them. It turns out the crack officers misread the wind and the leaflets ended up several blocks away.

If Pittsburgh wanted to believe in omens, that was one. Another one: the weather. It was New Year's Eve in Pittsburgh, and it was 63 degrees. We'd take that. That was *our* weather.

But the Steelers were a tough, young team, too. They were assembling the pieces of the group that went on a dynastic run later in the 1970s: Bradshaw. Harris. Mean Joe Greene. L. C. Greenwood. Jack Ham. Mel Blount.

And confident?

"We'll beat the Dolphins," Bradshaw said that week from a Pittsburgh hospital, where he battled a flu. "I'm sure we can move the ball and put some points on the board." Later he said, "Before San Diego and Oakland and now again, I've had this feeling. It's kind of like ESP and it's that we can't lose."

ESP, huh? We took it in without comment or rebuttal, as was our custom. And it's a good thing the way the game started. Down 7–0 for most of the first half, it took the kind of trickery we rarely used to get anything going on offense. Punting from the Pittsburgh 49, Seiple saw exactly what Keane had alerted him to. Only one Steeler was rushing. Pittsburgh coach Chuck Noll said it was the only time they rushed one player on a punt all season. Seiple immediately saw Bob Matheson blocking the rushing Steeler, too.

The rest of the Pittsburgh punt-return team was running downfield with their backs to him. It was just like in the film that Keane showed that week. Seiple didn't wait for coaching approval. He didn't hesitate even to think. He just took off running without knowing how far it was to a first down (5 yards). And he kept running.

His leg? It was so shot up with Xylocaine that it didn't even feel like it was there. Pittsburgh players didn't turn around. At one point,

Seiple appeared to be using three Pittsburgh players as blockers as he ran behind them. If any of them turned, that would have ended the run.

As it was, he ran 37 yards to the Pittsburgh 12-yard line. It was the kind of play our day—our season, considering the stakes—needed.

"We had position, momentum, everything when that happened," Noll said. "That play changed the game."

From there, after a run for a few yards, Morrall threw 9 yards to Csonka for a touchdown to tie it up. That was the extent of our offense that half. That's why Shula made the change. I made all the necessary preparations before the second-half kickoff. Plays to use. Players to watch. I felt great warming up, too.

But before I even got on the field in the second half, we were behind. Pittsburgh got a field goal and went up 10–7. So the anxious feeling on our sideline ratcheted up a notch. You could sense that we needed something good to happen.

As I ran on the field and into the huddle, there was a lot of emotion.

"Watch the offsides," someone said.

"Let's ram the ball down their throat," someone else said.

Everyone runs a huddle a little differently, and it was time for me to take control.

"Shut up, dammit," I said sharply.

Several players said later it was the only time they ever heard me curse. That's an exaggeration. But my aim was clear. I wanted to get their attention. Make everyone focused. It was time to stop babbling in the huddle, come together, and throw all our energy into the task at hand.

On third-and-five, I called for a simple throw I liked to make. Every quarterback has some favorite plays. This quick slant pass to Warfield was one of mine. Our linemen just had to engage the defensive linemen to keep their hands down. It was a quick drop-and-throw for me. One key is being perfectly accurate with the pass, which I had confidence in doing.

The other key was Warfield getting inside positioning on whoever was over him. In this case, it was Andy Russell, Pittsburgh's great outside linebacker. To this day, when Russell sees Warfield, he'll say, "I can't believe you got inside on me on that."

That was Warfield. In the biggest moments, he delivered. That play worked even better than hoped. I delivered the 5-yard pass to Warfield in full stride. He took it 52 yards. It was our longest play of the year in our biggest game of the year to that point. And it changed the game. It gave us life. Energy.

Shula fed that new confidence with a bold decision, too. Defensive tackle Mean Joe Greene had been named the AFC's Lineman of the Year just that week. That didn't go unnoticed by the second-place finisher, Larry Little. Greene was double-teamed all season by teams for good reason. But he wasn't double-teamed in this game. It was Greene vs. Little, mano a mano, in one of those games inside the game that everyone watched. Little said afterward that he went into a "deep concentration bag" for it.

"I know if I don't do the job on him, we won't win," he said. "If I do, we'll win."

On fourth-and-one inside the Pittsburgh 10-yard line, Shula didn't send out Yepremian. He wanted the touchdown. He demanded that we be the team we thought we were.

"You have to go for the short ones if you want to be champ," he said.

I debated what play to call. I had faith in Little. I called the play to run right over him—or, to take another view, right over Greene. Want to show who's the best lineman in the game, big fellas? You decide things. And, at least for that day, they did.

Little handled Greene.

Jim Kiick gained 2 yards.

We had a first down.

A couple of plays later, Kiick scored from 3 yards out to complete the kind of drive that was this offense's trademark that season. Even with the big throw to Warfield, the drive lasted 11 plays over 80 yards, had a series of gut-punching runs through a tough Pittsburgh defense, and ate up nearly 7 minutes. Oh, yeah, we had the lead, too. Our defense wasn't about to give that back.

When we got the ball again early in the fourth quarter, you could see that everything was back on track for us. In these two opening drives of the second half, we ate up nearly 15 minutes—about a quarter of the game! Noll said afterward that that's what he feared the most.

Both drives ended in touchdowns, too. This second drive was shorter—10 plays over 49 yards—but it ran exactly like the previous one. There even was a fourth-and-short call inside the 10. Shula went for it again. I ran the play over Little again.

Little beat Greene again.

First down. Again.

Hey, could we get a revote on AFC Lineman of the Year?

Kiick scored from 2 yards out this time. That put us up 21–10. And just as we got a sense that we were on our way, Bradshaw returned to the game, completed four straight passes for 71 yards, and Pittsburgh pulled to 21–17.

We took some time off the clock on offense. But not enough. Not the way I wanted. Bradshaw got the ball back again with more than five minutes left. But here's where poise and experience come into play.

Buoniconti read a play beautifully, just as he did his whole career, and intercepted Bradshaw.

Then, when Pittsburgh got the ball back in the final minute, Doug Swift intercepted Bradshaw.

It wasn't their time yet. It was ours. We were on the way to the Super Bowl for the second straight season. We had a nice New Year's Eve toast that night on the plane ride home. We heard Washington beat Dallas in the NFC to meet us in the Super Bowl.

And I thought how nice it was to be back in the game again—and how much had happened since our last Super Bowl. It seemed forever ago that Shula stood before us after that awful game in New Orleans with words that stayed with me: "We embarrassed ourselves out there today. We lost our shot at the championship, and that wipes out everything else we accomplished this season. There's only one way for something good to come out of this. That's if we use this experience to motivate us to get back here and win this game. That's the only way to erase the embarrassment of this loss in our mind."

And now we had the chance.

17

Perfection

In the days after the AFC Championship Game, Don Shula faced another decision. Everyone knew it. No one said anything. When I came out Tuesday for our first practice before the Super Bowl, he watched me closely.

"You come out of the game okay?" he asked.

"Yes," I said.

"You're ankle's fine? Everything's good?"

"Everything feels fine."

I didn't ask the obvious question. That wasn't my place. The next day before practice, Earl Morrall was sitting in the rocking chair by his locker when a locker-room attendant told him, "Coach wants to see you."

As he entered the office, Morrall knew the answer. He could see it on Shula's face before he even sat down.

"I'm starting Bob in the Super Bowl," Shula said.

This was Shula's way, man-to-man, direct, and honest. It was tough for Shula to say those words. It hurt Morrall to hear them. And as they sat there and discussed the situation for a few minutes, as Shula stressed how important Morrall was to this team, it was Morrall who had to swallow his well-earned pride and accept the decision.

"I feel I've contributed and I still want to contribute," Morrall said.

"We need you to go out and prepare like you always do," Shula said.

As the years passed, as our accomplishment added the weight of history, I've never thought Earl received proper credit for what he did that season. Everyone inside the team appreciated what he did. He was 11–0 as a starter. He was named first-team All-Pro, which tells you what people thought of his season in the immediate aftermath. He was an old-timer in the league and a newcomer to the team thrown into a pressure-filled situation, and he kept the machine rolling right along week after week right to the biggest game of the season.

And then he was back on the bench.

And forever a pro.

"I won't make waves or anything," he told Shula that day in the office. "I've seen how that works. The biggest thing we all want to do is win the game."

I've always appreciated that that's how he carried himself, too.

Years ago, there was a process to winning a Super Bowl. The first step was making the playoffs, then losing early in them. The second step was advancing to the Super Bowl and losing. Finally, you made it back to the Super Bowl, summoned all the knowledge and motivation of years past, and won the big game.

That's what Dallas did the previous year in beating us. It's what Baltimore and Kansas City had done, too. Now it's what we attempted as well. There's no explaining why things changed as the years moved on until today's results show there's little advantage to having experienced a Super Bowl. But there seemed to be a distinct benefit to having been there and lost in the early years.

Maybe our Super Bowl trips in the 1971 and 1972 seasons explain why that was. In 1971, in New Orleans, in our first trip to the Super Bowl, it was a circus. And that was just inside our hotel. Kids ran up and down the halls pounding on doors for autographs. Players' wives came in for the weekend and stayed in the team hotel. And the hotel management, as if not to miss out on the fun, put a live dolphin in its swimming pool, causing even more of a festive commotion.

What a zoo. What a time. What a lesson learned by everyone, too.

Our hotel in Los Angeles wasn't in Los Angeles. It was in Long Beach. It was quiet. It was isolated. And instead of having a dolphin in the pool, our windows looked out over an oil refinery.

Most players couldn't believe how far it was from the bright lights or the sunny beaches of the big city. Shula loved it. "The quietest Super Bowl yet," the *Los Angeles Times* called it by the end of the week, and on that point none of us was about to argue.

Fun could be had, if you wanted to find it. And plenty of players did early in the week. With no curfew Monday night, Larry Csonka and Jim Kiick started bar-hopping and ran into Jim Mandich, Jake Scott, and Dick Anderson doing the same. All of them piled into Anderson's rental car and took a tour of the area. Beverly Hills. Century City. They had dinner in Marina del Rey. They ended up in a bar where Kiick talked with Washington guard Ray Schoenke. Then they found another bar. And another. And then a massage parlor, surprised at how crowded it was in the middle of the night.

When they rolled back to the hotel, it was 6:00 a.m. and they headed to the restaurant for breakfast. There was Shula, up early and eating, before another big day of preparation.

Red-eyed and beer-breathed, Mandich sat down opposite Shula. "Morning, Coach."

Shula just stared.

By this second Super Bowl trip, no one had to be told to stay in line once curfew came down that Tuesday. We understood the stakes. And if we didn't, there were reminders everywhere about how big a game this had become. In its first trip to Los Angeles in the inaugural Super Bowl in 1967, Memorial Coliseum was nearly a third below its ninety-thousand-seat capacity. The $12 tickets were sold on game day for $6. As if to underline how new that game was to broader America, when a halftime interview with Bob Hope ran long, TV viewers missed the second-half kickoff. Sideline reporter Pat Summerall was ordered by a network producer to approach Green Bay coach Vince Lombardi and ask him to kick off the second half again.

"I'm not doing that," Summerall said.

The game was known as the AFL-NFL Championship that first year. It became the Super Bowl by the third one. It grew Roman numerals for the fourth one. Now, by Super Bowl VII, all the grand machinery was in place. The game was a sellout. The $12 tickets were being scalped that Super Bowl Week for $40. Hundreds of reporters showed up for Media Day.

And the hype was on.

"Charley Taylor never made any big plays off me the first times I've faced him," Dolphins cornerback Lloyd Mumphord said. "I've never had any trouble with their receivers."

"What about Billy Kilmer?" a reporter asked of the Washington quarterback.

"I like the way Kilmer throws the ball," Mumphord answered. "He doesn't throw with much zip, but he tries to throw it in there anyway. That gives you a pretty good chance to come down with it."

"So he likes to catch my passes?" Kilmer asked. "If he really likes it enough, maybe he ought to try out for our team next year as a wide receiver."

That was one day's firestorm. Another day's simple question brought another run of headlines.

"There is no man made of flesh and blood that I can't whip," Washington defensive tackle Otis Sistrunk said. "Larry Little has made a career of beating up defensive backs. I'm bigger than a defensive back."

"I think I can handle him," Little said. "In fact, I know I can handle him because there's nobody I can't handle."

"Sistrunk is just whistling past the graveyard," Bob Kuechenberg said.

These were words. Just words. And if there's one thing we learned from the previous Super Bowl, it's that words couldn't beat you. The game, we knew, didn't start until Sunday.

Alone in my hotel room, alone with Howard Twilley, a pen, and a notebook the Wednesday night before the Super Bowl, I finally turned on the film projector and studied Washington's defense. I dissected its playoff games against Green Bay and Dallas. I assembled the defensive puzzle pieces to fit our game plan.

Even with the two-week break to the Super Bowl, I wanted to follow my normal routine of watching the opposing defense on Wednesday before the game. The coaches showed film of Washington during the first week while practicing in Miami. We worked on some ideas. We saw a few things that could work. We practiced on a muddy field, joking how Shula warned everyone to stay healthy a minute before having us lie down on the cool mud for calisthenics. I phoned home and talked to my oldest son, Scott, whose big worry was that Dad might miss a planned trip to Disney World the next week.

But I waited until Wednesday to break down Washington's defense. From the outside, it was a great defense, allowing just a field goal in each playoff win against Green Bay and Dallas. It ranked third in the league in points allowed. It was full of smart veterans playing under the defensive mind of George Allen. And the more I watched the film, the more certain I was we'd pick them apart. I didn't just like what I saw flickering back and forth on the hotel room wall, I loved it. As Twilley and I sat there, winding and rewinding game film, Washington's defensive recipe was discovered. As I watched alone on Thursday night, it became obvious.

It was always in zone coverage on third-and-long plays.

It was always in man-to-man coverage on third-and-short plays.

It always double-covered the opposing team's best receiver when the offense crossed the 50-yard line and left the other receivers in man-to-man coverage. We could use that to our advantage. It always used their nickel back, Ted Vactor, in the same manner. We could use that, too.

It surprised me that a great coach such as Allen wouldn't change things more. I saw that defensive end Dion Talbert, a great pass rusher, could be run at inside. I saw that their excellent outside linebackers, Chris Hanburger and especially thirty-six-year-old Jack Pardee, were no match to cover Jim Kiick out of the backfield.

I saw how much freedom they gave an aggressive cornerback such as Pat Fischer.

"You know what I'm thinking," I said to Twilley as we watched Fischer.

"I hope it's what I'm thinking," Twilley said.

As time moved on, I understood that Super Bowls were easy games for which to prepare a game plan. It was the same idea the next season, against Minnesota's second-ranked defense. They had a set and successful formula. They weren't about to change that. Why would they?

The more I watched film of Washington that Wednesday and Thursday, the more confident I became. We had so much that would work against it. The trouble I had wasn't figuring which plays would work against a mighty defense. It was deciding which plays would work the best. The most important thing for me to do was to get the plays I expected to be successful out of my mind and onto paper. We had a great week of practice. We were prepared. By Friday night I began writing down the specific plays to use in the game. I sharpened the list Saturday. I probably redid the page that would go on the clipboard five or six times.

As I reviewed the plays, there was no doubt in my mind that we would win this game. And win it easily. I chuckled at the difference between a flashy personality such as Joe Namath and me. Namath guaranteed a victory before his Super Bowl in 1969. It made headlines, drew spotlights, and defined Namath's legend for generations to come.

Me?

I said little to reporters all week.

But inside, I swaggered.

Even before our first practice in Los Angeles, we moved our practice site. Don Shula took one look at the Los Angeles Rams' nice facilities, spacious locker rooms, and plush field and decided they wouldn't work. There was a school across the street. It overlooked the practice field.

"Too risky," Shula said.

That's because Washington coach George Allen lived by the phrase "If you're not spying, you're not trying." His antics weren't the stuff of football mythology. They were documented. Dallas caught one of his spies at their practice. Howard Schnellenberger, the Dolphins' offensive coordinator, was on Allen's staff with the Los Angeles Rams and told of being ordered to spy on a team practicing the day before the game. Schnellenberger didn't do it. He drove around for a while and told Allen he couldn't see anything.

Shula planned with that in mind. We rode a bus to the Rams' facility and changed in their locker room. We then reboarded the bus and rode to Orange Community College. It wasn't a short ride, and Jake Scott asked if we were going to scrimmage for the San Diego Chargers. A couple of guys told the bus driver to keep going, to Tijuana.

During our practices at Orange Community College, Al King, who filmed them for the Dolphins, and John Cheever, an equipment manager, searched the area for anyone hiding in trees with binoculars. If a helicopter flew overhead, we stopped practice. When we ran plays, we had an extra running back and receiver in the formation to confuse anyone who might be watching. There was reason for these precautions, even if I couldn't let it pass without comment to Shula.

"You know, Don, there's an old saying," I said. "Those who expect a guy to take advantage of a situation are the ones who know how to take advantage of a situation themselves."

Shula didn't smile. "I've never spied on anyone," he said.

Allen constantly thought his offices were bugged. He regularly had his practices checked for spies. He made Washington the first NFL team to hire a full-time security guard.

By this Super Bowl, Allen had developed a reputation for winning and making enemies with equal regard. Chicago coach and owner George Halas became upset enough to sue Allen, then a Bears assistant, for breaking his contract to accept the Los Angeles Rams head coaching job. Halas won in court, then let Allen go anyway. At the next NFL meeting, Halas shouted, "George Allen is a liar! George Allen is a cheat! George Allen is full of chicanery!"

Across the table, the Rams' owner, Dan Reeves, was growing embarrassed at his new hire until Vince Lombardi spoke up. "Sounds like you've got a helluva coach," the Green Bay Packer coach told Reeves.

After the Rams played in two conference championship games in four years, Reeves ended up firing Allen. "I had more fun losing," he said.

Difficult? Contentious? Complicated?

"George was given an unlimited budget and he exceeded it," Washington president Edward Bennett Williams once said.

"He got unlimited authority and exceeded it," Rams owner Carroll Rosenbloom said after firing Allen two preseason games into the 1978 season.

Allen stretched any boundary, tested every rule. He was fined $5,000 for trading draft choices he didn't have with Washington. He once denied the identity of his son, Bruce, to avoid a penalty for insulting a referee on the sideline. "The kid's not with us," he told the referee. "He must be one of those people the Eagles gave us as ballboys."

Allen became the first coach to stress a sixteen-hour workday. He regularly told reporters he slept on the couch in his office. For team meetings on road trips, he ordered new chalk and new erasers and had meeting rooms kept at 64 degrees to keep players alert. Ice cream was his favorite food—and became his nickname to players—because "he doesn't have to chew it. Chewing would take away his concentration from football," his wife, Etty, said.

Allen walked around the Redskins offices and asked secretaries, "What have you done today to help us win games?"

"The future is now," he said.

"One hundred percent isn't enough," he said.

"Every time you win, you're reborn; when you lose, you die a little," he said.

For all his personality, Allen was a winning coach who understood how to build a team. Nothing demonstrated that better than his work in Washington. Lombardi began the roster's reconstruction before dying of cancer in 1970. Allen then entered and completed its rebuilding by fashioning the defense in his personality. He traded seven draft choices and a veteran linebacker to Los Angeles for six of his favorite Rams, including the entire linebacking corps of Jack Pardee, Myron Pottios, and Maxie Baughn. He made another trade, with New Orleans, for aging quarterback Billy Kilmer. He imported so many players on the back ends of good careers that the Redskins had a new name by that Super Bowl: "The Over-the-Hill Gang."

Now he was in the Super Bowl for the first time. And he wanted to show how smart he was. He told reporters how he sent assistants to the stadium to chart the sun in the Coliseum to better prepare his punt and kickoff returners to handle the sunlight in their eyes.

That was amusing. A couple of other incidents proved just how uptight he was for the game. The first came when Jim Snowden, a

reserve tackle who was injured and ineligble to play, was caught breaking curfew. Allen was irate. He wanted to fine Snowden and send him
home. Snowden, who is black, was singled out unfairly because several
starters were with him, black teammates thought. They signed a peti-
tion. Team captains Charley Taylor and Len Hauss met with Allen.
Snowden stayed. The issue was defused. But emotions were tense and
remained so all week with Washington.

In his final meeting with the media on Friday, Allen complained
how talking to reporters was causing him to miss his "first meeting with
the team in twenty-three years." He whined, "Yesterday we had thirty-
one players in interviews for one and a half hours, and we had our
worst practice of the week."

"Aren't you sounding like a loser?" a reporter asked.

"I'm not thinking like one—is there anything else?" Allen answered.

"Do you want to leave, George?" another reporter asked.

"You guys wrecked our practices. At least let me have my meeting."

That was one way to handle Super Bowl Week. Shula, however,
showed there was another way. This is where having been there helped.
Shula had double the lessons, too, having been to the 1969 Super Bowl
with Baltimore and the previous year's game with the Dolphins. He
learned that if you fought against the outside demands, it turned Super
Bowl Week into a miserable time and infected the team.

In Super Bowl III, Joe Namath made a point of saying that Earl Morrall didn't stack up to quarterbacks in the AFL. "I don't know how Namath
can rap Earl," Shula said angrily. "Anyone who doesn't give Earl the credit
is wrong. But I guess Namath can say whatever the hell he wants to say."

That, he later thought, didn't help matters. He softened his
approach at the Dolphins' Super Bowl against Dallas. When former
Dolphins coach George Wilson was quoted as saying "any Joe Doakes"
could have taken that team to the championship, Shula joked the next
morning, "Hi, I'm Joe Doakes." But it seemed forced, unnatural.

By this third Super Bowl, he projected a calm, loose attitude to the
media.

"Good morning, Breakfast Clubbers!" he greeted reporters at one early session.

"It's good to see you distractions again," he said to the media another day.

He gave Washington ("Tremendous weapons") its proper due ("They're so strong up front"). But it was with the off-the-wall questions that Shula worked extra hard to demonstrate how relaxed he was.

"How could I enforce that?" he asked with a smile when a reporter asked if he'd allow his players to have sex in the days before the game.

"If it rains Sunday, we're going to forfeit," he answered when told that Washington hadn't lost in the rain that season.

"We'll let George film them," he said when asked if the Dolphins were filming practices.

While Allen held longer practices, bristled to the media, and wouldn't let players even see their wives the week of the game, Shula went the other way. Normal practices. Small jokes. Wives were there most of the week (though the Dolphins put them up at the Beverly Hills Hilton).

"I want you to prove to me on Sunday that my way is better," Shula said.

He was more active in meetings, demanding that players understand assignments, double-checking the details of strategy. But I appreciated that. It meant I didn't have to play that role. And his way won over the public. "Graceful humor," the *New York Times* called Shula's manner. "The good-natured Shula," the *Washington Post* called him, adding, he "sounded like anything but a coach who was paranoiac about the fear of losing his third Super Bowl."

That's the front he showed us, too. At one practice he said, "Well, we've seen the films of six of Washington's games this year. That leaves just ten more games for us to watch."

Pause.

And a chuckle.

It was a good act. It was a winning act. But it was just that, too. An act. All of it. Shula was worried sick about this game. Literally and physically worried sick. A flu bug made its rounds. Monte Clark got it. Bob Matheson. Shula, too, was sick even if he refused to acknowledge it.

There was too much work to be done, too many thoughts swirling in his active mind: his previous Super Bowl losses, the pressure of an undefeated season, the daily barrage of media, the nonstop debate about the game plan, and, on top of everything, his former boss Carroll Rosenbloom opening his mouth again.

"I've seen him freeze up in big games," Rosenbloom said of Shula that Thursday before the game. As if it wasn't enough to question Shula's mind, Rosenbloom lumped him with Allen, saying, "These are two coaches who broke all the rules in football."

Shula called NFL commissioner Pete Rozelle on Friday.

"You've got to stop this," he said.

Shula had another complaint with Rozelle, too. The commissioner told reporters just that day how Allen might be fined for hiding an injury to guard John Wilbur before the NFC Championship Game. Shula was angry. How could Rozelle announce this right before the Super Bowl? Didn't he know Allen would use this to rally his team? To further his us-against-the-world approach?

Rozelle said he hadn't fined Allen. That didn't matter to Shula. The damage was done. By Saturday night, Shula's mind raced when he took in the stakes of the game. He got out of bed. He paced around the room. He got back in bed.

"Sleep," he demanded.

This was one coach's order that wasn't followed.

I woke up early and hungry on game day.

Starving, actually.

I went to mass, then ate everything in sight at breakfast in the hotel. Steak. Eggs. Toast. Coffee. Honey. As I ate, Larry King, a Miami radio talk-show host and former Dolphins analyst, entered the restaurant. In his national talk shows in coming years, he occasionally related how relaxed I was by my asking him five hours before kickoff: "Do you think property values in Key Biscayne can keep going up?"

I was relaxed, too. We all seemed to be. Or most of us. When Jake Scott got on the bus a few seconds late because he was giving friends some tickets outside the bus, Shula barked at him about being late.

"What's the matter, you thinking about going down as the coach with the most losses in Super Bowl history?" Scott asked.

Shula didn't turn. "Just be ready to play," he said.

Shula took it as a good sign: Jake was Jake. Feisty. Argumentative. In other words, he was ready. That was one of the questions earlier in the week. He separated his shoulder against Pittsburgh. Or sprained it. Or bruised it. The reports kept varying. But oddsmaker Jimmy "the Greek" Snyder singled out Scott's injury for raising Washington from a two- to a three-point favorite. And he wasn't alone in picking Washington. Everyone was. It was the most amazing thing, our being undefeated during the year and underdogs for the Super Bowl. The common knock was that we hadn't beaten anyone significant other than Kansas City and Minnesota, at the start of the year. Our response was that we beat everyone on our schedule.

"The prediction here is that the fearsome Redskins defenders will force Shula to wait for his reward," *Time* magazine's Pete Axthelm wrote. *Sports Illustrated*'s Tex Maule said Washington would win "by at least 10 points and perhaps by as many as 21." Jim Murray of the *Los Angeles Times* said, "The Redskins are sure to hand the Dolphins their shoes and ask that they bring them back by morning shined and leave them outside their door."

After the following season, after we won our second straight Super Bowl, Mercury Morris entered a Los Angeles bar and, almost immediately, the manager asked, "Are you Mercury Morris?"

A man wanted to see him. The manager led him back to a dark and secluded place. A well-dressed man greeted him there and thanked him, too. "I made a lot of money when you won sixteen games in the regular season and everyone was picking against you," he said.

Frank Sinatra.

Hearing everyone pick Washington over us, I chuckled again that I should have "guaranteed" a win. But that wasn't my personality. Riding the bus to the game, I sat next to Norm Evans. We didn't talk about the game or any detailed strategy. We talked about our families. How our kids were doing. What fun ages they were at. That's how comfortable we felt.

Shula already gave everyone the first few plays of the game. "Counter 32 Straight" was the opening play, a fake up the middle one way to Larry Csonka and a handoff the other way to Jim Kiick. That was a double surprise for Kiick. He not only started over Mercury Morris for just the fourth game this year, he also got the call on the first play. Washington would be keying on Csonka, Shula figured. Kiick might just spring a big gain. Kiick was so wound up by the news that he fell asleep on the locker room floor before the game, just as he usually did.

Another good sign.

Shula gave a straight and simple talk about our last three years together, as a team, a family. He talked of the work and the sacrifice. He talked of our playoff loss to Oakland in 1970 and our Super Bowl loss to Dallas in 1971.

"We've waited in line," he said, "and now it's our turn to take the cake. We've worked too hard to lose this one."

After a year of waiting, after a season of dominance, after a week spent thinking we were the better team, I went on the field, called that first play, handed off to Kiick, and . . . he gained two yards.

So much for them keying on Csonka. The next play—"25 Lag Give-It"—was a handoff to Csonka. Two more yards. On third down, I threw a short pass to Csonka that lost a yard. And so we went nowhere on our first possession. And in came the punting unit, which meant that the game had arrived at its first strategic crossroads.

Part of the greatness of Allen was being on the cutting edge of ideas. He was the first coach to have a full-time assistant on special teams. Marv Levy, who later made his name taking Buffalo to four Super Bowls, ran Washington's special teams that season. Preparing for Green Bay in the NFC Championship, Allen and Levy noticed that the Green Bay center raised the ball off the ground on punts before snapping it. Allen thought the ball could be slapped away in such a snap. He even called the NFL supervisor of officials, Art McNally, who informed Washington that it was illegal to slap the ball. They didn't try it in that game. But when Allen noticed that Dolphins snapper Howard Kindig lifted the ball in the same manner, he couldn't resist the temptation a second time. Maybe the referee didn't know the rule. Maybe he wouldn't be watching closely. Who knew if he'd even see the play?

It was worth a shot, Allen figured.

So as Kindig went to snap the ball for the first punt of the game, Washington's Howard McLinton slapped at it. The ball tumbled free on the ground. Players jumped after it. Other players stood in confusion. Officials blew whistles. A Washington player landed at the bottom of the pile with the ball. But what was the call? Fumble? Penalty? Kindig was furious and screaming at the referees.

"Kindig was so nervous the ball slipped between his hands," announcer Curt Gowdy said on national television.

For several minutes, the officials huddled. The crowd buzzed. Players waited. Finally, the correct call was made. Washington interfered with the snap. Shula wanted a 15-yard unsportsmanlike-conduct penalty. Instead, a 5-yard offside penalty was called. Fourth down was replayed, and this time Kindig snapped the ball with no interference, and Larry Seiple punted it 50 yards.

For each team's initial two possessions, no blood was drawn. I felt like a boxer feeling out Washington's defense. I studied the film. I knew what they were supposed to do. But I actually had to see them do it. And when those first two possessions confirmed everything I saw on film, I was ready. I knew how to attack. I knew what we could do.

On our third possession, Kiick carried twice, for 11 yards. I completed an 18-yard pass to Warfield. Soon we faced a third-and-four situation at Washington's 28-yard line. The ball was on the left hash mark. This is where the hours of film work and game preparation came into play.

On the Saturday night before each game, the coaches brought me a self-scouting report. It was a list of all the plays I had called in the previous few games. This was the list the opposing defenses worked off and studied. If I was always calling the same play on first down inside the 20-yard line, this list would show that. The defense would know that. And I would know the defense knew it. An intricate mind game inside the football game was set up. And these were the games I loved.

This third-down situation was exactly what Twilley and I prepared for after watching game film in the hotel room. We knew what defense Washington would be in. They never changed their defenses, right? And they knew what play we often ran in that situation: a simple down-and-out to Twilley for the first down. And we knew they knew that.

So we practiced a little wrinkle on the play: Twilley ran his simple down-and-out. I took a quick, five-step drop and set up as if to throw. If Washington's cornerback had done his homework, he'd come flying to stop that short pass. And with two weeks to prepare for this game, who didn't do their homework? That's what professional football is about, right?

That's why we practiced Twilley then turning upfield and me throwing him the ball on a longer pattern.

"You've got to sell the short route," I told Twilley.

"I know that," he said.

"Don't get too quick and go."

"I'll make him bite."

We worked on that play overtime in practice. Fifty times, Twilley ran it. Fifty times I threw it. Maybe more. Now, in the huddle at the Super Bowl, I looked at him and called the play we'd invested so much effort in: "66-D-Q."

As we came to the line, I saw that it was just as we'd drawn it up. Pat Fischer, one of the game's best cornerbacks, was lining up on Twilley. It was almost too perfect. Fischer, in his twelfth year, wasn't big, at 5-9 and 170 pounds. He had lasted this long in the game because of his smarts and aggressiveness. Those were just the traits this game of chess worked best against.

At the snap of the ball, I took my five-step drop. Twilley went downfield five steps and then ran out five steps as he looked for the ball. Fischer had read the scouting report. He accelerated to jump Twilley's route. Twilley then made a perfect move upfield to break open. The protection for me was perfect, and I had a good, simple throw toward the end zone.

So often these things don't work out as you draw them up. You have to adjust a play. You never have the chance to use it. Or, if you do have that chance, something unexpected happens. A breakdown. A penalty. But here, in the first quarter of the Super Bowl, was a moment when all the hard work and preparation paid off on the biggest stage.

I threw the ball.

Twilley caught it.

Fischer actually made a good play in hustling back to knock Twilley into the end zone. But that didn't matter. Twilley was so excited about scoring the touchdown that he jumped up and patted the official, Tom Kelleher, who lived in Miami, on the butt.

"Howard, don't do that again," Kelleher said a few minutes later, embarrassed.

We were up 7–0. We felt in control. And a few minutes later, as if to show that the planets were aligning, we found ourselves in another situation straight out of our game plan.

The film work showed that after you crossed the 50-yard line Washington always put double coverage on the best receiver and played man-to-man elsewhere. Well, we had just crossed midfield. What's more, the ball was on the right hash mark, meaning Paul Warfield could line up to the wide side of the field alone and work on

Washington's double coverage. Warfield made a Hall of Fame career doing that. Oakland's Al Davis used to come up to me at the Pro Bowl and ask, "How does Warfield beat double coverage?"

"I don't know," I answered.

But I knew. This play showed how. We had practiced it during the week, too.

I called "66 Dig Split Post" in the huddle.

As I came to the line and saw the chess pieces set up, I thought, This is too good. I'm dreaming, right? Washington's defense set up again just as the film studies showed. This play had touchdown written on it.

Tight end Jim Mandich and receiver Marlin Briscoe were on the short side of the field. They went down 15 yards and ran square-in routes. That occupied Washington's strong safety and cornerback on that side and kept them out of Warfield's way.

Warfield lined up to the wide side, released up the field, engaged the cornerback, and cut right in front of him—"across his face," as they say in football. Since Warfield made that cut with surgical precision, that effectively took the cornerback out of the play. That left the free safety, Roosevelt Taylor, who we saw could be moved a step or two out of position with run fakes. That was my job. Warfield would take care of the rest. Taylor was thirty-five. He was no match for the best athlete in the game.

All week long, George Allen stressed in Washington's meetings how they were concentrating on Warfield. He set up defensive schemes to double-team Warfield all over the field. He didn't want Warfield to have a catch. Not one. Word of this even filtered back to Warfield. Let someone else beat us, Allen said. He even introduced a move called "the Axe," where a Washington defensive back would sprint toward Warfield as a play began and roll into him to knock him down.

Warfield played his part perfectly on this particular play. The cornerback, Mike Bass? Warfield cut across his face and shook him off like a loose shirt. The safety, Taylor? Warfield was 5 yards behind Taylor at the end of the route. I couldn't miss that throw if I tried. Warfield caught the ball and sprinted easily into the end zone.

"He could've crawled in," Gowdy said on television.

I looked for penalty flags, didn't see any, and trotted upfield, thinking we were on our way to a great afternoon. Then I heard a whistle. And saw a flag.

"What is it?" I asked the referee.

Briscoe moved early on the play. The touchdown was lost. There aren't many times I got upset over a mistake. This was one. Briscoe knew better than anyone that if he didn't hear the signal to line up wide as a receiver, just to watch for the snap of the ball. He was in such a rush to move off the line and engage Fischer, one of his boyhood heroes in Omaha, Nebraska, that he blew the play.

Shula benched Briscoe for the rest of the game. Briscoe felt so bad about his mistake that he couldn't celebrate the win. It pushed him to work that off-season and lead the Dolphins in catches in 1973. But none of that returned points to the scoreboard against Washington.

Fortunately, the No-Name Defense was playing up to its billing. In his film studies that week, Bill Arnsparger watched the Washington offense play the New York Giants. He was struck by the play of nose tackle John Mendenhall. He treated Washington's All-Pro center, Len Hauss, like a door to be opened and shut. He stymied Washington's vaunted inside running game. Arnsparger made a point of showing this film in the team meeting to get the full attention of Manny Fernandez. He didn't overplay it. Fernandez, he knew, was a smart player. He would see the possibilities for himself. Occasionally, when Mendenhall made an especially dominant play, Arnsparger rewound the film and replayed it without comment.

Washington's strategy played out exactly as Arnsparger hoped. Just as Dallas did in the previous Super Bowl, it concentrated on neutralizing Nick Buoniconti with its guards. Hauss blocked Fernandez one-on-one. Or didn't block him, as the case played out. Fernandez had spent the season fighting double- and even triple-teams as the nose tackle in the "53" defense. Having to beat one man was like a walk in the park.

Fernandez used his quickness to elude Hauss and hit running back Larry Brown in the backfield. He used his strength to shed Hauss and meet Brown at the line. He wasn't alone. Dick Anderson knocked Brown's helmet off with one hit. Vern Den Herder stopped him for no gain. Bill Stanfill figured he was having a nice game himself, though he noticed that every time he moved in for a tackle, Fernandez already was there. Fernandez was everywhere. Brown ended the game with 22 carries for 72 yards—a full yard below his 4.3-yard average per carry that season. Fernandez ended the game with 17 tackles (11 solo). It was the most dominant performance by a defensive lineman in Super Bowl history. It also was lost on the one person with the influence to record such feats for history.

Sport magazine's Dick Schaap had the lone vote for the game's Most Valuable Player award. He slept off a late night during the game. As it ended, he noticed Jake Scott's two interceptions and named him the MVP. He didn't even know that Fernandez had 17 tackles. "I'm going to have a second set of keys made for Manny Fernandez," Scott said upon receiving the Dodge Impala that went with the award. (He traded the Impala in for a pickup truck. He also said, "I'm going to have a third set of keys made, too. I'll give them to Billy Kilmer.")

With Washington's running game stopped, it began to throw in the first half to generate some offense. That's when Buoniconti and Arnsparger showed their homework. Kilmer liked to run a simple pass pattern to Brown out of the backfield. Buoniconti saw no film of Kilmer reading the middle linebacker before throwing the pass. Buoniconti knew just what to do when that play showed itself. Arnsparger, too, knew that Washington would identify Bob Matheson before each play as the wild card to locate. So on a third-down play at the Dolphins' 49-yard line—as deep as Washington had penetrated, late in the second quarter—Arnsparger had Matheson stay put. He blitzed Doug Swift through the middle. Kilmer just so happened to call for the pass to Brown out of the backfield. Buoniconti took a step to the left at the snap of the ball. That gave Kilmer the false impression that the linebacker was moving away from Brown's route. Washington guard John Wilbur looked for a blitzing Matheson, who wasn't coming. Swift sprinted through the middle untouched. Kilmer had no time to check on Buoniconti a second time. He lofted the ball to Brown. Just as he pivoted to throw, Buoniconti reversed field and cut in front of Brown to intercept the pass.

And he began running.

And running.

Buoniconti kept going until he toppled out of bounds at the Washington 27. I immediately looked at the clock. A minute and 51 seconds remained in the half. That was more than enough time to do some good work.

Kiick ran for a couple of yards. Csonka did for a couple more. On third down, I went to another of those plays gathered in film work. Warfield and Twilley went to the left side. That cleared out the right side for Mandich, who was a great receiving tight end. Crisp routes. Soft hands. Tough. All that was on display here as he made a diving catch at the 2-yard line.

Kiick took it from there, running up the middle and stretching the ball over the goal line before disappearing in a mass of bodies.

"He's in!" I screamed.

"No, no!" Washington players were yelling.

The crowd roared. The officials ran in to the pile. No signal. They began sorting out bodies. Their arms went up.

"Touchdown!" Gowdy yelled on television.

There were 18 seconds left in the half and we were up 14–0 after Garo Yepremian's extra point. In two quarters, everything in our arsenal was working. Power. Deep threats. Great defense. Game preparation.

"Attaway," Shula said as we came to the sideline.

As we walked into the locker room at halftime, there was a feeling we were in complete control of the game. There also was a nagging thought that we should have put the game away by this point. Shula said we were halfway to our goal. One more half, he said. That's what I felt, too. Allen, not straying from his demand for drama, told his players, "We've got thirty minutes to live!"

Washington took the second-half kickoff and immediately showed an adjustment. After passing seven times in the first half, Kilmer passed on seven of his first nine plays. He drove to the Dolphins' 17-yard line. There, on third-and-10, he went to pass for an eighth time and was sacked for a 7-yard loss by Manny Fernandez. Who else? Fernandez was doing everything else this day. From there, a 32-yard field goal attempt went wide right. No blood was drawn.

As I came out for our first possession of the second half, my plan was to be smart and conservative. Up 14 points? With Washington's offense shut out? Give the ball to our great backs. Let our great offensive line take over the game. I handed off three times to Csonka. It didn't do the trick, as we had to punt. But the plan was clear: don't lose the game by taking unnecessary risks. I completed all six of my passes in the first half, felt great, and some quarterbacks wouldn't want to shut down the passing game. I understood that. I threw just five passes in the second half, completing two. That gave me scrawny numbers in the game: eight completions in 11 attempts for 80 yards. But isn't the idea to win? Why let ego get in the way? In the 1973 AFC Championship, I threw six passes against 53 running plays. We won, 27–10. In that Super Bowl, I threw seven times (completing six for 73 yards) and the same 53 running plays. That's still a Super Bowl record for fewest pass attempts. We won, 24–7.

That was our formula. Get an early lead. Play great defense. Run the ball, run the clock, and run happily into the locker room.

I called three running plays to Csonka on our first possession. Then we punted. I called seven straight running plays on our second possession. Morris gained 12 yards on one. Csonka busted one for 49 yards on his way to 15 carries for 115 yards rushing that day. We pushed it all the way to the 2-yard line. There, with Washington bunching up,

I called a pass to Marv Fleming, our great tight end. Fleming had won two Super Bowl titles with Green Bay and now was in his second Super Bowl with the Dolphins. So in five of his nine seasons Fleming played for a championship (and was on his way to winning his fourth in five). Reporters asked that week who would win if his Green Bay teams met this Miami team. He broke it down analytically, talking of each team's power running games and defensive strengths. Then he gave the kicker: "Whoever had me would win."

On this play, Fleming ran his pattern—faking to the middle and then cutting to the corner. It was the same play we ran earlier in the year against Buffalo. Fleming didn't just score on that play but to his delight found a $10 bill in the end zone. He came off the field holding it high, smiling.

Now he was open again.

And I made a bad throw.

Or Washington safety Brig Owens made a great play. Call it what you will. I threw the ball for what looked like a sure touchdown. Only I underthrew it a bit. Owens cut in front of Fleming to intercept it. Another mistake. More points we didn't get. These were adding up.

As I came to the sideline, Shula said, "We needed to get three points out of that."

"I know that better than anyone," I answered.

Still, we were in charge. The clock was our ally. And as if to show that it just wasn't going to be Washington's day, Kilmer assembled another good drive midway through the fourth quarter. Brown had a couple of good runs. Kilmer threw some nice passes. They moved to the Dolphins' 10-yard line. It took them more than seven minutes to get there, though, as they plodded along with a lot of small gains. That was fine with us. Washington tight end Jerry Smith broke free in the end zone. Kilmer threw a nice pass to him. Then, to underscore whose day this was, the ball did something unexpected. It hit the crossbar of the goalpost, which sat at the front edge of the end zone. Talk about getting a break. Jake Scott then created one on the next play by intercepting Kilmer's pass—Jake's second interception of the day—returning it 55 yards to the Washington 48-yard line.

"Yeeeeeah!" Shula shouted on the sideline.

There were five minutes left. The day, the game, the championship were ours now. The outcome was so obvious that hundreds of fans began leaving. We methodically began running the ball and running out the clock. Csonka gained seven yards. Kiick gained four, then three. Csonka got the ball up the middle again, and Washington was playing that so heavily he didn't gain a yard.

We were at Washington's 34 now. I knew we needed to get closer for a field-goal attempt. This is when the quarterback has to think like the coach. Yepremian, as good as he was, performed differently outside 40 yards. Most kickers did in this era, when fields weren't perfect and conditions weren't climate-controlled, as in so many cases today. Yepremian made seven of eight field goals between 30 and 39 yards that year, I knew. But between 40 and 49, he was just four of eleven. Right now he was looking at a 42-yard field goal.

We need to get closer, I thought. Washington was stacking the line now. On third-and-seven, I called a pass to Twilley. Incomplete. That's one I wanted back. It didn't make Yepremian's job any easier. Still, I walked off the field, saw there was 2:07 left in the game, and was certain this day was ours.

Joe Robbie, from his owner's suite, saw an aligning of history. He sent a messenger to the press box with word that this field goal could give the Dolphins a 17–0 victory in a 17–0 season. The symmetry struck his soul.

Earl Morrall had the same thought as he came on the field to hold for Yepremian's kick.

"All our numbers are coming together," he said to himself.

The curtain went up on the strangest Super Bowl play ever.

Yepremian wasn't thinking of big-picture items such as numbers lining up or the perfect season. He thought of details: the wind, the measured setup, and, most of all, the elevation he wanted on the ball. All day long he had been line-driving his kicks for some reason. He couldn't figure out the reason. Was it footwork? Technique?

"Am I holding the ball wrong?" Morrall asked in warm-ups.

"It's not you," Yepremian said.

Even on simple stuff such as the two extra points earlier in the game, the trajectory was low. No one else noticed. They were good, weren't they? But Yepremian noticed. He wondered. And he concentrated on changing that, though from 42 yards he needed to balance elevation against distance.

He said his prayer. He gave a quick nod to Morrall, signaling that he was ready. Morrall, kneeling on the ground, extended his fingers to Kindig, signaling that he was ready.

The snap was perfect.

The hold was perfect.

The kick was . . .

"Blocked!" Gowdy screamed on television.

Yepremian's fears came true. He kicked the ball too low, a line drive into Washington's defensive tackle William Brundige's outstretched arm. The ball ricocheted back, bouncing behind Yepremian. He chased after it. He bent down and grabbed it on a small bounce.

"Yepremian has it!" Gowdy yelled.

Now he had to decide what to do with it. Fall? Run? On the first practice of the next summer, Don Shula ran a drill: A field-goal kick went bad. The ball was bouncing free. He instructed Yepremian to fall on it and do nothing more. Just fall on it. Yepremian did so that practice and sprained his ankle. He missed four days of practice. So maybe nothing good could come of this play, no matter what Yepremian decided.

The day before the Super Bowl, Yepremian passed some time in practice throwing passes with the coach's son David Shula. Twenty yards. Thirty yards. Yepremian showed he had a capable arm, at least for a kicker. Now, as he picked up the blocked field goal, he took a couple of steps running with it. As chaos gathered around him, he saw a white jersey running in the flat. He thought it was Larry Csonka, considering that was Csonka's area to move toward on a botched field goal attempt. In that instant, Yepremian made a small decision that changed the game and, ultimately, his future.

He decided to throw the ball.

Morrall still was trying to block Brundige. Yepremian still was on the run. He was off-balance. He made a small jump, tried to throw, and the ball slipped out of his hand. It went like a puff of smoke into the air. No one knew how to react in that split second.

"Ho-ho!" Gowdy laughed.

"Ha-ha!" analyst Al DeRogatis chuckled.

The misthrown ball landed on Yepremian again. Brundige was nearly on top of him now. Yepremian thought to smack it out of bounds. Instead, he patty-caked the ball back into the air.

"There's a pass!" Gowdy yelled.

"Ha-ha!" DeRogatis chuckled.

In full stride, Washington cornerback Mike Bass grabbed the ball out of the air. Suddenly, Brundige was a blocker. He knocked Morrall to the ground. Suddenly, Bass wasn't frustrated by a day of covering Warfield or being knocked around by Csonka. He was running with the football. He moved to the sideline. He saw lots of green grass and the end zone in sight. The only person with an angle on him was—him again—Yepremian. A small man unaccustomed to the combat of football, Yepremian made an amateur's swipe at Bass. He missed.

"He's running for a touchdown!" Gowdy screamed.

Immediately, the rout was gone. Immediately, the game was on after the play that has come to define the game. I stood on the sideline and, like everyone watching, couldn't believe it. I was stunned. But the way my mind works, I began preparing for our coming possession and what we needed to do to win the game.

Shula never drifted from coach mode. "Next time, just fall on it," he said as Yepremian came to the sideline.

Yepremian went to the end of the bench. Teammates approached him with messages as disparate as the involved personalities.

"What a chicken-shit play," Bob Kuechenberg told him.

"We lose this game, I'm gonna kill you, you little cocksucker," Nick Buoniconti said. "I'll hang you by one of your ties."

"Garo, don't worry about it," Norm Evans said. "God loves you, and our defense will stop them."

The God-loving Evans then did something he never did another time in his twelve-year career. He prayed for a victory. "Dear God," he said, "don't let us lose this way."

Losing was one thing. But losing because of this?

"What a kooky play that was," Gowdy said on national television.

"Not only that, Curt, but who was he throwing to?" DeRogatis said. "Garo just threw it up in the air . . . had no idea. Maybe thought he was back—well, they don't do that in soccer, either."

The Garo jokes began.

"He just might be thinking now about a new tie pattern," Gowdy said, referring to a men's tie business Yepremian had started.

This is how it would be forever for Yepremian and, in the immediate aftermath, he was a broken man. That night at the celebration party, he felt a stabbing pain running down his right side. His brother, Krikor, helped him back to his hotel room and put him in an ice-water bath. Stress, he concluded. The emotional pain and physical depression set in for weeks. He became a recluse. He refused to leave his home in Miami. He tried to cope with his sudden fame as an unintended comedian. He wondered if he had a future with the Dolphins.

Finally, a letter arrived from Shula. It said how important Yepremian was to this team. It emphasized the ways in which he had contributed to this championship. It demanded that he enjoy the bonus money and come back ready to help the team to a second title the next season.

A few decades later at a charity golf tournament, Yepremian was signing autographs beside Shula. Some fan mentioned what a great coach Shula was. Yepremian chimed in that it was true and, beyond that, he was a great person.

"He wrote the most important letter I ever received," Yepremian said.

Shula looked at him. Letter? What letter? Yepremian tried to jog his memory. Shula was certain. He never wrote a letter. In their discussion, they came to understand that the coach didn't write that letter. As sometimes happened, the coach's wife, Dorothy, wrote it and signed her husband's name.

That winter after the kick, the letter changed Yepremian's attitude. He allowed himself to get in on the joke. A Miami car dealer started a "Garo for Quarterback" club. He laughed at it—and got a new endorsement. He was a guest on comedian Bob Hope's show that winter. He laughed at himself—and became a lovable figure.

"President Nixon made me throw the pass," he said. "Since I don't have citizenship papers, I thought I'd better throw it."

He was flooded with offers to speak. He did so with great humor and humanity. Four decades later, he not only is defined by that kooky play, as Gowdy called it, but the play has served him nicely, too. He remains in demand to talk, especially during Super Bowls. There was a "Where's Garo?" promotion for a cellular phone company during one Super Bowl in which nearly a thousand people followed clues to find where he was.

All this has led to a split among Dolphins. Some shake their heads about profiting from a play in which he looked scared. Me? I have no problem. Yepremian played a vital role in our success. I think of the kicker whose field goal won The Longest Game against Kansas City for us. I think of the kicker who made a 51-yard field goal at Minnesota without which our undefeated season would never have happened.

Maybe I'd think differently if we had lost that Super Bowl. It was our job not to let that happen. Washington elected to kick the ball deep rather than attempt an onside kick. I came on the field at the two-minute warning thinking how best to burn time off the clock. We needed a first down. After Morris ran for three yards, I decided we couldn't go into a shell. I called a simple but hopefully surprising pass play to Warfield down the left sideline. It worked: it went for 11 yards. The play was against the boundary and ended out of bounds, but we got the first down. We started running the ball. Washington started using time-outs. On third-and-seven, there was a decision to make. Knowing our defense had controlled Washington, we decided to run the ball. Morris got the call on a sweep. He gained three yards and Washington used its final time-out. One minute, twenty-three seconds remained.

After the punt, there was a minute and fourteen seconds left. I was counting every one from there. Kilmer got the ball at his 30-yard line and threw incomplete on first down. Sixty-nine seconds left. He over-threw Charley Taylor on second down. Sixty-four seconds. A swing pass to Brown that Stanfill snuffed out for a 4-yard loss meant the clock wasn't stopping. Forty-five, forty-four, forty-three . . .

One more, one more, I thought.

On fourth down, Kilmer looked downfield. But in a picture symbolic of our team effort, Stanfill and Den Herder met on top of him. He went down. They celebrated on top of him, hugging and yelling to the point when the referee had to say, "Come on, get off him."

The offense had to come out on the field, but one snap and it was over. It was the prettiest countdown I ever heard.

"Ten . . . nine . . . eight . . ."

We were hugging each other on the field.

". . . seven . . . six . . . five . . ."

Shula was lifted up for the ride of his life.

". . . four . . . three . . . two . . ."

Shula pumped his fist. He let with a whoop. Players joined him. Fans circled him. One fan shook his hand and . . .

"Hey!" Shula said.

. . . took his watch. Shula jumped down from the ride and ran after the kid. He caught him and grabbed his watch. The guy made all the right decisions on this day.

It was a blur on the field after that. We hugged. We smiled. All our work and sacrifice were rewarded in the best way possible. For all of us except Marv Fleming and Earl Morrall, this was a new experience. Our first championship. Nothing felt like it again.

In the locker room, when it was just this team together one final moment, Shula spoke about how proud he was and how much we should enjoy this championship. No one talked of the undefeated season. It was the title we cherished. The ring. This moment when we were the best.

As captain, I then stood up to award the game ball. Shula stood beside me.

"This is a tough decision, because so many people played well," I said. "We could give this to Jake, with those two big interceptions."

I paused as players applauded and yelled.

"Manny deserves the game ball, too," I continued. "Seventeen tackles. What a game."

More applause. More yells.

"And Csonka had 115 yards."

I went through a couple of other candidates. Warfield. The offensive line.

"This is a tough game ball to award," I said.

I looked around as if trying to decide. Everyone laughed. Everyone knew. I tapped Shula on the shoulder with the only game ball he wanted all season—the one he spent a career working toward.

"This is for you, Coach," I said.

Four decades later, I still hear those cheers.

Index